How to Read Ethnography

How to Read Ethnography is an invaluable guide to approaching anthropological texts. Laying bare the central conventions of ethnographic writing, it helps students to develop a critical understanding of texts and explains how to identify and analyse the core ideas in order to apply these ideas to other areas of study. Above all it enables students to read ethnographies anthropologically and to develop an anthropological imagination of their own. Combining lucid explanations with selections from key texts, this excellent guide is ideal reading for those new to the subject or in need of intellectual refreshment.

- Includes excerpts from key ethnographies
- Offers balanced and progressive reader activities and exercises
- Provides reading exercises, a glossary and full chapter summaries
- Teaches an independent approach to the study of anthropology.

Paloma Gay y Blasco and **Huon Wardle** are lecturers in social anthropology at the University of St Andrews.

How to Read Ethnography

Paloma Gay y Blasco and
Huon Wardle

 Routledge
Taylor & Francis Group

LONDON AND NEW YORK

First published 2007
by Routledge
2 Park Square, Milton Park, Abingdon, Oxon OX14 4RN

Simultaneously published in the USA and Canada
by Routledge
711 Third Avenue, New York, NY 10017

Routledge is an imprint of the Taylor & Francis Group, an informa business

© 2007 Paloma Gay y Blasco and Huon Wardle

Typeset in Sabon by Taylor & Francis Ltd.
Printed and bound in Great Britain by CPI Antony Rowe, Chippenham, Wiltshire

British Library Cataloguing in Publication Data
A catalogue record for this book is available from the British Library

Library of Congress Cataloging in Publication Data
A catalog record for this book has been requested

ISBN10: 0-415-32866-7 (hbk)
ISBN10: 0-415-32867-5 (pbk)
ISBN10: 0-203-39096-2 (ebk)

ISBN13: 978-0-415-32866-1 (hbk)
ISBN13: 978-0-415-32867-8 (pbk)
ISBN13: 978-0-203-39096-2 (ebk)

Contents

Acknowledgments

We are very grateful to Catherine Alexander for her useful and insightful comments on the last draft of this book. We also thank Keith Hart and Joanna Overing for their incisive comments on various chapters, and Jane Cowan for her suggestions regarding our treatment of her piece. Deema Kaneff came to our rescue at the very end when a small family crisis meant we were about, once again, to be late with our delivery. As always, we are in debt to her. We are very grateful to Juan Serrano and Iona Dobson who relieved us of some childcare duties and gave us much needed time to complete the project, also to Mhairi Aitkenhead and Orchid Liu who worked very hard preparing the excerpts. Finally, it was thanks to Lesley Riddle, Senior Editor at Routledge, and to her determination, that we got on with the job.

We are grateful for the permissions to reprint excerpts from the following texts:

In Chapter 1: Bird-David, N. (1990) 'The Giving Environment: another perspective on the economic system of gatherer-hunters', *Current Anthropology* 31(2): 189–96.

In Chapter 2: Pages 74–88 from Cowan, J. (1990) *Dance and the Body Politic in Northern Greece*, Princeton: Princeton University Press.

In Chapter 3: Fortune, R. (1947) 'The Rules of Relationship Behaviour in One Kind of Primitive Society', *Man* 47: 108–10.

In Chapter 4: Pages 400–9 from Lévi-Strauss, C. (1984) [1955] *Tristes Tropiques*, trans. John and Doreen Weightman, Harmondsworth: Penguin.

In Chapter 5: Firth, R. (1964) [1954] 'Foreword' to *Political Systems of Highland Burma: a study of Kachin social structure*, by Edmund Leach, London: Athlone Press.

In Chapter 5: Leach, E. (1964) [1954] 'Introductory Note to the 1964 Reprint', in *Political Systems of Highland Burma: a study of Kachin social structure*, London: Athlone Press.

In Chapter 6: Di Leonardo, M. (1987) 'The Female World of Cards and Holidays: women, families and the work of kinship', *Signs* 12(3): 440–53.

In Chapter 7: Pages 24–42 from Wardle, H. (2000) *An Ethnography of Cosmopolitanism in Kingston, Jamaica*, New York: Edwin Mellen.

In Chapter 8: Hart, K. (2006) *African Enterprise and the Informal Economy: an autobiographical note*, available at http://www.the memorybank.co.uk/papers/african_enterprise

Paloma Gay y Blasco and Huon Wardle
University of St Andrews
April 2006

A note on the use of words in bold

Throughout the book some words are highlighted in **bold type**. The meaning of these words, or our usage of them, is explained in the Glossary. Words are usually highlighted in bold only the first time they appear in the text or the first time they appear in a particular discussion.

Introduction
The concerns and distinctiveness of ethnography

This book is a guide to reading ethnography aimed at those new to the subject or in need of intellectual refreshment. In it we lay bare the central, often implicit, codes, conventions and concerns of ethnographic writing, and explore how anthropologists use them to create and transmit knowledge about diverse experiential worlds. We provide readers with the skills to analyse ethnographic texts, and guide them through an investigation into distinctive qualities of anthropological knowledge.

Anthropology textbooks have traditionally taken one of two approaches: either they introduce students to the core themes and concepts in anthropological writing to date or they summarise the theoretical standpoints of the various schools of anthropological thought. Our perspective is different: rather than presenting information, we focus on enabling our audience to read ethnography critically and to think anthropologically. We do this by submitting ethnographic texts to the anthropological gaze, and unpacking them as we would any other cultural product. By teaching our readers how to analyse ethnographies anthropologically, we help them to understand what kind of knowledge ethnography is, as well as to develop an anthropological imagination of their own.

Our starting point is the conviction that ethnographic writing constitutes a valuable and distinctive way of asking and answering a recurrent question – 'what does it mean to be human?' Writers of ethnography approach this issue in a unique manner, taking their field experiences as their starting point and framing them in terms of anthropological standards, concepts and debates. The ethnographic arguments that result draw from, and contribute to, wider flows and eddies of the human conversation. Of course, there is a striking multiplicity of modes of writing and even conceptualising ethnography. Some authors view anthropology as a science and ethnography as the tool that helps it deliver objective representations of society. For others, ethnographic writing is akin to literature and art, and introspection and self-reflection should predominate over the search for objectivity. Yet others attempt to find a middle ground, stressing the subjectivity of their accounts but nonetheless trying to produce communicable knowledge of particular social and cultural worlds. But, in spite of these and other variations, we argue that there are more than superficial resemblances between what different anthropologists achieve in their writing. There are key concerns and techniques to written ethnography present across a continuum of aims and values and styles. It is these elements that form the basis for anthropological dialogues and expressions of difference, thereby providing an intellectual core to our discipline. And it is by uncovering these commonalities, and by investigating this tension between diversity and cohesion, that in this book we explore what makes ethnography a distinctive way of knowing and representing the world.

By the same token, it is by learning to identify how these concerns and techniques play out in specific texts that you will learn how to read ethnography. Reading ethnography involves more than being able to glean information about a particular group, an activity, or a theory: it entails taking an anthropological approach to ethnographic texts. And this implies being able to elucidate how a text embodies the aims and cultural assumptions that support anthropology as a discipline; how an ethnography adheres to, or attempts to challenge, the shared codes and conventions of the ethnographic genre; and how it evidences the social and cultural conditions under which it was produced. It is the breadth of response across these three domains that gives us very different ethnographic writings, but which also provides a unity that distinguishes ethnography from other ways of recounting human experience such as novels, travel accounts, or even texts produced in sister disciplines like sociology or human geography. By negotiating these three domains, writers of ethnography make their own distinctive contribution to the discipline and establish their originality.

The problem is that these aims and assumptions, these codes, conventions, and conditions are rarely made explicit in ethnographies themselves. They are often difficult to identify, not just for readers, but for writers too. In Tony Crook's words, ethnographic writing, like other knowledge practices, is governed by a 'powerful aesthetic that is taken for granted' by its practitioners (2006: 358). Although the capacity to reproduce this aesthetic is demanded of all writers of ethnography – in other words, they must write ethnography that looks and feels right – Crook tells us that 'the skill is never explicitly put into words' (*ibid.*). Authors learn to write ethnography by trial and error, and also by repeated exposure to other ethnographic texts – that is, by reading ethnography. But what is true of the capacity to write ethnography is also true of the ability to read it: students of anthropology are not usually taught how to read ethnographies; they are expected to develop the know-how by themselves, and the cycle perpetuates itself. Most importantly, the ethnographic text tends to be treated as either a vehicle for the transmission of information or a mere literary production: it is rarely considered as an apparatus for the creation of knowledge.

In this book we consider the role of ethnographic writing in the production of anthropological knowledge, addressing a series of questions that are fundamental, not only to reading ethnography, but to anthropology at large. What are the shared concerns and understandings that make communication and debate among anthropologists of the most different persuasions possible? How can readers identify how these concerns mould ethnographic texts? And also, what are the technical and stylistic principles upon which our discipline is based? How do writers of ethnography reproduce these in their work? The structure of the book follows our unravelling of these questions. Chapters 1, 2 and 3 examine what we believe are the basic concerns addressed in all ethnographic texts. These are:

(i)   the concern with understanding different cultural or social life worlds by reference to each other, that is to say, through comparison;
(ii) the need, which follows from the comparative outlook, to contextualise; to show how the differences thrown up through comparison have meaning within a relevant mutual framing of context and detail;
(iii) the objective of showing that the life world in question displays elements of pattern or logic that helps explain why people might act in this way, or speak in that. This is a deepening of the process of contextualisation.

Chapters 4 and 5 proceed to examine the distinctive stylistic devices, techniques of processing information and modes of argument that anthropologists use to address the concerns we have just described. We focus on (i) how anthropologists portray lived experience; and (ii) how they shape this portrayal through positioning the ethnography as an argument. Chapters 6, 7 and 8 open up the discussion by considering the social and cultural settings within which ethnographies are produced. We examine (i) the relationship between ethnographic texts and their audiences; as well as (ii) the creation of an authorial or authoritative ethnographic voice that this involves. This discussion in turn leads to a consideration of (iii) how ethnographic texts relate to each other and to disciplinary conversations, big and small. In the Conclusion we argue that ethnographic writing delivers a distinct kind of knowledge. We explore in detail what this knowledge involves and the continuing importance of ethnography for a conversation about what it means to be human.

Ethnographic concerns

Writers of ethnography attempt to make the ways of living and thinking of particular groups of people intelligible to their readers, no matter how foreign or incomprehensible, or how familiar and taken-for-granted, these practices may appear at first. Faced with a new field of language and behaviour, anthropologists unavoidably start by setting it against what they are familiar with – that is, they compare. They compare what they see and live through in the field against their own lives, ideas and expectations. Because they write for an audience, they perforce set their object of study against parameters comprehensible to their readers. And, because they write within a tradition, using anthropological knowledge and debate as their point of reference, they also compare what they learn about the people they study against the knowledge of other groups that they have obtained through their familiarity with anthropology as a way of thinking, talking and writing. Thus, not only are ethnographic descriptions always comparative, but the very concepts and analytical tools that anthropologists use to mould these descriptions and construct their arguments are also premised on, and designed to enable, comparison. And so in Chapter 1 we examine this centrality of comparison to the anthropological worldview, outlining the various kinds of comparisons writers of ethnography make, and how to identify their role in a particular text.

If comparison is the first stage and strategy through which writers of ethnography attempt to make sense for their audiences of very different ways of knowing and behaving, contextualisation, the topic of Chapter 2, is the second. In order to explain actions and meanings that may initially appear inexplicable – either because their foreignness challenges explanation or because they are so familiar that explanation appears superfluous – all writers establish social and cultural contexts for them. They ask their readers to lay aside their immediate response and instead learn to appreciate the specific instance as it takes its place in, or embodies in itself, a particular context. As with the weave of a cloth, the smallest detail is only meaningful when considered as an aspect of a pattern, but the pattern itself is an elaboration of integral details. In Chapter 2, then, we consider the ways context is deployed in ethnographic writing, examining how writers of ethnography establish the distance between significant detail and contextual frame, and how they understand and interpret one by reference to the other.

The work of explaining lived experience with regard to context depends on the awareness that human life is inherently relational in character – that it is built out of relationships, for example between husbands and wives, among workmates, between leaders and followers, and so on. In Chapter 3 we explain how ethnographers examine the many different relationships we all engage in, investigating what they tell us about broader social and cultural dynamics. Writers of ethnography aim to abstract a pattern of relationships from one-off statements and ways of behaving, and go on to use this abstract delineation to make sense of specific instances and details. They also look for the relationships – both links and discontinuities – between different areas and levels of experience, for example between what people do and what they say they do, between

activities and rationalisations. And they often focus on their own relationships with others during fieldwork in order to gain further analytical
perspective on a context.

The distinctiveness of ethnography

In order to initiate the study of others, then, writers of ethnography must
compare. In order to unveil the purposes and significance of an activity or
a belief, they must contextualise. And for this same reason, they must also
consider meaning and action relationally, understanding how their interplay shapes the quality of life among a particular group of people.
Comparison, contextualisation of a life world, and an exposition of the
relationships involved – these are the central prisms through which writers
of ethnography look at the world. And yet, none is unique to ethnography.
Below, we include excerpts from two very different books, both novels,
whose authors attempt to create for their readers particular social and
cultural worlds by deploying these same three strategies.

In the first excerpt, from *The Age of Innocence*, Edith Wharton (2006
[1920]) tells the reader about the New York upper class into which she
was born. The novel is set in the 1870s, and in the passage below Wharton
describes a dinner attended by Newland Archer, a young man from a
respectable family, and Countess Ellen Olenska, the disgraced woman he
has fallen in love with:

> The dinner was somewhat a formidable business. Dining with the van
> der Luydens was at best no light matter, and dining there with a Duke
> who was their cousin was almost a religious solemnity. It pleased
> Archer to think that only an old New Yorker would perceive the shade
> of difference (to New York) between being merely a Duke and being
> the van der Luyden's Duke. . . . It was just for such distinctions that
> the young man cherished his old New York even whilst he smiled at
> it. . . .
>
> When the men joined the ladies after dinner the Duke went straight
> up to the Countess Olenska, and they sat down in a corner and
> plunged in animated talk. Neither seemed aware that the Duke should
> first have paid his respects to Mrs Lovell Mingott and Mrs Headly
> Chivers, and the Countess have conversed with that amiable hypo-
> chondriac, Mr Urban Dagonet of Washington Square who, in order to
> have the pleasure of meeting her, had broken through his fixed rule of
> not dining out between January and April.
>
> (Wharton 2006: 43–4)

Wharton's ironic narration provides a meticulous anatomy of New York
upper-class society. She emphasises the peculiarity and arbitrariness of New

York moral conventions as witnessed by Archer, who is able to reflect on them but who nonetheless submits to their restraining effect. Wharton uses Archer's relationship with Countess Olenska to highlight for the reader the distinctiveness of old New York; conversely, Archer's life is given meaning by reference to this distinctiveness. Detail and context are carefully inter-twined as interpretation. Wharton uncovers for us the organising principles behind the specific relationships that she describes, allowing us to understand the life of old New Yorkers in general and, more specifically, Archer's motives and behaviour (the moral values that he has internalised and cannot ultimately escape; his inability to leave his wife). The end result is a compelling reconstruction of a world premised on the awareness that mores are culturally specific even as they appear absolute and necessary to those who live by them.

A similar emphasis on the cultural specificity of morality also runs through the next excerpt, from Richard Morgan's (2002) *Altered Carbon*. Morgan imagines a future in which human consciousnesses are storable and transferable from one body (or 'sleeve') to another. In the excerpt below the protagonist, a hitman called Takeshi Kovacs, has just witnessed the reunion of a young black man, newly downloaded into a white middle-aged body, with his wife and children. Kovacs remembers his own father:

> The cleaning robot trundled off and I went back to the graffiti. . . .
> [H]igh on the bench's backrest and chiselled upside down, like a tiny
> pool of inverted calm in all the rage and desperate pride, I found a
> curious haiku in Kanji:
>   Pull on the new flesh like borrowed gloves
>   *And burn your fingers once again.*
>   . . . I rolled my head to an empty quadrant of the hall. My own
> father had walked right past his waiting family and out of our lives
> when he was re-sleeved. We never even knew which one he was,
> although I sometimes wonder if my mother didn't catch some splinter
> of recognition in an averted gaze, some echo of stance or gait as he
> passed. I don't know if he was too ashamed to confront us, or more
> likely too set up with the luck of drawing a sleeve sounder than his
> own alcohol-wrecked body had been, and already plotting a new
> course for other cities and younger women.
>
> (Morgan 2002: 234–5; original italics)

Like Wharton, Morgan plays with comparison, and *Altered Carbon* revolves around the notion that there might be infinite social and cultural possibilities. By recounting Kovacs' life, Morgan highlights to us the idiosyncratic character of our own world, and it is our intuitive under-standing of our own society that works as the final reference point for the imagined future of the novel. We are presented with a complex of actions and expressions that are only meaningful against very specific social and cultural patterns familiar to ourselves. Once again, the protagonist's moods and choices are used to explain the singularity of his society, but in turn can only be understood if this society itself is contextualised, its relational pattern exposed.

If cultural comparison, contextualisation and analysis of relationships are so important to other kinds of writing about human experience, such as fiction, why have we argued that they are what makes ethnographic writing distinctive? Because they take a particular shape in ethnography, and because they are deployed for a very specific, and distinctly ethnographic, end. Read through the excerpt below, from Henrietta Moore's (1986) ethnography *Space, Text and Gender*, a study of a social group called the Endo who live in Kenya. In her book, Moore presents an argument about how the relationship between Endo men and women is mediated by their symbolic use of space. Here she focuses on a crucial element of Endo spatial thinking, the hearth and, more specifically, the ash that comes from it.

> The following incident involved two girls from Sibou village, and was observed during the early morning cleaning of the house and compound:
>
> Chepkore is removing ash from the fireplace. Using a flattened tin, she scoops the ashes into a wooden container and leaves the house to go to the ash placement. On the way she meets a friend, Jerop, and, in jest, she tilts the ash container towards her friend. Jerop starts back and laughs.
>
> This simple sequence of events appears unsurprising to a Western observer. Gestures of mock aggression, particularly involving substances considered 'messy' or 'dirty', are recognisable indicators of a degree of friendship and intimacy. However, this particular sequence of events can only be understood with reference to a series of associations linked with the element of ash. The Endo say that only woman can remove ash from the hearth: a statement which confirms the identity of the woman with the home, hearth and cooking. It is, however, at the same time an implicit recognition of the destructive 'power' of ash – a power which derives from an association between ash and the socially and sexually destructive aspects of womanhood. Ash in its destructive capacity is harmful to men and to male interests. It would, therefore, be unthinkable for a man to remove ash from the hearth. When Chepkore 'threatens' her friend with the ash, the same destructive connotation is invoked. The destructive quality is compounded by the fact that ash is also associated with sterility. This link is made by the simple fact that if a girl wishes to refuse marriage, then she will cover herself in ash. The Endo say that this act signfies her desire for the 'death' and/or sterility of the proposed union.
>
> (Moore 1986: 117)

Moore goes on to describe further, positive, connotations of ash, including its linkage with female sexuality and creativity, and its significance within a picturing of the fertility of the clan as a whole. She finishes by drawing some theoretical conclusions from the fact that, for the Endo, ash can mean many different things:

> I have shown that, as a symbol, ash has distinct polysemic qualities and can be used to represent a number of different concepts and perceptions, in a variety of contexts. However, this multivocality is not the product of an inherent ambiguity of meaning which permits constant metaphorical expansion. The 'meaning' of ash cannot be reinterpreted in any particular context, just because it is so brimful of ambiguity that it at once means everything and nothing. The metaphorical extension of meaning is only possible on the basis of recognition of a more literal meaning. This literal or primary meaning gives access to a series of secondary meanings or significations.
>
> (Moore 1986: 118)

Here Moore is using her Endo material to enter a long-standing anthropological conversation regarding symbols, how they work, and what roles they play in social and cultural life. She deploys concepts – multivocality, polysemic, metaphorical, context – whose meanings have been honed through debate, and she puts forward her analysis as a contribution to this discussion. The distinctiveness of her position is clear to readers who are familiar with the ideas and theories that Moore is discussing.

At this stage – and all these features will be explored in greater depth as this book unfolds – we can contrast Moore's ethnography with the two novels above on a number of points. First, this particular ethnographic text is driven by explicit comparison: Moore tells the reader that, beyond typical Western assumptions, a further field of associations needs to be addressed and she lists them as items to be taken into account. Second, in the ethnography the process of contextualisation and interpretation is likewise opened up primarily for intellectual consideration rather than for intuitive-aesthetic appreciation as in the novels. We are, in effect, being asked to try out the feasibility of Moore's analysis and not merely of her description. By the same token, Moore presents us with evidence in that her account is being put forward as partial substantiation of an overall argument. Last, in her writing Moore responds to the theoretical viewpoints and ethnographic descriptions of other anthropologists and takes an authorial stance with regard to these. The result is that, as readers, we are not asked to suspend our disbelief in order to engage with the alternative world on offer here, as we are in *Altered Carbon* and *The Age of Innocence*. On the contrary, we will hold the ethnographer answerable for the factuality of what she says, even while we use our aesthetic and imaginative senses to enter her account. As we argue in the Conclusion, this basis in true knowledge is crucial but it is also only one aspect of ethnographic knowledge taken in the round. By providing a full account of an experiential life world, ethnography can also deliver a provocation to established ways of understanding what it means to be human. And beyond this, it can have a liberating role, freeing us to think outside our ingrained expectations concerning society, the self and human nature.

Shaping ethnography

Ethnography, then, is never just recollection: it is a reflection on, an examination of, and an argument about experience made from a particular standpoint, one that responds to questions which have their roots in the history of anthropological thinking. Because ethnographic writing involves a reshaping of experience in order to address anthropological conversations, all ethnographers need to consider the gap between the text and the lived reality that they try to explain. There is a tension between the chaos and diversity of experience and the transcription of that experience in a text, between life and analysis, that every author must deal with. Moreover, because ethnographers set out to make anthropological claims, because they draw on anthropological concepts and discussions, there is always a distance between the knowledge of experience put forward in ethnography and the local ways of knowing and making sense of the world that the ethnography is trying to explain. All ethnography, then, is moulded by the inevitability of dealing with the gaps between life and text, and between local and anthropological perspectives. And all ethnographers need to make decisions as to how to represent these gaps and how to bridge them.

In Chapter 4 we discuss how anthropologists transform experience into analysis by way of narrative, and how their narrations of the immediacy of everyday life are shaped by the need to deliver ethnographic knowledge and contribute to anthropological conversations. We discuss how contrasting narrative styles serve different ends in ethnographic texts, from highly uniform descriptions of collective life to fleeting notations of a personal response to particular situations. These varied kinds of account emerge from their authors' particular engagement with anthropology and its history, and as such are mediated by anthropological debates and concerns. Narratives of the immediate, thereby, function as the building blocks of anthropological claims to knowledge.

We go on to examine in Chapter 5 the processes through which, in ethnographic texts, experience becomes evidence and evidence is conjoined as argument. We show that ethnographic arguments, and hence ethnographies themselves, are always positioned relationally *vis-à-vis* others. The argument of an ethnography, which sometimes becomes condensed in the form of a key concept, is invariably presented with regard to the arguments of other anthropologists. The use of conceptual or jargon terminology in ethnographies has to be understood with this in mind: anthropologists use conceptual terminology in order to make their fieldwork experience relevant to a broader anthropological conversation.

It is, then, by drawing on anthropological debates, concepts, and analytical tools that writers of ethnography make sense of what they have seen and lived through in the field. No matter how close anthropological styles and aims may be to those of non-anthropologists, and in spite of the many undeniable continuities between ethnographic and other kinds of writing, it is this framing of ethnography within anthropological debate that sets it apart from other genres. The recognition that ethnographic texts always engage anthropology as a body of knowledge and discussion, that they take on their wider meaning as contributions to a broader anthropological conversation, is taken up in detail in Chapters 6, 7 and 8.

In Chapter 6 we explore the relationship between the ethnography and the broader context within which it is written, taking as our starting point the idea that the two, the text and its context, are in fact inseparable. Because ethnographies are written by individuals who are socially and culturally situated and engaged, the context is always part of the text's very fabric. We analyse the interweaving of text and context by examining the ways ethnographers present their writings for an assumed audience. We also examine how the intellectual climate at the time an ethnography is written shapes its production from fieldwork onwards, and finish by considering wider social, cultural and political milieus and their impact on the production of ethnographic texts.

Because ethnographers are social actors writing within particular sociocultural contexts and for specific audiences, ethnographic authorship has to be seen as relational. And indeed, in Chapter 7 we argue that it is out of constellations of relationships in the field and in the academy that writers emerge as authors – that is, as agents with the capacity to know, represent and analyse. And yet, in ethnographic texts this authorial agency is not always openly displayed or asserted: it is often hidden and disclaimed. So we trace the ambiguation of agency in ethnographic texts and argue that it works to reaffirm the authority of the author. Ultimately, the ethnographer as author will be answerable for their text as knowledge.

Chapter 8 places these issues again within a wider framework. Ethnographies exist as contributions to larger anthropological conversations. Certainly, for the anthropologist, their ethnography will exist as only one kind of utterance amongst others – lectures and tutorials, graduate supervisions and informal chats. Here we explore features of this anthropological dialogue. While the history of anthropology is often taught as the supplanting of one kind of theoretical **paradigm** by another, and anthropologists typically write as if this were the case, the actual circulation of anthropological knowledge is much less squarely cut. A richer understanding is gained by exploring the ethnography as the expression of relationships that an ethnographer has entered into at certain times and the pattern of intellectual commitment thereby formed. Rather than looking at the ethnography from the top down, as the product of a school of thought, we explore the continuing movement back and forth between personal intellectual commitment and the bigger and smaller conversations of anthropology.

How we wrote this book and how to use it

This book was written by two practising anthropologists/ethnographers: Paloma Gay y Blasco, whose primary research has been with and about Roma in Spain; and Huon Wardle, who has worked in and on urban Jamaica. One is of Spanish, the other of English background, both of us teach anthropology in Scotland. We mention this to emphasise the differing perspectives we inevitably bring to this book, and the degree to which these are blended in it. Just as ethnographic writing is always part of conversations, this book itself is the result of a dialogue between us in which we evaluate, not only the writings of others, but our own sense of ourselves as anthropologists and writers of ethnography. We have wanted to convey this feeling of an open-ended conversation through our organization of this book, particularly through the way key themes are introduced from one perspective and then re-explored within others as the text unfolds. It should be stated that we have not always agreed on what the priorities of ethnography or anthropology are, and this is still true even as we add the last words and corrections.

The core chapters in the book, 1 through to 8, are made up of excerpts from ethnographies published in English, in-depth commentary on these excerpts, and a cumulative argument derived from both. Here we are not primarily concerned with exposing the chronology of anthropological ideas, nor with putting forward another discussion of schools of thought in anthropology and their contrary perspectives on social life. Instead, and as we have already explained, we are looking for the common thematic and stylistic elements characteristic of ethnography. And so in each chapter we mix together texts of very varied theoretical orientations, written at different times by academics from diverse scholarly traditions.

Even though we have cast our net wide, we have inevitably and often fallen back on ethnographic selections that were familiar to us, written by anthropologists whose work we know well, sometimes made known to us by people who have taught us anthropology, or with whom we have collegial relationships. In other words, many of the ethnographies highlighted in this book were authored by figures we consider important or interesting given the pattern of our lives as professional anthropologists. Others we simply have found illustrate a point or a trend particularly well. We can hardly claim, then, that the ethnographic extracts we base our discussion on here are representative in some general or absolute sense; the amount of ethnography written by anthropologists and its thematic and historical diversity precludes that. Instead we have created a **heuristic** picture based partly on our response as readers, partly on our expectations as anthropologists and partly on our practice as ethnographers. Likewise, given a central strand of our argument, we cannot pretend that the scope of this book stands somehow outside the delimited pattern of social relationships characterising our lives as academics. And there are bound to be people who will primarily react to what is written here in terms of what has not been included. Our claims for it are based in its combination of perspectives, which, all told, provide a revised way of understanding ethnography.

This has consequences for how what we have written may best be put to use. Included here are extracts from many different ethnographies. Readers can simply browse these alongside the relevant analysis, perhaps using them as starting points for further research. Each of the eight main chapters also deals with a specific theme and exists in a relatively self-contained form. So, readers interested specifically in, say, comparison or ethnographic argument may wish to focus on those chapters (Chapters 1 and 5 respectively) taking in viewpoints on the same issues from other books and articles. *How to Read Ethnography* has, however, been written as an accumulation of perspectives and scales of vision, moving from the concerns that can be uncovered within an ethnography, to an understanding of the place of ethnographic knowledge within broader anthropological discussions.

Following each of the main eight chapters are eight long excerpts from ethnographic texts, accompanied by activities. These longer excerpts can be taken (and are worth taking) by themselves and of course can be studied for purposes outside the objectives of this book. However, they are primarily intended here as illustrative of the themes discussed in specific chapters and are aimed at providing a thought tool for testing out some of the ideas raised there. Before each selection we have described the ethnography in brief, and provided some questions that we feel will help the reader to focus their reading.

We have tried here to cut through tightly intertwined understandings of, and expectations concerning, ethnography, laying these out to view. Our goal with this book is thereby to give ethnography its due and its place. Ethnography is not the only way of understanding the human condition, though in the last century it has become a very important one. It is, however, worth understanding the specific parameters of ethnography as a kind of knowledge. And it is worth respecting this specificity.

Comparison

The ethnographic outlook

> Imagine yourself suddenly set down surrounded by all your gear, alone
> on a tropical beach close to a native village, while the launch or
> dinghy which has brought you sails away out of sight.
>
> (Malinowski 1978 [1922]: 4)

This is how Bronislaw Malinowski described the beginning of his fieldwork
among the Trobriand Islanders of Papua New Guinea, which he undertook
during the First World War. In this short sentence Malinowski tells us that
anthropological fieldwork is an adventure, an unusual event separated
from the humdrum of everyday life, characterised by the sense of heightened awareness of our surroundings we feel when arriving at an unknown
place. *Imagine yourself suddenly set down surrounded by all your gear,
alone*, not sure where to go or what to do next, hesitantly looking around,
struck by how different everything is from what you know well and yet
already searching for clues that will tell you what life is like in this alien
environment. At this point you cannot help but compare all you see, hear
and feel against the accumulated total of your previous experiences. Like
all humans, you make sense of what you learn through contrast and
comparison. Moreover, as an anthropologist, you are trained to search for
and interpret difference, that is, to compare (Gingrich and Fox 2002: 20).

This sense of separation from normal life that typifies anthropological
fieldwork is essential too to ethnographic writing. Writing ethnography
also revolves around carving times and spaces out of the continuity of
experience, as in Malinowski's statement above, and investing them with
special significance, showing them to reveal something important about
the quality of social life among a particular group. In the following excerpt
from her account of life in Gerai in Western Borneo, Christine Helliwell
reflects on the sense of unfamiliarity she first experienced when confronted
with the sounds of daily life in the longhouse:

> While living in the Gerai longhouse, I wrote many letters back to
> Australia in which I described myself as part of a 'community of voices'.

Although this perception was not, at the time, finding its way into my notebooks it was, nevertheless, the most apt way I could find the central quality of longhouse residence. Voices flow in a longhouse in a most extraordinary fashion; moving up and down its length in seeming monologue, they are, in fact, in continual dialogue with others. . . . Within the longhouse, voices create a powerful sense of community.

During my first two months in Gerai, while living with a household in its longhouse apartment, I was unable to understand why my hostess was constantly engaged in talk with no one. She would give long descriptions of things that had happened to her during the day, of work she had to do, of the state of her feelings and so on, all the while standing or sitting alone in her apartment. To a Westerner . . . her behaviour seemed eccentric, to say the least. It was only much later, on my second field trip, that I came to realise that the woman's apparent monologues had always had an audience, and that they were a way of affirming and recreating ties across apartments that made her a part of the longhouse community. In addition, I recognised with time that she had been responding to questions floating across apartment partitions that I, still bewildered and overwhelmed by the cacophony of sound that characterises longhouse life, had been unable to distinguish. . . . Even now the memory of such conversations fills me with emotion; it is they which most clearly define longhouse life for me, and which distinguish that life from the Australian one to which I have since returned.

(Helliwell 1996: 138–9)

Helliwell describes an almost physical feeling of disconcertedness when faced with the Dayak way of living in a house. Her description illustrates how comparing and contrasting what we find against what we already know or remember is an automatic or unavoidable process, an inescapable element of our encounter with others. More importantly, her account shows that it is by setting up her expectations as a Western woman against her actual experiences in the longhouse that Helliwell realises that there is something anthropologically significant about living in a Dayak house. If you reread the excerpt above, you will see that a series of factors help transform Helliwell's immediate and unavoidable awareness of difference into knowledge that is distinctively anthropological (as opposed to touristic, journalistic or literary for example). First, she deliberately explores the distance between herself and her informants drawing on a series of reflexive, comparative categories that are essential to anthropology: 'now' and 'then', 'here' and 'there', 'I' and 'them', 'fieldworker' and 'informant', 'ethnographer' and 'subject'. Second, she analyses her sense of difference between life in the West and in Gerai looking for patterns and regularities: it is the relationship between the idiosyncratic and the regular that Helliwell, like all writers of ethnography, is interested in. So she tells us that her friend's monologues were not eccentric as they seemed at first but rather a distinctive Dayak strategy of 'affirming and recreating the ties across apartments', and hence of creating a 'sense of community' in a Dayak way. Lastly, Helliwell recounts life in Gerai in such a way that she addresses – obliquely in this excerpt, directly elsewhere in her article – a well established anthropological concern with explaining the processes through which communal life is created.

Comparison between the self and 'the Other' lies at the core of Helliwell's article, and is also the axis on which all ethnographic writing revolves: all ethnographers use themselves or their knowledge of their own societies as their starting point for understanding and writing about others. How exactly they do this, however, varies enormously and reveals much about an author's theoretical and stylistic standpoint and about their aims and purposes in a particular piece. Thus Helliwell takes a very personal approach grounded in her own experience which she recounts in an autobiographical way. She talks about the 'first two months in Gerai', about her later return to the field, about feeling initially 'bewildered' and about how '(e)ventually I, too, was able to appreciate and make sense of this tapestry of sound, and to recognise individual voices as they wove together with others in the air' (1996: 139). Helliwell's focus on experience is in fact essential to her **phenomenological** approach to anthropology and to her argument in this article. Attending to how people live in and use Dayak houses, she explains, helps us to move beyond an unhelpful Western distinction between public and the private spheres of experience and, as a result, to understand better the making of Dayak communities.

By contrast with Helliwell's emphasis on her own self, other authors construct an idealised picture of Western culture or society which then they use as their baseline for comparison. In order to do this, they may turn to other academic accounts of life in the West or of Western ways of thinking produced either within anthropology or in other disciplines such as political science, sociology, or psychoanalysis. At the opposite end to Helliwell's on the continuum between personal experience and abstraction is Marilyn Strathern's account of folk Western notions about the relationship between persons and objects, which she uses as part of a comparative analysis of gender and property relations among two groups in the Highlands of Papua New Guinea. Among the Daulo there exist women-only savings- and exchange-groups and networks, but in Hagen only men are involved in these kinds of activities. Because in Hagen wealth is classified as male 'valuables', the money that women generate through their work is channelled into male collective enterprises. In as much as women hand over their money to men without recognition of the hard work that has gone into creating it, from a Western perspective women seem to be exploited. Women's labour appears to be unvalued and their rights in their produce unrecognised: indeed, Hagen has been analysed in these terms by other ethnographers. By contrast, Strathern asks

> What compels us to talk of labour being undervalued or of rights not recognised? Embedded in our notion of 'property' is that of 'rights' exercised over others or at the expense of others, constructs I have used myself. . . . But (this notion) carries certain assumptions. . . . As subjects people manipulate things; they may even cast others in the role of things insofar as they can hold rights in relation to these others. In the Western folk antithesis between treating somebody as 'a person' and 'as an object', a person is defined as an acting subject, recognisable by his or her rights, which should therefore include control over the products of labour. . . . Discussion of social relationships in terms of control over property, I would argue, is also a covert discussion of how far this or that category can act as 'persons'.
>
> This conflation may work for us, and for other cultures too. In the Highlands, however, ideas of personhood are not necessarily bound up with a subject-object dichotomy nor with its attendant issues of control.
>
> (Strathern 1984: 162, our brackets)

In Western thought, rights over property reflect the activity of a person in generating that property. To ignore someone's ownership rights is to treat that person not as an active subject but to manipulate them as if they were an inanimate object. The Daulo seem to recognise the link between women's work and the property rights generated by it; Hageners do not. What, though, if the problem here is not with the Hageners' exploitation of women's work, but the misapplied Western distinction between active subject and inanimate object?

Strathern's movement between the Daulo, the Hageners and the West is aimed at demonstrating how difficult it is to extrapolate conclusions from one case to another. Comparison in her article plays a dual role: it highlights what is specific about Melanesian ways of thinking, and also uncovers the premises or assumptions that underpin the anthropological analysis of gender relations in the area. These premises, as Strathern emphasises, depend on Western-specific ways of thinking about hierarchy and inequality, and do not account adequately for what happens either in Mount Hagen or among the Daulo.

Helliwell's and Strathern's excerpts give support to Mark Hobart's statement that comparison 'underpins – explicitly or implicitly – almost all the ways of talking about other cultures. Whether we are studying agriculture or food, narrative or myth, Divinity or witches, we are comparing our popular or technical categories with other people's' (1987: 22). In other words, writing ethnography is an act of communication, always between 'us' and 'them', often across multiple cross-cutting contexts: writers of ethnography move between themselves and the people they study, between the latter and their own society, and between these two and their 'second-hand' knowledge of yet other groups that they have gleaned from long-term exposure to the discipline. At the core of this multi-levelled exercise in translation lie not only observation, abstraction and the reaching of conclusions (for example, about community-making among the Dayak or hierarchy and inequality in Melanesia), but the creation and deployment of novel concepts (such as 'community', 'gender' or 'property relations'). These concepts act as bridges between very different ways of living in, perceiving, or talking about the world.

In the rest of this chapter we take as our starting point the central place that comparison occupies in the anthropological enterprise of apprehending and translating social and cultural difference. We will focus on (1) how to identify comparison in a text, even when no comparisons are at first sight present; (2) the roles that different kinds or styles of comparison play in ethnographic texts; and (3) how comparison contributes to the creation and revision of core anthropological concepts.

Summary points

1   Writing ethnography is an act of translation and hence of comparison, and ethnographers mediate or translate across multiple contexts or arenas.
2   All writers of ethnography use themselves and their knowledge of their own society as a starting point for understanding and representing others.
3   Some ethnographers make experiential comparisons, others rely on abstract representations or models.

Identifying comparison

Helliwell's and Strathern's excerpts in the previous section are explicitly comparative and easy to identify as such. Not only do these authors use comparison as a way of generating anthropological insights about particular groups, they also deliberately address the problems involved in cross-cultural translation. Unlike Helliwell and Strathern, however, many ethnographers choose not to write explicitly about themselves or their own societies or even about the comparative processes through which they arrive at their conclusions about a particular group. They often also refrain from talking about other societies as described by other anthropologists. This means that, at first sight, many ethnographies appear to involve only the ethnographer as author and the people he or she is portraying. In these ethnographies contrast and comparison are still present, but only obliquely, as a sub-text, a hidden script or an unacknowledged background that nonetheless shapes how descriptions and arguments are put together. This kind of implicit comparison is very well illustrated by Sharon Hutchison's depiction of father-child relations among the Nuer:

> Nuer were not of the opinion that a steady supply of sperm was necessary for the healthy growth of the foetus. Consequently, a man considered it his right to suspend sexual relations with his wife at any point he wished following conception. Although some men continued to have sexual relations with their wives during early pregnancy, most men abstained after about month five or six. Men also distanced themselves from the delivery process, which they considered to be repugnant and polluting and attended only in emergencies requiring immediate sacrificial or medical intervention. Indeed, a father would not so much as hold his newborn child for a period of a month or two after birth. Rather, several men confessed that they would feel awkward holding such a small child because they realised that they had nothing significant to offer 'since all the child wants is the breast'. The weaning taboo, which prohibited sexual contact with lactating women, further distanced the father from both mother and newborn child.
>
> (Hutchison 1996: 177)

At first sight this is not a comparative statement. Nowhere here or indeed in the nine-page long section on 'Blood-links: the mother-child relation', from which this excerpt is taken, does Hutchison explicitly refer to other groups or to her own experience of living in the West. And yet, the opening sentence ('Nuer were not of the opinion that a steady supply of sperm was necessary for the healthy growth of the foetus') would be meaningless outside a comparative framework: Why mention what the Nuer *do not* believe in, when, most likely, Hutchison's readers do not believe it either? What is the role of this, at first sight rather peculiar, negative statement? This sentence, like the rest of the excerpt, only makes full sense to an audience who know that there are many other groups (for example, in Papua New Guinea), who *do* consider that a steady supply of sperm is necessary for the growth of healthy foetuses and who link their beliefs to attitudes and taboos similar to the ones Hutchison outlines for the Nuer. She is thus not only describing the Nuer, but implicitly setting them up against these other groups, and both drawing from and adding to the pool of anthropological knowledge of ideologies of conception and personhood, and of the practices through which fathers in societies throughout the world ensure the wellbeing of young infants. Last, she is also writing with a series of longstanding anthropological debates in mind, and contributing to them. These are debates that go back at least to Malinowski's 1920s writings on the Trobrianders and that address issues as fundamental to the development of anthropological theory as the nature of kinship and the social meaning of fatherhood. In other words, this is not just a conversation between Hutchison and her readers, or between Hutchison, her readers and the Nuer: there are an undetermined number of other 'ghost' contributors taking part.

All ethnographic writing is comparative in the implicit sense illustrated by Hutchison's excerpt: all ethnographers write with knowledge of other groups and of key anthropological debates or discussions in mind, and this knowledge and disciplinary context unavoidably shape the questions ethnographers ask while in the field and when analysing their material, as well as how they present their descriptions and conclusions to the reader. Likewise reading ethnography is an exercise in comparison in this implicit sense: in all likelihood Hutchison's readers will have had access to other ethnographic descriptions, both of the Nuer and of other groups, and will be making their own connections, establishing their own contrasts and comparisons, whilst reading her account. Richard Fardon (1990a) emphasised the key role that anthropological literature as well as accounts produced in other disciplines have in shaping what ethnographers write. He challenged the notion that ethnographic writing is a dialogue which involves solely 'the self' (writer) and 'the Other' ('her' people) and instead explained how

> [E]thnographies are also reworked versions, inversions and revisions of previous accounts. . . . The authorship of ethnographic accounts and of fieldwork experience while individual is also enabled, *inter alia*, by the example of precedent writings in academic culture, by the presuppositions of a broader, usually western culture, and, crucially, by the terms on which members of a host culture allowed the ethnographer to know them.
>
> (Fardon 1990a: 22)

It is thus best to conceptualise ethnographic writing as a conversation that is inherently comparative and which takes place across times and places. As Gudeman and Rivera (1990) explain, this conversation involves several participants – the author, the people he or she is describing, other anthropologists past and present, as well as the latter's descriptions of the same or other groups. The notion of ethnography as conversation is essential to our argument in this book and we continue to develop it throughout the chapters that follow.

Summary points

1   All ethnographers approach the people they study with knowledge of other groups in mind.

2   Although comparison always shapes ethnographic texts it is often not explicit or visible: it may rather be implicit.
3   Ethnographic writing is akin to a conversation with many participants, rather than merely a dialogue between ethnographer and subjects.

Roles and aims of comparison

Ethnographic writing is inherently comparative because it always explains particular ways of living and thinking by reference to others. However, it should be clear by now that not all ethnographic texts are comparative in the same way: above we have dealt with, amongst others, experiential versus abstracted and implicit versus explicit styles of comparison. The next question we need to examine is, what roles do different kinds of comparison play in particular ethnographies? What can you learn about an author's aims and standpoint in a text by paying attention to their use of comparison? Below you will find an excerpt from Margaret Mead's (1963) [1935] classic, *Sex and Temperament in Three Primitive Societies*. The book is organised around the comparison of three neighbouring Papua New Guinea groups, with the Arapesh receiving a greater deal of space and attention than the Mundugumor and the Tchambuli. After describing sequentially and in detail the sex/gender system of each group, Mead concludes

> We have now considered in detail the approved personalities of each sex among three primitive peoples. We found the Arapesh – both men and women – displaying a personality that . . . we would call maternal in its parental aspects, and feminine in its sexual aspects. We found men, as well as women, trained to be co-operative, unaggressive, responsive to the needs and demands of others. . . . In marked contrast to these attitudes, we found among the Mundugumor that both men and women developed as ruthless, aggressive, positively sexed individuals, with the maternal cherishing aspects of personality to a minimum. Both men and women approximated to a personality type that we in our culture would find only in an undisciplined and very violent male. Neither the Arapesh nor the Mundugumor profit by a contrast between the sexes. . . . In the third tribe, the Tchambuli, we found a genuine reversal of the sex-attitudes of our own culture, with the woman the dominant, impersonal, managing partner, the man the less responsible and the emotionally dependent person. These three situations suggest, then, a very definite conclusion. If those temperamental attitudes which we have traditionally regarded as feminine – such as passivity, responsiveness, and a willingness to cherish children – can so easily be set up as the masculine pattern in one tribe, and in another be outlawed for the majority of women as well as for the majority of men, we no longer have any basis for regarding such

aspects of behaviour as sex-linked. . . . [M]any, if not all, of the personality traits which we have called masculine or feminine are as lightly linked to sex as are the clothing, the manners, and the form of head-dress that a society at a given period assigns to either sex.

(Mead 1963 [1935]: 279–80)

It is obvious from this short excerpt that it is on comparison between the three groups, and between the three groups and the West, that Mead's project in *Sex and Temperament* is built. It is only by drawing on the combined evidence provided by the 'three situations' that Mead can confront the Western assumption that men's and women's emotional attributes and social roles are linked to their biology and can argue instead that they are culturally specific and hence variable. She needs the Arapesh (the group she knew best), the Mundugumor and the Tchambuli equally, because each challenges Western gender stereotypes in a different way: while the Tchambuli display an almost direct inversion of Western sex roles, Arapesh men and women are uniformly maternal, and Mundugumor men and women uniformly aggressive. Together, they afford an extremely neat array of alternatives all found in close proximity to each other, 'conveniently within a hundred mile area' (1963: I). In a **positivistic** manner typical of the 1930s, Mead writes her ethnographic account as an exposition of scientific data: as she explains, 'the seemingly "too good to be true" pattern is actually a reflection of the form which lay in these three cultures themselves' (1963: I). That is, she is giving us observed facts and not readings. Her role is to elucidate and not to interpret and it is the data themselves that, Mead argues, lead her to a 'very definite conclusion' and push her into constructing a grand theory of gender roles.

Mead wants to debunk an extremely widespread and entrenched Western belief that explains social arrangements in terms of biological universals. The alternative she proposes, however, is equally universalising: if gender roles can vary so significantly in such a small area, and if none of the permutations that Mead uncovers corresponds to the Western pattern, then gendered temperaments and roles must be universally variable. Everywhere, she argues, gender roles and temperaments are determined by the social and cultural context, not by the body. An opposite comparative strategy can be distinguished in the following comments on Spanish Roma (or Gitanos) by Paloma Gay y Blasco. Here, comparison is not being used in the service of large-scale generalisation. Instead, Gay y Blasco compares in order to highlight distinctive and particular features of Spanish Gitanos *vis-à-vis* a group with whom they share some broad similarities:

How relevant attitudes towards the past are for understanding the particular processes through which groups of people come to act and also to see themselves as such has already been demonstrated by

Carsten's analysis of 'forgetting' among Malaysian islanders. Describing a reluctance to talk about the past reminiscent of these Gypsies, she (1995: 318) explains how 'forgetting is an important part of the creation of shared identity', because '[p]ieces of knowledge which are not passed on have a kind of negative significance in that they allow other images of shared identity in the present and the future to come to the fore'. 'Identity' works here as a short-hand to refer to both relatedness and links to place, and hence points more widely to key features of the social and political organization.

Whereas among Carsten's Malaysian islanders 'forgetting' emerged in conjunction with widespread migration at the edges of the Southeast Asian state (1995: 326ff.), as I discuss below among the Gitanos the main points of reference are economic, social and moral marginalisation, resistance to cultural and political assimilation and, in particular, radical intra-community fragmentation and dispersal. Moreover, whilst in the Malaysian case it is siblingship in the present and the future that works as the idiom through which attachment to place and to others is constructed (Carsten 1995: 323), in Jarana the sense that Gitanos share with each other who they are is premised on the current performances of individual persons and the extent to which these are seen to adhere to the *leyes Gitanas* (Gitano laws) – the highly reified Gitano gendered morality.

(Gay y Blasco 2001: 632–3)

In this article comparison has been used sparingly: the Malays do not appear again and other groups (mostly other Roma) do so even more briefly. The author does not aim at producing a universalising or broad-ranging theory of remembering and forgetting, but at elucidating in detail how the Gitanos of a small neighbourhood in Madrid deal with the past. The Malays have been chosen because the questions and analysis put forward by Carsten provide a useful point of departure for Gay y Blasco's own exegesis: their reluctance to talk about the past is 'reminiscent of the Gypsies' but its form, context and roots are very different. Gay y Blasco moves from describing in the first paragraph the similarities between the two groups and between Carsten's and her own interpretation, to focusing in the second paragraph on the disparities. The comparison allows her to escape the limitations of arguments specific to the Roma or Spain and to place her questions and ethnographic material within a broader field of debate. And the contrasts and disparities between the two groups open the way for the detailed ethnographic account that follows and that forms the core of the article. Comparison here is used, almost in passing, as a staging point for description and analysis. And by contrast with Mead's positivistic stress on the objectivity of the data, it is the mutual shaping of material and interpretation that is emphasised.

Summary points

1   Comparisons can play a variety of roles in a text.
2   Two common uses of comparison are to aid generalisation and to highlight difference.
3   Focusing on the role comparison plays in a text can tell you much about an author's aims and about their theoretical standpoint.

Comparison and the creation of ethnographic concepts

We have talked about ethnographic writing as a conversation between different parties: the ethnographer, the people they study, and other authors and texts. In this conversation, an anthropologist's awareness of earlier descriptions, both of 'their' people and others, shapes the questions they take to the field as well as their accounts and analyses. Out of a multitude of anthropological conversations of this kind, and hence of implicit and explicit comparison as described above, emerge through time what are known as ethnographic concepts. These are terms (such as **matrilineal** or **nomadic pastoralist**) that are used to organise ethnographic material according to criteria that this material shares with other examples. Ethnographic concepts are essential to the anthropological enterprise because they help us make other people's ideas and practices understandable in *distinctively anthropological* (as opposed to simply Western or personal) terms. These concepts are tools for explanation and translation, rather than mere descriptions of what we see 'out there'. As we will discuss in more depth in Chapters 2 and 5, ethnographic concepts emerge not just out of field observation, but also out of abstraction and analysis and are rooted, in particular, in processes of comparison.

Ethnographic concepts start off as analytical tools used in the exegesis of specific ethnographic problems and often grow out of debates linked to particular geographic regions: for instance, **matrifocality** was first developed to account for features of Caribbean family organisation but later took on a more general use cutting across regional boundaries. Other concepts such as **gatherer-hunters** have more general application to begin with. In both instances, particular concepts and particular groups of people often become so closely associated as to be mutually defined. Geographically bound concepts travel, because although they are generated out of the need to explain a social or cultural phenomenon in one place, they are then found useful or are challenged when applied to a different region or to the same group or phenomenon later in time (Fardon 1990). Obversely, when anthropologists discuss an apparently general concept such as 'gatherer-hunters', very often they have in mind geographically specific ethnographic knowledge about, say, the Hadza or the

Kwagiul. All these processes and movements involve implicit and explicit ethnographic comparison at the level of both description and analysis.

The idea of the **segmentary lineage** exemplifies the key role that comparison plays in the career of a concept as it moves from a geographically specific, to a more wide-ranging, usage. In *The Nuer* (1969) [1940], E. E. Evans-Pritchard described tribes that were divided politically into segments that were themselves divided into ever smaller sub-sections. The coherence of the tribal system depended on groups allying themselves in their political conflicts against other groups, thereby creating integration between segments and across levels. Evans-Pritchard's model, constructed to make sense of Nuer kinship and political organisation, was debated and refined through comparison with other societies, mostly in Africa but also elsewhere. Out of this debate emerged **lineage** theory, which dominated British social anthropology during the 1940s and 1950s and which guided the interpretation of societies in areas as wide apart as the Middle East, China and South America. By the mid-1960s the segmentary lineage model and its cross-cultural applicability was challenged and alternative theories came to dominate studies of kinship and politics. In the passage below, Maurice Freedman uses and critiques Evans-Pritchard's account in order to throw light on his Chinese material:

> Evans-Pritchard's classical work on the Nuer set anthropological minds working on systems of symmetrical segmentation and exercised a dominating influence on ideas about lineages. The Nuer was concerned with a society in which social homogeneity and the absence of political centralism could be shown to be associated with a kind of political and legal order made possible by the balancing of segments. . . . But the newer work on lineages in centralised political systems has led to an understanding of how, when power is exercised from the centre, a different conformation of segments appears. . . . The essential point about the Chinese case is that political and economic power, generated either within or outside the lineage itself, urges certain groups to differentiate themselves as segments and provides them with the material means to persist as separate entities through long periods of time.
>
> (Freedman 1966: 38–9)

So Freedman tells us that the Nuer model provides a useful starting point for analysis, but that it needs to be modified to incorporate both the Chinese centralised state and the social stratification of Chinese society. Nonetheless, today it is still easy to come across ethnographic accounts that depend very heavily on Evans-Pritchard's model of Nuer lineages. Below, we have placed an excerpt from *The Nuer* (on the left) side by side with an excerpt from Aud Talle's (1993: 92–4) account of Somali lineages, part of an article on female infibulation:

Within this segmentary structure of agnatic affiliation, the various groups are in opposition to each other but are at the same time joined by common descent, matrilateral ties and marriage relations. Traditionally, the lineage groups at a 'primary level' (of six to ten generations depth . . .) are exogamous; but practices vary considerably and there seems to be an overall trend towards marriages being contracted even within this group.

(Evans-Pritchard 1969 [1940]: 137–8)

The Somali population is divided into a few large patrilineal clans of several hundred thousand members each. Subgroups or smaller segments of these function as corporate groups economically and politically, whose internal relationships are set within an egalitarian, pastoral ideology. To the individual, these smaller groups are of more practical relevance than the clan . . .

(Talle 1993: 92, 94)

Talle does not quote Evans-Pritchard and does not refer to the Nuer. And yet, it is obvious that a very similar notion of the segmentary lineage guides her understanding of the kinship and political organisation of Somali society. This, in turn, provides the underpinnings for her analysis of female infibulation. Setting the two excerpts side by side points to a very widespread phenomenon in ethnographic writing: particular ways of conceptualising and representing ethnographic material become solidified in the anthropological imagination, and go on providing the argumentative starting point for texts produced long after the original models were questioned or discarded. In other words, through intradisciplinary debate involving comparison, anthropological knowledge becomes formalised and reified in the form of concepts that, albeit subject to revision and rejection, tend to be surprisingly resilient. One reason for this resilience is that, by grounding analysis in shared core concepts, new insights and ethnographic arenas can join the anthropological conversation. Thus, challenging debates about infibulation can be considered anthropologically because Somali ethnography can be recognised in terms of the segmentary lineage.

Summary points

1 Ethnographic concepts are the formalised result of ethnographic comparison often closely tied to a particular ethnographic region.
2 When applied in a new ethnographic locale, ethnographic concepts provide a basis for new comparisons.

3   Ethnographic concepts serve to stabilise anthropological knowledge, allowing new material and ideas to enter the anthropological conversation.

Concluding remarks

In this chapter we have explored the key role that comparison plays in the production of distinctively anthropological knowledge. We have shown that anthropologists always build portrayals of the people they study by comparison with themselves, with what they know about their own society, and also with other anthropological accounts of other peoples. Ethnographic comparisons can be explicit but are very often implicit, and can be used for diverse purposes. Above we have discussed comparison to aid generalisation and to highlight cultural distinctiveness, but you will come across other uses in the course of your studies.

We have emphasised that writing ethnography is not merely about describing what we encounter in the field, but about abstracting, interpreting and analysing. In this sense we would suggest that is not possible to separate the data that is being compared from the analytical constructs ethnographers have put together in order to interpret it and analyse it. Indeed, in this chapter we have presented the ethnographer's borrowings of, and challenges to, concepts as a process of comparison leading to new angles of vision on cultural experience. If it is not possible to separate ethnographic material from ethnographic interpretation, a key question arises. When anthropologists compare, what is it that we are comparing? Are we comparing realities 'out there'? Are societies and cultures 'objects', 'things' amenable to scientific investigation? Or are we comparing our own interpretations, the models we build to translate what we observe? In other words, what is the object of anthropological knowledge? These are the questions that we will deal with in Chapters 4 and 5, when we consider how anthropologists transform their extremely personal and idiosyncratic relations in the field into models and patterned accounts of the lives of other peoples.

Chapter 1 – activities

In the excerpt below from *The Giving Environment*, Nurit Bird-David analyses the understanding of the environment and the economic system of the Nayaka gatherer-hunters of South India, comparing them with those of neighbouring groups and of other gatherer-hunters. Read the excerpt carefully and respond to the following questions:

1   Give examples of how Bird-David uses explicit comparison to establish an argument about Nayaka exchange.

2   Can you distinguish implicit comparisons of the kind discussed in this chapter?
3   How does Bird-David connect the broader conceptual discussion at the beginning of her argument with her specific ethnography?
4   What similarities and differences might we draw between the comparative approach taken here and that taken by Mead in the example discussed in the chapter above?
5   By way of the comparisons she has made, what new concept is Bird David introducing to anthropological conversations?

Bird–David, N. (1990) 'The Giving Environment: another perspective on the economic system of gatherer-hunters', Current Anthropology 31(2): 189–96

For the past 25 years anthropologists have been interested in the relation between man and environment in reference especially to gathering and hunting societies. They have viewed these as 'societies which by definition share the characteristic that their members obtain their food and other requirements directly from wild natural sources' (Woodburn 1980: 95). Approaching the environments of these societies in terms of Western ecological criteria, they have examined how food collectors have adapted to them. For example, on discovering that giving without expecting an equivalent return is more common among food-gathering peoples than among any others and is a feature of most food-gathering societies, they have explained it is a way of reducing risk – a kind of 'collective insurance against natural fluctuations' . . . (Ingold 1980: 144) . . .

This account, however, invoking modern economic and ecological ideas, is unlikely to be acceptable to food-gathering people themselves, for their own ideas about their environments are summed up by /Xashe, a !Kung man from Mahopa: 'why should we plant, when there are so many mongongos in the world?' (Lee 1979: v). Furthermore, it makes little sense of these people's demand for generosity and practice of what has been recently described as demand sharing (Barnard and Woodburn 1988: 12; Peterson 1986: 1). Why do they make constant demands for sharing and not require people to produce more (cf. Barnard and Woodburn 1988: 11)? Why do they have this 'collective insurance against natural fluctuations' when they have little difficulty in obtaining their material requirements and desires, setting these well within their capacity to achieve and allowing themselves much leisure (Sahlins 1968: 85–9; 1972: 1–39), and when some of them have access to alternative sources from farming neighbours?

[. . .]

Because the traditional approach has reached its limits with respect to certain important issues, in this paper another perspective on gatherer-hunters' economic arrangements is explored. This perspective suggests that gatherer-hunters are distinguished from other peoples by their particular views of the environment and of themselves and, in relation to this, by a particular type of economy that has not previously been recognised. They view their environment as giving, and their economic system is characterised by modes of distribution and property relations that are constructed in terms of giving, as within a family, rather than in terms of reciprocity, as between kin.

This perspective is offered in reference to the south Indian gatherer-hunters called Nayaka, among whom I conducted fieldwork during 1978–79 and again in 1989, in three ways. First, Nayaka are contrasted with their cultivator neighbours, the Bette and Mullu Kurumba, who hunt and gather extensively. Second, a similarity is shown in passing between the Nayaka versus their neighbours and other forest gatherer-hunters (e.g. the Mbuti Pygmies and the Negrito Batek) versus their respective neighbours. Third, a hypothesis concerning gatherer-hunters in general is offered.

[...]

Giving environment and reciprocating environment

Nayaka differ considerably from Bette and Mullu Kurumba in the way in which they view their shared environment. The differences are reflected amongst other things in myriad everyday verbal expressions and actions, in kinship terms, and in ritual.

In general, whereas the Bette and Mullu Kurumba, like the Malay-speaking neighbours of the Batek Negritos and the Bantu-speaking neighbours of the Mbuti Pygmies, see themselves as living 'not in [the forest], or by it, only despite it ... opposing it with fear, mistrust and occasional hate' (Turnbull 1976 [1965]: 21), and attempt to 'carve out an island of culture in the sea of nature' (Endicott 1979: 53), the Nayaka, like the Mbuti and Batek, view themselves as living within the forest (Endicott 1979: 10; Mosko 1987). Nayaka look on the forest as they do on a mother or father. For them, it is not something 'out there' that responds mechanically or passively but like a parent; it provides food unconditionally to its children. Nayaka refer, for example, to the spirits that inhabit hills, rivers, and rocks in the forest and to the spirits of their immediate forefathers alike as *dod appa* ('big father') and *dod awa* ('big mother') and to themselves in that context as *maga*(n) ('son') and *maga(l)* ('daughter'). They believe that dod appa and dod awa look after them and provide for their needs. If Nayaka misbehave, as parents do these spirits inflict upon them aches and pains, removing them when they express regret and promise to mend their ways; they never punish by withholding food.

Similarly, the Mbuti Pygmies refer to the forest as giving 'food, shelter and clothing just like their parents' (Turnbull 1976 [1965]: 19). In a ritual performed by youth on their return to their forest camp after two months' participation in the initiation ceremony of their neighbours (a ceremony concerned with detaching children from their parents and attaching them to the ancestors), their first act is to sit on the laps of their mothers, showing 'that they still consider themselves as children in the forest world' (Turnbull 1976 [1965]: 65; cf. Mosko 1987).

This perception of the forest as ever-providing parent may be contrasted with the construction of nature as reciprocating ancestor. In this latter model, suggested for cultivator and cultivator-hunter groups in Africa (Gudeman 1986: ch. 5), nature is viewed as providing food in return for appropriate conduct. When the descendants make offerings and follow the customary code of behaviour: the ancestors bless them with success in their hunting and in cultivation. If the descendants fail to satisfy the ancestors, harvests and hunts fail.

The Bette Kurumba (like the Bemba and the Bisa of Africa) view nature as ancestors. Both Nayaka and Bette Kurumba worship the deity Hetaya, but each insists that its Hetaya is different from the Hetaya of the other (von Fürer-Haimendorf 1952: 28). For the Nayaka, Hetaya means 'birth-giver' (p. 24), that is, a parent. For the Bette Kurumba, Hetaya means 'the old man who died first' (p. 27), that is, an ancestor. Furthermore, Nayaka make offerings to their Hetaya upon gathering fruit, catching game, and collecting honey and after the harvest (p. 24), that is to say, in thanks for what Hetaya has given them. Bette Kurumba make offerings to their Hetaya at the time of the first sowing (p. 26) that is, in a bid to secure blessings for a successful harvest. Mullu Kurumba also pray to their gods before they go out hunting (Rooksby 1959: 361–2; Misra 1971: 58) and consider failure and success in hunting in terms of divine approbation or disapproval (Rooksby 1959: 373).

Nayaka's view of the forest as parental is reflected in their view of themselves a siblings. While the nuclear family is the primary social unit, all groupings beyond it are referred to as sonta, which means something like an aggregate of relatives as close as siblings. The people who live in one's own hamlet are one's sonta, and in other contexts so are all Nayaka who reside in the locality. Nayaka project themselves as members of a joint household in other metaphorical ways. They call all children in the local group maga(n) ('son') and maga(l) ('daughter') and all older people cikappa(n) ('little father') and cikawa(l) ('little mother'). (The Mbuti, incidentally, have a similar usage (Turnbull 1983: 33)). In general, Nayaka attach equal weight to ties on the mother's and on the father's side and can be broadly described as a bilateral society.

In contrast, Bette and Mullu Kurumba have groups aggregated about patrilines and, in some restricted context, matrilines. They conceptualize the constituent social groups as descendants of particular ancestors. Their view of nature as ancestors is in harmony with their view of their society as constituted of patrilineal exogamous clans, wherein elders and their descendants are tied to each other by complex obligations (Misra 1971: 41; Rooksby 1959: 238; von Fürer-Haimendorf 1952: 21, 26).

The ethnographic details above all point to the metaphor 'forest is parent' distinguishing the Nayaka from their neighbours, who hold the primary metaphor 'nature is ancestor'. In relation to the material dimension of the relation between people and the environment, 'forest is parent' entails a view of the environment as giving, like a parent, while 'nature is ancestor' entails a perception of the environment as reciprocating, like an ancestor. The local economic models that are centered around these two metaphors I sum up by the phrases 'giving environment' and 'reciprocating environment'. Drawing on these, it is possible to achieve a fresh perspective on various economic aspects of Nayaka life.

Giving and requests to be given

The metaphor 'forest is parent' and its entailment 'Nayaka are siblings' imply that food is shared as among siblings (especially within the same household). Nayaka give to each other, request from each other, expect to get what they ask for, and feel obliged to give what they are asked for. They do not give resources to each other in a calculated, foresighted fashion, with a view to receiving something in return, nor do they make claims for debts.

   [. . .]

The difference in distribution processes is strikingly seen in the way in which game is divided. Among Nayaka game distribution is a ceremonial act of giving which emphasises the importance of sharing and implies nothing about the any personal obligation of recipients towards the providers of the meat. Nayaka distribute game equally to all other Nayaka in the hamlet. The hunter who returns with game passes it on to another man, and this man, sometimes helped by the hunter, divides each part of the animal into small pieces. The butcher places the pieces in piles, each of which will be distributed to a household in the hamlet, the pile received being proportionate to the household's size. Children are given almost the same share as adults. People stand around the butcher while he works and help to assess the quality and volume of the growing piles. They constantly make suggestions as to where the butcher should place each piece of meat. Mere presence in the hamlet entitles a person to a share, and this includes the old and the infirm, who can never reciprocate. The hunter receives a share just like anyone else's, though he usually gets the skin (cf. the similar practice among the Batek [Endicott 1988: 117]).

In contrast to the Nayaka, the Mullu Kurumba share large game in a celebrational act of reciprocity that emphasises the importance of exact repayment. Hunters receive meat in return for their help in the hunt according to specific rules. For example, in one type of hunting, game distribution takes the following form: The person who detects the track of an animal and calls others to the hunt receives a foreleg. The one whose arrow or bullet first hits the animal receives the head, the flesh contained between the five ribs counted from the neck, the liver, and the other foreleg. The one who first approaches the dead animal gets half of the meat between the lungs and the pelvic bone, and so on, with a total of eleven categories of helpers (Misra 1971: 110).

In sum, Bette and Mullu Kurumba view nature as ancestors who reciprocate with them and themselves as kin, and they are linked with each other through acts of reciprocity and requests for reciprocity over time. Nayaka view the forest as a parent who gives them food and themselves as siblings, and they are engaged with each other through giving and requests to be given that do not obligate them on the morrow.

The environment that gives to all

The same themes come to the fore in questions of ownership of land. Nayaka believe that the forest as parent gives wild resources to all Nayaka, that is, that all

Nayaka are born with rights of direct personal access to land and unearned resources. For Nayaka, not even preparatory work entitles the labourer to an exclusive right over a resource in situ. For example, in order to fish, Nayaka block a section of the river, put poison in the water, and then catch the fish by hand. The preparatory work takes three to four hours, yet other people may catch the intoxicated fish in the water alongside those who did the work (the situation among the Batek is similar [Endicott 1988: 114–15]).

Nayaka recognise particular groupings that are associated with particular localities. These groupings are formed around families who are thought to be the descendants of those who first settled in the area, and the male descendant of the first family is called *modale* ('first, oldest'). The economic implications of this association can best be understood in relation to the metaphor 'forest is parent', which entails that land is not an object that can be owned but something that people can be closely associated with and related to. The particular relation 'parent', which is not necessarily the same as 'genitor', entails furthermore a relation that is not ascribed but practised, not closed but adoptable.

This relation is re-established once a year or at least once every few years, during a 24 hour festival. Throughout the day, the celebrants, who refer to themselves as *maga(n)* and *maga(l)* ('children'), and the spirits of local forefathers and the local forest, addressed as *dod appa* and *dod awa* ('big father' and 'big mother'), converse through the mediation of shamans. My taped records of such conversations on three separate occasions show that they are elaborations on the responsibility of the celebrants 'to follow the ways of the big-parents' – the spirits – and the responsibility of the latter 'to look after the children' – the celebrants. At the end of the day people and spirits share a meal that has been cooked on one hearth.

The *modale's* main responsibility is to organise the annual feast in his locality, but all Nayaka who live there and in the surrounding areas may and normally do contribute to the provisions and attend the feast. They all thus establish their rights to collect wild resources in the locality, for by their contribution they reaffirm their ties with the *modale* as siblings and thereby their attachment to the local forest as children. The *modale* occupies a pivotal point in the relation between particular groupings and particular localities, but he is neither an owner nor a boss; he is in this context the first, the eldest child and sibling.

Among the Mullu and Bette Kurumba, in contrast, land is associated with households, many of them composite. The *mupan*, the head of the composite household, allocates land to the heads of the constituent families, who later inherit it, establishing their direct association with it (Misra 1971: 74–5; von Furer-Haimendorf 1952: 29–30).

[. . .]

Gatherer-hunters and the giving environment

Drawing on the cases of Nayaka, Mbuti, and Batek, I have shown that gatherer-hunters, although they may not be strictly distinguished from other peoples (especially their neighbours) in terms of their bases of subsistence, do have a distinct economic system. It relates to the particular view of the environment that is entailed by their primary metaphor 'forest is parent'. The immediate question that arises is to what extent these groups represent gatherer-hunters in general, for they are all inhabitants of tropical and subtropical forests and all have an immediate-return system and trade extensively with their neighbours. I suspect that Nayaka (and Mbuti and Batek) present a variation on a theme that is characteristic of gatherer-hunters in general. I offer the hypothesis, which is being explored and will be assessed elsewhere, that gatherer-hunters share the characteristic that their members' views of the environment are centered around metaphors that commonly draw on primary kin relations, though not necessary just on the 'parent' relation. These metaphors entail a common view of the environment as giving, though in varied ways.

The further hypothesis then follows: that insofar as they commonly view the environment as giving, gatherers-hunters share core features of the economic system that I have discussed in reference to the Nayaka (varying in other respects, partly in relation to the varied family relations that constitute the cores of their local economic models). What they share most conspicuously is an economic system that is constructed in terms of giving. Even in its most institutionalized and formalised form, distribution amongst gatherer-hunters, for example, is, I suspect, still constructed in terms of giving. The !Kung *hxaro* (Wiessner 1977, 1982); for instance, although it is described as an exchange system, always includes family members (Wiessner 1982: 70); the transactions are normally conducted in the idiom of giving and requests to be given (see Draper 1978: 45); the objects of transactions are personal possessions (Wiessner 1982: 70–1); and these objects carry no mystical obligations of reciprocity (cf. Barnard and Woodburn 1988: 22).

Conclusions

My narrow argument has been that there is a strong case for distinguishing between gatherer-hunters and their neighbours, though the distinction in terms of mode of subsistence may not be clear-cut in that the former pursue cultivation of a sort and the latter pursue gathering and hunting. The difference between them relates to their distinct views of the environment that they share, which center around different metaphors: 'nature is parent' and 'nature is an ancestor'. The gatherer-hunters' economic system, constructed in terms of giving in relation to the metaphor 'forest is parent', implies that people have a strong ethic of sharing and at the same time practise demand sharing; they make demands on people to share but not to produce more.

The wider argument is this: whilst economic systems that are constructed about reciprocity have been discussed extensively by numerous anthropologists since Mauss (1954 [1911]), the kind of economic system that the Nayaka exhibit has not yet been recognised. On the whole (but see Price 1975), giving has not been analytically distinguished from reciprocity, and even Sahlins, for instance, regarded gatherer-hunters' 'sharing' as a kind of reciprocity – in fact, as a prime example of generalised reciprocity (1972: 193–4). There has been a great deal of work on the gift economy and the commodity economy and the relations between them. I argue that there is a need to explore a third kind of economy, which may be found universally, to varied extents and in varied realms, just as the other two are (see Appadurai 1986).

References

Appadurai, A. (ed.) (1986) *The Social Life of Things*, Cambridge: Cambridge University Press.

Barnard, A. and J. Woodburn (1988) 'Introduction', in *Hunters and Gatherers, vol. 2: property, power, and ideology*, eds T. Ingold, D. Riches and J. Woodburn, Oxford: Berg.

Draper, P. (1978) 'The Learning Environment for Aggression and Antisocial Behaviour among the !Kung (Kalahari Desert, Botswana, Africa)', in *Learning Non-aggression: the experience of non-literate societies*, ed. A. Montagu, Oxford: Oxford University Press.

Endicott, K. (1979) *Batek Negrito Religion: the world view and rituals of a hunting and gathering people of peninsular Malaysia*, Oxford: Clarendon Press.

——(1988) 'Property, Power, and Conflict among the Batek of Malaysia', in *Hunters and Gatherers, vol 2: property, power, and ideology*, eds T. Ingold, D. Riches and J. Woodburn, Oxford: Berg.

Gudeman, S. (1986) *Economics as Culture: models and metaphors of livelihood*, London: Routledge and Kegan Paul.

Ingold, T. (1980) *Hunters, Pastoralists and Ranchers*, Cambridge: Cambridge University Press.

Lee, R. B. (1979) *The !Kung San: men, women, and work in a foraging society*, New York: Cambridge University Press.

Mauss, M. (1954) [1911] *The Gift: forms and functions of exchange in archaic societies*, London: Cohen and West.

Misra, R. (1971) *Mullu-Kurumbas of Kappala*, Calcutta: Anthropological Survey of India.

Mosko, M. (1987) 'The Symbols of "Forest": a structural analysis of Mbuti culture and social organisation', *American Anthropologist* 89: 896–913.

Peterson, N. (1986) 'Reciprocity and the Demand for Generosity', paper presented at the 4th International Conference on Hunting and Gathering Societies, London, England.

Price, J. (1975) 'Sharing: the integration of intimate economies', *Anthropologia* 17: 3–27.

Rooksby, R. L. (1959) 'The Kurumbas of Malabar', Ph.D. dissertation, University of London.

Sahlins, M. (1968) 'Notes on the Original Affluent Society', in *Man the Hunter*, eds R. B. Lee and I. DeVore, Chicago: Aldine.

——(1972) *Stone Age Economics*, Chicago: Aldine.

Turnbull, C. M. (1976) [1965] *Wayward Servants: the two worlds of the African Pygmies*, Westport CT: Greenwood Press.

——(1983) *The Mbuti Pygmies: change and adaptation*, New York: Holt, Rinehart and Winston.

Von Fürer-Haimendorf, C. (1952) 'Ethnographic Notes on Some Communities of the Wynad', *Eastern Anthropologist* 6: 18–32.

Wiessner, P. (1977) '*Hxaro*: a regional system of reciprocity for reducing risk among the !Kung San', Ph.D. diss., University of Mich., Ann Arbor Mich.

——(1982) 'Risk, Reciprocity, and Social Influence on !Kung San Economics', in *Politics and history in band societies*, eds E. Leacock and R. Lee, Cambridge: Cambridge University Press.

Woodburn, J. (1980) 'Hunters and gatherers today and reconstruction of the past', in *Soviet and Western anthropology*, ed. E. Gellner, London: Duckworth.

——(1988) 'African Hunter-gatherer Social Organisation: is it best understood as a product of encapsulation?', in *Hunters and Gatherers, vol 1: history, evolution, and social change*, eds T. Ingold, D. Riches and J. Woodburn, Oxford: Berg.

People in context

In 1901 British colonial troops overran the West African kingdom of Asante, amalgamating it into the colony of Gold Coast (now Ghana). Twenty-six years later, Captain Robert S. Rattray, anthropologist and officer in the British administration in West Africa, published an ethnographic monograph, *Religion and Art in Ashanti*. Rattray was concerned to present a holistic account of Asante social life, including elements of tradition that had been suppressed under imperial rule just over a quarter of a century before. In the following passage of his monograph, Rattray begins to establish how the human sacrifices that had formerly occurred on the death of a king can be understood by placing oneself within the experiential world of the Asante.

> One aspect, however, of these funeral rites of the Ashante king has attracted much attention. This is the so-called 'blood-lust', and the consequent apparently indiscriminate slaughter of victims ... I am sure ... that my older friends, venerable greybearded folk who themselves were actors in these events, will not object to the English public knowing the facts, which will help, I hope, to free the Ashanti from the stigma of having been bloodthirsty and ferocious savages before we took over the government of their country. I am now aware that there were motives other than blood-lust and cruelty, which ought to be known and taken into account before we pass judgement on the scenes of slaughter which seem to have been inseparable from great national mourning. Europeans seem to have an innate fear of the unknown beyond the grave; this the psycho-analyst calls *thanatophobia*, which is aptly designated as our 'passionate, absorbing, almost bloodthirsty clinging to life'. It will not therefore be easy to persuade the average person that there was something underlying all this spilling of blood, that ought to excite, if not admiration, at any rate a feeling that should be remote from disgust or pious horror.
>
> (Rattray 1927: 104–5)

Rattray proceeds to present evidence that both the (now 'greybearded') executioners and those executed accepted the legitimacy of human sacrifice, because it fitted within their understandings of life, death and particularly the way in which the afterworld was organised. Not only did executioners feel the necessity of sacrificing 'victims', but 'victims' also went willingly to their deaths. Rattray asks that readers suspend judgement until they know more about the totality of Asante culture. He demands that his reader relinquishes crude stereotypes ('ferocious savages') and examines deeper aspects of his or her own emotional equilibrium ('*thanatophobia* . . . bloodthirsty clinging to life'). His argument depends on the claim that we cannot fully judge one cultural element without reference to the whole or wholes of which it is part. Even something as overtly extraordinary as human sacrifice can be understood if considered against the overall context of which it is an element. As we will discover as this chapter develops, this sense of culture or society as an overarching totality is by no means shared by all ethnographers. Nevertheless the process of placing-in-context that Rattray demonstrates here remains at the centre of ethnographic writing.

Whether it results from fieldwork in an African kingdom, amongst crack dealers in New York or in the company of bureaucrats in the World Bank, an ethnography is an exploration of a world of experience. The reader of ethnography is invariably being asked to displace some personal knowledge and expectations about their own world in order to understand what it is like to live within a quite different framework of knowing, behaving, and participating in events. A key dimension of ethnographic writing involves establishing the grounds on which the reader can suspend disbelief or even moral outrage about certain kinds of unfamiliar behaviours and understandings. There are two complementary movements that follow from this. One is broadly holistic, to create an appreciation of the overall cultural context or contexts within which particular details – a disturbing cultural practice, for instance – exist. The other is specific, to show how these details both throw light onto and are illuminated by this larger picture.

The world of the ethnography, then, is revealed through telling detail, and detail finds its significance within broader or narrower framings of context. We can explore this point further using Rhoda Metraux's (2000 [1953]) description from the 1950s of her attempts to build an analysis of certain kinds of statements made by Haitians and by herself in the Caribbean island of Haiti.

1   Gede is here. (Gede is the name of a God.)
2   Gede is dancing in the head of Ti-Jo. (Ti-Jo is a man.)
3   The milk mounted to her head and made her crazy. (Said of a woman believed to be insane.)

4   The mother gave her cold to her baby. (Said by myself, an American.)

The first and the third of these sentences are, for the Creole speaker, simple statements of fact. The first means that the god, Gede, has possessed a man or a woman and is now literally present, dancing and enjoying himself. The second sentence is a synecdochic phrasing of the same fact. The third sentence is an explanation of cause and effect: a nursing mother was so badly frightened or angered that the milk liter-ally mounted to her head and made her insane. The fourth sentence, an explanation which I offered to some Haitian peasants, was greeted with disbelief and anxious amusement; since it was incredible that any mother would make her own child sick . . .

The first three sentences and the response to the fourth provide clues to the Haitian Creole perception of the world. But the sentences can be interpreted . . . only if the analyst's initial point of reference is not his own system of perception but rather (his own system held in suspense) the context in which the Creole images occurred.

(Metraux 2000 [1953]: 389–90)

The ethnography as a complete text is built up by drawing together varied elements, situations, behaviours, statements and responses within an understanding of 'the context in which . . . [these] images occurred'. Metraux implies that there are many other 'clues' to Haitian culture that she could have worked with here in addition or instead of the ones selected. She realises that certain features that were unique to these state-ments (tone of voice, accompanying gestures, for example) have been lost as they have become elements within a broader interpretation of this 'context' ('Haitian Creole perception of the world'). She tells us that quite diverse kinds of cultural material, including an anthropologist's own inter-jections, can provide a point of entry which widens out into the contextualised appreciation of another experiential framework.

Anthropologist Roy Dilley remarks that the 'etymology of the word "context" suggests derivation from the Latin verb *texere*, "to weave". The related Latin verb *contexere* carries the meaning "to weave together", "to interweave", "to join together" or "to compose"' (1999: 4). The metaphor of context-creation as weaving is helpful. When we look at woven cloth, we recognise the distinct colours and shapes as a design, we see the cloth as a whole, but we probably pay less attention to the specific threads from which it is constructed. Ethnography is premised on the idea that contextu-alisation can provide us with an explanation of the scattered and sometimes puzzling details that make up human social experience by showing these as elements of the 'weave' of society or culture. We need to lay aside our immediate response and instead learn to appreciate the specific instance as it takes its place within a broader design. The creation of context is the process in which sociocultural specifics are ordered and combined within a more or less integrated larger picture. This mutual dependency between levels of analysis is sometimes referred to as the interpretive or hermeneutic circle (Hodge 1944: 27; Dilley 1999: 14–17). As we shall see, there are qualities of ethnography itself that complicate any move to close the circle of interpretation and contextualisation.

We will begin this chapter by exploring how the creation of an account of people in context involves identifying or differentiating the qualities that characterise their lives as social actors with particular positions and roles, different from those of others. The second section, then, discusses the movement between these levels and how they are integrated. While the interpretive integration of themes in the ethnography is essential to making meaning out of cultural elements, there is inevitably a balance between the inherent diversity of fieldwork experience and the move toward homogenising ethnographic experience in order to interpret it. The last section explores that balancing: all ethnographers contextualise, but what counts as context may vary substantially between ethnographies.

Summary points

1   Ethnography emphasises the provision of cultural context over immediate assessment of particular cultural details.
2   Since it gives an entry into an experiential world distinct from our own, ethnography implies certain kinds of suspension of judgement.
3   Detail in ethnography has meaning as a part within a broader interpretive framework or set of frameworks.

Differentiation as the basis for interpretation and explanation

In a short ethnographic analysis of fishermen, Barth (1966) outlines the special **role** of the 'netboss' on a Norwegian fishing vessel. He argues that the person who has the status of netboss is enabled to do and say things that he could not do and say if he held another position on the boat, for example, as an ordinary crew member. That is, he *differentiates* the specific features that characterise the 'netboss' in a situation where there are a range of activities underway:

> The netboss acts out a very different role [to the skipper]; he is spontaneous, argues and jokes, and gives evidence of inspired guesswork, flair and subtle sensing. He is recognized, and lives up to his reputation, as being unafraid of the consequences of his actions; he can brag about gambling and drinking bouts. All these dispositions are regarded

as qualifications for his skill in sensing the herring and daring to cast at the critical momentary optimum. At the same time his joking behaviour is a constant denial of any claim to authority on the bridge in challenge of the skipper and is in this respect in marked contrast to the institutionalized pattern of gross and continual cursing and assertion of authority on his part during the net-casting operation . . .

[I]n the development of the netboss, there is evidence that his scope was more limited, and his role-play less marked a generation ago. . . . At that time, being netboss . . . lacked the *prima donna* character depicted above. With increased capital investment, echo and asdic equipment, the present netboss emerged as a kind of logical opposite to the skipper – two roles which could formerly be combined.

(Barth 1966: 8–9)

The status of netboss, with its expectation of a charismatic ribald and foul-mouthed performance, is not written in stone: it has been generated, argues Barth, by broader changes in Norwegian fishing technology and practice. These changes have influenced the way two divergent kinds of **agency** have been established (control of the boat by the skipper versus control of fishing operations by the netboss). Clearly, Barth's ethnography has begun with diverse personal experiences during fieldwork on a fishing boat. In the process of understanding these experiences, the figure of the netboss has emerged from the general scene as ethnographically significant. By focusing on this figure, contextual features of the situation have become more clearly defined, the actions of the netboss outlining themselves sharply within a scenario in which other distinctive roles are in play. In particular, we have learnt about the specialised ways in which hierarchy, competitiveness, and egalitarianism are managed in the technologically complex situation of the fishing boat. And, by clarifying the institutionalised behaviour of the netboss, Barth is also able to set against this figure changes and continuities in Norwegian fishing. Here, then, the interpretation of ethnographic detail and wider context work in tandem, increasing our appreciation of both. The result is a concise but vivid entry into an ethnographic world in which different kinds of behaviour are comprehensible within a clear framing of context.

Identifying and differentiating the positioning of particular people as actors within a specific cultural context is fundamental to ethnography. But ethnographers also differentiate when analysing other social and cultural phenomena, such as characteristic ways of talking, moral principles shared by a group, or recognisable kinds of physical behaviour. By 'differentiation' we mean, then, the way certain features are distinguished and highlighted as having an integral importance within the overall interpretation, while other aspects are left in the background. Ethnographers concentrate on and isolate those specific features that bear on the question in hand, describing only those aspects of experience that they think are significant for understanding a practice, a belief or a people. These dimensions are given greater explanatory weight so that once again, detail throws light on context and vice-versa.

Although his focus is very different from Barth's, like him Paul Antze (1987) engages in differentiation in his study of an Alcoholics Anonymous group. Whereas Barth focused on the figure of the netboss in order to understand the combination of technology and social practice in Norwegian fishing, Antze wishes to throw light on American culture at large and, in particular, on how medical understandings are incorporated into everyday common sense. He does this by exploring the idea of being an alcoholic as a culturally specific role in American society, and how the organisation Alcoholics Anonymous has impressed its own meanings onto this role. In the following paragraph he examines the particular emphasis placed by Alcoholics Anonymous on the idea that alcoholism is a medical condition, a form of sickness:

> To be an alcoholic is first of all to be a sick person. What does this mean? Today the notion that alcoholism is a disease is so widely accepted that it seems wrong to accord the belief any special signifi-cance of an ethnographic nature. One tends to dismiss it as a simple reflection of popular medical knowledge. To do so, however, would be a serious mistake. The disease model of alcoholism was still far from being fashionable when AA first proclaimed its view in 1937. E. M. Jellinek (1960) has shown in fact that this perspective owes much of its current popularity to AA's own therapeutic success, and the resulting influence the group has acquired with both physicians and the public at large. Medical research, on the other hand, is still very far from confirming the appropriateness of a disease model in explaining the compulsive drinking syndrome.
>
> (Antze 1987: 155)

So taken-for-granted is the idea that alcoholism is a sickness, argues Antze, that it is difficult for Americans to think of 'the alcoholic' without thinking in medical terms; in terms of alcoholism as a disease that causes alcoholic behaviour. And the status 'alcoholic' in American society has taken its meaning from the pattern of ideas and activities in the Alcoholics Anonymous programme.

Antze's interpretation reminds us of the hermeneutic circle that carries the reader from the specific behaviour or role to wider levels of cultural meaning and back again. In the process he questions the unthinking accep-tance of the status 'alcoholic' as natural and obvious by probing and contextualising that idea. He shows that the significance of the role needs to be reconsidered as a type of feedback loop whose success is dependent on the willingness of participants to define their experiences in the terms put forward by the institution, Alcoholics Anonymous. In order to reach this level of interpretation, the idea of 'the alcoholic' has been carefully delineated as a distinctive cultural meaning with its own history and consequences within an overall framework of explanation.

Ethnographic writing works by throwing reality into contrast, by isolating and consolidating certain kinds of quality and by clarifying the borders around particular aspects of reality. Ethnographic interpretation and analysis, that is, revolves around contrastive differentiation. In this way we move from generalised comments about life on a Norwegian fishing boat to a description of a triangle of inter-communicating roles – netboss, skipper, crew – and from that to an explanation of certain kinds of behaviour. Or we take a status such as that of alcoholic and, by setting it against a reconsidered contextual background, we essentially reinterpret its meaning.

Summary points

1   The elaboration of the world of the ethnography involves processes of differentiation, for example the contrastive highlighting of characteristic roles or statuses.
2   The differentiation of social positionings within a context enables an appreciation of the kinds of social capacity or agency specific to these statuses.
3   The contrastive differentiation of particular aspects of ethnographic reality is what creates the basis for interpretation/explanation as opposed to simple description.

Individuals and groups – levels of integration in the ethnographic life world

We have seen that a key aim of ethnography is to show the lives of particular people contextualised and differentiated within an experiential life world. But the process of differentiation goes beyond demonstrating the characteristics and agency of a particular social status or role such as the netboss or the alcoholic. Forms of social personhood of these kinds themselves acquire further meaning once framed within an account of how people act within larger groupings and organisations. Having isolated the relevant features that make up a role, an activity, or a concept, there is then the process of showing the way social activity is integrated in particular situations and in the overall picture created by the ethnography.

A . . . [Thonga] debate or discussion is conducted in very different lines from those to which we are generally accustomed, nothing ever being put to the vote. The chief presides. A proposition is put forward in short sentences, generally interrogative, by one of the counsellors. The assembly listens in silence until the mover concludes with an energetic 'ahina', being the equivalent of 'That's all right'. . . . Another individual elaborates the matter further, saying: 'Did you not hear what he said? He said so and so.' This is the way of seconding the motion. The debate proceeds, and little by little, objections are brought forward and the assembly comes to a decision.

It often happens that the chief does not say a word; when he sees that the counsellors are agreed and if he has no objection, he merely shows his assent by nodding his head. So the decision is arrived at without any vote being taken. The voice of the majority has not been ascertained by any show of hands, but is generally perceived by intuition in a very remarkable way, and grave counsellors, who have been squatting in a circle throughout the discussion, jump to their feet and disperse, knowing perfectly well what has been decided.

(Junod 1962 [1912]: 434–5)

In this account of the South African Thonga from 1912, Henri Junod attempts to assess a subtle mode of arriving at agreement which seems to depend on 'intuition in a very remarkable way'. What is absent in this case is a distinction that is primary in Western ideas about group interactions; that the decision of a group is the bringing together of the individual perspectives of its participants and that, ideally, this is signalled by a showing of hands. Here, by contrast, the group appears to have subsumed the individual perspective and yet each participant is able to intuit what the consensus is. The implicit strand of comparison running through this passage – comparison between Western and Thonga group dynamics – recalls themes raised in Chapter 1. The value of Junod's description is in its reminder that the circle of contextualisation and interpretation in ethnography may well lead us away from familiar understandings of the relationship between individual and society and, in the process, undermine our implicit expectations about both. Either way, the ethnographer is engaged in articulating the kinds of group which provide context for the lives of the people in question, as the following description and analysis by William Foote Whyte (1943) also demonstrates.

The Nortons and the Italian Community Club functioned at different social levels, and they were organised upon fundamentally different bases. At the same time, they were representative of a large part of Cornerville society. Most of the generalisations to be made about the Nortons could be applied equally well to a number of other corner gangs . . . One evening in the fall of 1937 I was standing on Norton Street talking with Chick Morelli, Phil Principio, Fred Mackey and

Lou Danaro, when Frank Bonelly and Nutsy came along and took up a position next to us. I was standing between the two groups. I talked with Chick, Phil, Fred and Lou, and I turned to talk with Frank and Nutsy. There was no general conversation. . . . At no time did Chick or Phil communicate directly with Frank or Nutsy . . .

Although they had frequently seen one another on Norton Street, Chick and Phil and Nutsy and Frank belonged to social groups having no intimate contact with one another. Lou, Fred and I 'fitted' with both groups and could therefore serve as intermediaries . . .

The intermediaries could function only when the gap separating the two groups was sufficiently narrow. When the gap widened beyond a certain point, there were no longer men capable of bridging it.

(Whyte 1943: 94–6)

In this excerpt, Whyte analyses organisational features of the Italian street corner gangs he worked with in 1930s America. An intriguing feature of the account is the way in which he indicates each individual by name and sketches out the chance encounter bringing them together (see Chapter 4). At the same time, he makes clear that the interactions involved can only be understood contextually by reference to the larger groups that Chick, Nutsy and the others are part of. Chick Morelli and Nutsy do not talk to each other because they are invisibly divided from each other by what they perceive to be, and enact as if it were, a boundary. When, at the end of this excerpt, Whyte talks of the 'gap separating the two groups' he is using a spatial metaphor to describe the social 'distance' between people whose status depends on their being tied into different sub-groups within an neighbourhood-wide organisation. The metaphor works well because Nutsy and Frank do indeed place physical distance between themselves and Chick and Phil – the smaller situation mapping onto the larger. A principle purpose of ethnography, then, is not only to characterise clearly the capacities and activities of the people who are relevant to the life world of the ethnography, but, at the same time, to show the importance of the interconnections between these distinct kinds of people – the framework of integration. As a result, much analysis in ethnography is given over to explaining how the two, divisions and connections between kinds of people and activity, are created, maintained and challenged.

Summary points

1 Ethnography gives further contextual meaning to particular lives by demonstrating their integration within more inclusive social forms.
2 Ethnography shows how personal agency is not just dependent on the capacities inherent in roles or statuses – status responds to levels of organisation within the social whole.

3   Ethnographers aim to show how parts of the social pattern are not only differentiated but also how they are interconnected.

Diversity versus integration

Ethnography is built on fieldwork. The experience of fieldwork is inherently diverse in its potential. That is to say, the many human encounters the ethnographer is exposed to during fieldwork with their unlimited variety and subtlety of tone of voice, verbal imagery, behaviour and gesture, emotional interest and aversion, could lead to a Babel of different kinds of contextualisation and analysis. That it does not is because ethnographers tend to apply a relatively limited range of questions and concepts to their material – questions and concepts that have emerged during the development of the discipline and which have enduring significance. This does not solve the problem of diversity versus contextualisation, though, which every ethnographer has to meet pragmatically in their writing.

In his ethnography of life in an English village, Wanet, Nigel Rapport (1993) describes how his fieldwork experience led him to focus on the diversity of individual worldviews rather than on a shared cultural context. Villagers like Sid and Doris, two of his key informants, were characterised not by occupying recognisable roles within an established cultural framework but rather by their very distinctive personal ways of making meaning out of the world. Sid and Doris continually searched for relevance in what the other said, achieving, in the process, moments of 'partial overlapping'. But ultimately, they found significance within their own subjective 'loops' of reasoning made up of oft repeated phrasings and motifs, using these to integrate different 'selves' in different situations. He argues strongly against reducing these individuals to their ethnographic context so that the inherent diversity of personal character disappears as people become 'ideal speaker-actors' (1993: 180):

> [T]here were obviously large differences between some of the assumptions held by Doris and those held by Sid. Not only were their own loops of opinion highly diverse but between Doris's loops and Sid's there was only partial overlapping – they could not easily be said to be always living within the same commonsensical worlds. For another thing . . . I did not find I could tie Doris's or Sid's different selves and opinions to seemingly objectively or overtly different situations. Their diversity could not be explained in terms of regular work-roles as opposed to play . . . or talk between peers as opposed to that between people of unequal status.
>
> (Rapport 1993: 123)

Rapport views individual consciousness as having a holistic coherence that the wider cultural context cannot have. The fact that individual worldviews can only achieve partial overlap means that there is diversity built into human communication. Rapport has, of course, contextualised Sid and Doris by arguing that what defines their various utterances is their inherent individuality and the cycles of expression that sustain it within a village setting. He accepts that ethnography as an intellectual activity inevitably involves selecting and shaping the kind of information that the ethnographer is attempting to understand. And, in Rapport's analysis individuals give meaning to the larger cultural context. However, in a further turn of the circle of interpretation, he denies that individuality can be envisioned as deriving its full meaning from cultural context. To argue this would obliterate the specific kind of diversity he is attempting to bring to the fore.

To emphasise the point we are making here about the process of contextualisation versus the diversity of fieldwork experience, it is useful to compare Rapport's ethnography with one where similar issues are contextualised in a different way – in this case a discussion of Western versus Indian approaches to mental illness. In his example, Stanley Tambiah (1990) has deliberately excluded much of the diversity of immediate experience in order to compare two cultural contexts in which two ways of being a person operate. Noteworthy here is that what Rapport describes as inherent to human individuality – self-contained consciousness integrating many lesser selves – Tambiah understands as part of the wider context of Western thinking about selfhood.

> Let us say for the purposes of sharp comparison that there exists a certain *Western* theory of the mental illness . . . predicated on the notions of bounded self. . . . Humans exist as bounded beings, who are self-centered, and society is only a collection of individuals, and society exists to promote the interests of these individuals. Such individuals extend a limited number of drawbridges which connect them with the outside. . . . [T]herapy . . . concentrates on the 'internalized' and 'interiorized' processes of the self. Thus a self . . . is seen as splitting into multiple smaller selves or parts, which become cut off from one another, a kind of failure of internal communication . . .
>
> The Indian cosmos [by contrast] is seen as constituted of . . . flows . . . between communities and groups, between families, between persons, and finally within individuals. . . . The empirical individual is therefore seen as porous and open to outside influences all the time. . . . [T]herapy naturally addresses itself to . . . the orienting of the patient to having solidary relations with other significant persons. It does not, as Western therapy might do, attempt to raise the patient's level of internal consciousness, self-reflexivity, and memory of the past, nor to manipulate his feelings of guilt and shame in any conscious way.
>
> (Tambiah 1990: 133–4)

There is a striking similarity between what Rapport describes as the inherent diversity of individuality *vis-à-vis* cultural context and Tambiah's description of the *Western* psychological understanding of the individual. In Rapport's description, consciousness masters its various selves within overall loops of reasoning. There is only partial overlap between individual consciousnesses. In Tambiah's discussion, the Western view of the self is one in which there are a 'limited number of drawbridges' linking the 'interiorized' processes of self with those of others. The bounded self may become split into 'smaller selves or parts' requiring reintegration.

There is the basis of a controversy here that there is no space fully to develop. To what degree has the high-level approach taken by Tambiah lost sight of a fieldwork experience in which human diversities predominate (consider phrases such as 'for the purposes of sharp comparison')? To what extent may Rapport have imported a pre-contextualised 'Western' consensus about the meaning of individuality into his analysis, presenting it as if it was inherent in reality itself? The sense of diversity deriving from fieldwork experience is not, of course, limited to the diversity of individual consciousness but has potentially much more extensive ramifications. The broader point for the present discussion is that there cannot be any absolute distinction between diversity and context: the relationship depends on the questions the ethnography is trying to answer. Even those ethnographers who emphasise human diversity as a principle will need to weave certain kinds of context together in order to make that argument, will have to differentiate the features that constitute this diversity. The kind of compromise arrived at becomes a starting point for creative disciplinary debate.

Moreover, in written ethnography (as opposed to fieldwork experience itself) diversity of experience as lived exists always in a balance with processes of intellectual integration created by the need for a clear framing of anthropological questions. Take the following example from Monica Hunter's analysis from 1937 of relationships between Bantu farm workers and white farmers in South Africa:

> Relations between servants and employers vary considerably. On some farms the personal relationship is very friendly, servants and employers having known each other for long, and getting on well together. Sometimes the farmer takes an interest in his people's school, attending concerts, and occasionally contributing to the teacher's salary. Some farmer's wives make wedding cakes when a son or daughter of the farm marries; some are brought gifts of green maize and other fresh produce grown by their servants' wives. On other farms there is mutual irritation and fear. One employer told the writer that he never went near the servants' huts without a revolver; another said: 'I think sometimes that we are cutting our own throats by stopping beer

drinks. If they (Bantu servants) had them they would kill each other. As it is now they are increasing, and will come and kill us'.

(Hunter 1937: 397)

The cautiousness with which Hunter approaches her analysis ('some . . . sometimes . . . some. . . . On other farms . . . ') goes with the fact that she is approaching a new kind of subject matter. While, by the late 1930s, a substantial amount had been written on 'traditional' Bantu social life, relatively little had yet been published on the lives of people, displaced by colonialism, who were now working on European-owned farms. Hunter is careful not to assume that there is a common cultural framework that all the farms share. On the contrary, the farm situation holds the potential for profound mutual misunderstanding and potential violence. This does not stop her from drawing her essay to a close with a generalising statement: 'in spite of extreme poverty and severe restrictions upon his liberty the African farmhand yet manages to preserve his self-respect and to enjoy the company of his neighbours' (1937: 404). The emphasis on diversity here indirectly serves the purpose of demonstrating the additional uncertainty of life for Bantu workers within the context of poverty and loss of liberty.

We can explore the balancing of diversity and context further by looking at a recent investigation by Bruno Latour (1996) of French technology and technologists. Latour's ethnography, *Aramis, or the Love of Technology* is focused not on a single culture but on a project, the unfulfilled attempt during the 1980s to bring into being a new automated transport system, 'Aramis', for Paris. Latour examines Aramis by moving between the perspectives of the interested parties – technicians, politicians economists and others – each with their own priorities and imaginings of the future. He also includes Aramis' perspective as a fictional countervoice, destabilising the truth claims of the others. The style of presentation is playful and jerky, with radically divergent perspectives shown by the use of distinct typefaces and other visual/authorial tricks. Each group, though focused on an apparently shared project, vaunts its own framing of reality; at certain points attempting to displace the reality assertions of the others; at others, making compromises in order to sustain its own vision as the project moves toward realisation.

Was I obliged to leave reality behind in order to inject a bit of emotion and poetry into austere subjects? On the contrary, I wanted to come close enough to reality so that scientific worlds could become once again what they had been: possible worlds in conflict that move and shape one another. Did I have to take certain liberties with reality? None whatsoever. But I had to restore freedom to all the realities involved before any of them could succeed in unifying the others.

(Latour 1996: ix)

Rattray or Metraux, discussed at the beginning of this chapter, talk of a singular culture or experiential world and ask us to treat that world as having its own valid priorities. By contrast, Latour wishes to show inter-mingling realities and partial solutions. He describes diverse possible worlds converging within a single unrealised project. But perhaps the distinctness of approach is not as great as it seems. In Latour's work, the diversities of these 'scientific worlds' with their differently combined elements – including ideas about the future – are best understood once framed within the totality of the project that brings them together. Latour asks the reader to relativise the claims made by the occupants of one or other 'world', to avoid giving validity to one worldview, to pay attention to the competition between realities that brings these worlds together. In other words, here are standard ethnographic techniques answering a new question. Latour argues that the world versions of the different actors are malleable and emergent – poor performance will lead to failure in the everyday. Like Rapport's description of Sid and Doris' cycles of reasoning, he wishes to show how the worldviews of these interest groupings are sufficiently stable that they retain self-similarity over time. Diversity acts within particular contextualising constraints, and has a particular argu-mentative role in his analysis.

Summary points

1   The diversity of human experience as lived presents a challenge to the contextualisation and integration of the ethnography.
2   Integration and diversity are inevitably balanced in the attempt to address particular ethnographic questions.
3   The idea of diversity can be deployed within the ethnography to chal-lenge accepted ideas and to lay the groundwork for debates.

Concluding remarks

Like many other primitive peoples the Lele have no systematic theology, nor even any half-systematised body of doctrines through which their religion can be studied. As practised by them, it appears to be no more than a bewildering variety of prohibitions, falling on certain people all the time, or on everybody at certain times. For the people who obey them, there is presumably some context in which these prohibitions make sense. But what is intelligible in them is not extracted from the rituals and presented in the form of myths and doctrines. Like all ritual, they are symbolic, but their meaning must remain obscure to the student who confines his interest to the rites themselves. The clues lie in the everyday situations in which the same sets of symbols are used. . . . By learning the symbols in their secular context we can find a kind of backdoor approach to Lele religion. We need to appreciate their idea of propriety, their ideals of womanhood and manhood, and of personal cleanliness, in order to interpret their rites.

(Douglas 1975: 9)

Ethnography goes beyond pure description in its desire to interpret and explain. It is a precept of all ethnography that the 'bewildering variety' of human experience, to use Douglas' phrase, can be interpreted if the issues can be framed and contextualised appropriately. Douglas establishes the basis for her contextualisation in the same breath as her comments on the lack of system in, and the variability of, Lele religious ideas. In order to explain Lele prohibitions, the secular use of symbols must be distinguished from the ritual use, different roles such as manhood and womanhood must be differentiated, and an analysis that compares and integrates these distinct levels and roles must be created.

If Douglas manages the issue of diversity versus integration in one way, we have seen that other ethnographers have pursued other approaches. The process of setting in context, fundamental as it is to ethnography, does not provide of itself any unchallengeable technique for creating anthropological knowledge. Each ethnography instances a struggle between detail and generality and a continuous back-and-forward alternation between the two. To interpret is to take part in an overall circular movement in which each significant element emerges as evidence from the general diversity once it has been framed within a context; this context is meanwhile refined with regard to the evidence which supports it. Again, as we will see in the next chapters, there are many ways of establishing ethnographic experience as evidence relevant to particular debates.

Chapter 2 – activities

In the excerpt below from *Dance and the Body Politic in Northern Greece*, Jane Cowan contextualises and interprets a new development in provincial Greek social life, the *kafeteria*, for what it tells us about changing gender relations in the town of Sohos. *Kafeteries* (similar to British coffee bars) first appeared in Sohos in the late 1970s. Until then, Sohoians visited coffee shops or *kafenia*, which catered exclusively for men, or *zaharoplastia*, which sold sweet pastries and drinks, and were directed at women and families. There was a strong gendered division of public sociable space that related to Sohoians' ideas about masculinitiy and femininity. In the newer *kafeteries*, by contrast, unmarried women socialized with men. In this part of her book, Cowan first contextualises the *kafeteria* as a new kind of cultural space, then presents five voices commenting on the *kafe-

teria and changing gender ideas and relations. Each voice represents a distinctive perspective on women, their agency and their personhood. In this edited excerpt we have included two of these five voices. Read the excerpt and respond to the following questions:

1   Why is the *kafeteria* as an institution important for understanding gender relations in Sohos?
2   How does a sense of the context as a whole emerge from the detail Cowan presents in this excerpt?
3   What part does the demonstration of diversity play in Cowan's argument?
4   What kinds of different roles and forms of agency does Cowan highlight through the voices she presents?
5   Can you see elements of a 'hermeneutic circle' at work in Cowan's account? Pick out some examples.

Cowan, J. (1990) Dance and the Body Politic in Northern Greece, Princeton: Princeton University Press, 74–88.

When Women Drink Coffee in the Kafeteria

One of the Sohos' three *kafeteries* is patronized almost exclusively by the high-school crowd, and though this space is male territory during certain times of the day, groups of girls often congregate here after school. They socialize both among themselves and with their male classmates. The dominant clientele of the other two *kafeteries* is youths and men in their prime. Scattered among the dominant group on any weekday afternoon, however, are one or two clusters of girls. They are almost without exception unmarried. They buy juice, a soft drink, or a Nescafé® and talk for a while, joking and laughing among themselves and with other acquaintances they may see in the *kafeteria*. Yet they always appear conscious of the eyes of the men around them. They arrive and leave in groups of two or more, never alone.

As an establishment that does not fit neatly into the familiar classification of gender and space, the *kafeteria* is a topic of discussion among Sohoians. Such discourse ostensibly concerns the moral tone of the place, but its subtext revolves around the nature and moral capacities of the categories 'man' and, more especially, 'woman'. 'Is it a good thing, or not, for girls to pass their time in the *kafeteria*?' Sohoians disagree. Amid the polyphony of opinion is the ideological struggle to define gender. As I listened and sought to analyze what I heard, five voices, each of which articulated a distinct position on women and the *kafeteria*, stood out. Three upheld the dominant gender ideology, though for different reasons. The remaining two challenged it – one begrudgingly, the final one with conviction.

[...]

The wife of Stellios

Stellios believes that a woman would wish to go to the *kafeteria* for one reason only: to pursue a sexual adventure. (Note his explicit reference to a married woman, reinforced in his reference to the fate of children.) Stellios believes that this compelling attraction cannot be resisted. In his view, women demonstrate that they are good by repudiating such a place, indeed, by not wanting to be there at all, as he indicated in telling us about his wife's reaction:

Jane:	Tell me, did your wife come to the speech?
Stellios:	No, she heard about it – I was sleeping – and she told me about it. So I say, "Why don't you go with the neighborhood women?" She laughs. "To do what?"
Jane:	Why didn't she want to come?
Stellios:	"To do what?" She says. I say to her, "Maybe you have some kind of complaint about the situation at home?"
Amalia:	Ah bravo! Why do you think that just to come and listen means she must have some complaint?

His wife, Stellios tells us, ridicules not only the *kafeteria* and the speech on women's issues, but indeed, the entire implication that she is dissatisfied with her personal situation at all.

This is the third voice. In some sense it is fitting that though the voice is that of a woman, a wife, it is uttered by a man, for a married woman's voice is the feminine voice most invested in male discourse and most tongue-tied and ambivalent (see Irigaray 1974). Although we must not forget that this third voice is a quotation (presented by her husband) of a woman who is not present, the attitude her words convey is not unfamiliar. A married woman – when speaking to her husband or to other women – may well deny any interest in going to a woman's meeting or in going out for coffee. She may even mock those who do. Indeed, this is precisely what Anna, herself married, who had attended the Women's Day discussion and who joined our conversation briefly, described as befalling her and the woman, also married, with whom she came.

> We were walking down the road, on our way here, and some women asked us, 'Where are you going?' We were afraid to answer. 'We're going to the gathering,' we called out to them. 'Come on with us!' But as soon as we said this, they started to make fun of us, saying: 'What's so wrong with things that you want to go to this meeting? What will the men say?' Yet, in fact, when we were talking at home, our husbands had themselves said, 'Go, listen, see what happens.'

To which Amalia replied:

> It is the *women* who say, 'What are you going to do?' Many women are like this. They think that a woman who comes here to listen is not acting right. That she wants to go against her husband. That she is stupid.

Stellios' wife, the townswomen Anna encountered, and Amalia's 'many women,' all invoked through quotation rather than present to speak for themselves, seem to say something similar: that the desire to go out to the *kafeteria*, whether to attend a speech or to drink a cup of coffee, is illegitimate. It challenges the implicit contract in which the married woman exchanges her good behavior for her husband's protection and respect.

Yet is repudiation of an interest in going out (a moral act) equivalent to a lack of desire? Younger married women often complained to me that they felt bored and restricted and they wished there were places a woman could go to get out of the house. They admitted that there was now a much greater freedom to go out with their husbands to clubs or to attend the formal dances sponsored by local civic associations. Indeed, they knew that their expectations for entertainment were comparatively greater than were their mothers' and grandmothers'. Yet they felt that in terms of everyday socializing, their right to enjoy certain small pleasures was not acknowledged. Such women often disparagingly noted the taboos against their movement in public as indicative of the community's grinding conservatism. 'In other places,' they remarked, 'married women can go out for a cup of coffee, but here *Po po po!*' They thus indicated – but with some contempt – the disapproval that would greet them were they to act out this desire. In so doing, they marked the quality of the desire as unrealizable, fantastic, in relation to the world they inhabited.

[. . .]

Married women bear a particular burden with respect to both the reality and the public image of family unity. To the extent that a woman's identity is domestically defined, her sense of competence, self-worth, and satisfaction may be strongly tied to how well she carries out her domestic responsibilities, including the emotional labor of managing familial relationships. At the same time, the public perception of her family's situation may be as important to such a woman as her own assessment and experience of it. Married women have very real interests in preserving the image of a harmonious family, for inasmuch as the woman is perceived as responsible for the house, any family and marital problems reflect negatively on her. This can be a cause for real suffering. As women often repeated to me, 'People will say that "the woman is to blame."' Consequently, though some women may genuinely have no desire to go to the *kafeteria*, such a statement cannot necessarily be taken at face value. The denial of interest articulated in the third voice is contradicted by many women's private confessions that they would like to go but do not out of fear of possible consequences: gossip, censure, mockery, angry scenes at home, verbal or physical retaliation from a husband or parent-in-law, or problems for their family. This married woman's voice, coming from women as well as attributed to them, upholds the dominant gender ideology because, ironically, it is against her interests (as a wife, mother, and a lady of the community, a *kiria*) to assert her interests (as a woman, an autonomous person). And the woman's response to this intractable contradiction may involve not so much real acceptance but rather, a form of what Connolly calls 'anticipatory surrender' (1983: 91).

The first three voices, despite their complexities and ambivalences, reaffirm the validity of the segregation of unrelated men and women in public leisure space. Although the voices articulate this in part by assigning a moral quality to the *kafeteria* as a space, at the crux of their arguments is a particular conception of the female person and the meaning of her actions in the world. In this view, the female person actively 'taking her pleasure' in the *kafeteria* constitutes a metaphor for an aggressive pursuit of sex. Thus, Stellios speaks of her as the archetypal and insatiable temptress; Katina defines the girl as a sort of 'victim of pleasure'; and the third voice invokes the proper married woman as one who 'repudiates' this sort of pleasure.

[. . .]

Soula and Amalia

The fifth voice is constituted by those of the two girls, Soula and Amalia. Though they have commented throughout on others' interpretations, they share a distinct vision of what a female is, and this they articulate in both what they say and what they do. First, they go to the *kafeteria*. Amalia, an unusually sophisticated student in her last year of secondary school, and Soula, the daughter of parents who in local terms are rather progressive, are striking as individuals, but in coming to the *kafeteria* they are not unique. To be sure, girls constitute a small minority among the customers, and their presence remains controversial. But the townspeople identify the *kafeteries* as a meeting place for young people and they recognize, though they may disapprove, that girls increasingly spend time there.

Significantly, the use of the *kafeteria* by girls was viewed with relatively greater tolerance, grudging though it was, than that granted to married women. Their children's reality, parents admitted, was not the one they had known as children. They also recognized that girls have a comprehensible interest in seeing and being seen by young men. Being seen is, of course, an ambivalent process. Parents may quarrel with their daughters over what the latter 'have been seen' doing there – such as smoking or flirting – whether this is rumor or fact. But the consequences for an unmarried girl are less serious – from the parents' perspective – than for a married woman.

It is also clear that despite its indisputably sinful connotations, the *kafeteria* carries prestige as a symbol of modern sophistication and civilized luxury. In a community that prides itself on being a bit of a bustling metropolis in comparison with the small sleepy villages surrounding it (yet one that is always painfully aware of its backwardness compared with the modern city of Thessaloniki), the *kafeteries* are part of the Sohoians' claim to being progressive. This explains, at least in part, why I, even as a woman, was taken to one on my first day by Mihalis, and why the mayor, an urban-bred and progressive man, arranged for the Women's Day speech to be held there. It is a lever that the girls use, as well, when they want to legitimize their presence there.

The conception of female personhood that Soula and Amalia defend is informed, first and foremost, by their understanding of a feminist discourse that emerges in the media and in the political agenda of the two major left-wing parties. It is informed, too, by the social position they occupy by virtue of their age and gender. Neither Soula nor Amalia is committed, in terms of interests or obligations, to a nuclear family in the same way that a married woman is. They are thus freer to articulate an ideal of the female person as autonomous and self-determining. Soula is indignant about the incessant and, to her, unreasonable demands for moral accountability that girls face in the village. She laments that girls constantly censor their own actions because of fears of public disapproval:

> In the village, the one thing that everybody thinks about, whether it's to marry, to get engaged, to separate, or for the girl to do whatever, is *other people*. What will people say if I smoke, what will people say if I get engaged after I turn twenty, what will people say if I get engaged and break up, what will people say if I marry and get divorced, what will people say? They never say, what shall I do to make myself happy?

This complaint will sound familiar to anyone who has spent time in a Greek community of almost any size. But the assertion that a girl's own individual needs and desires ought to be recognized as legitimate is not typical.

Soula and Amalia insist that a woman should make decisions about how to act not on the basis of 'what people say' but on the basis of her own needs, desires, and interests. They see the concern with reputation as hypocritical and conformist, and they deplore the fact that women organize their lives in terms of it. They do not believe that a woman betrays her husband when she expresses an interest in a women's meeting or in a cup of coffee with her friends. Their sense of what they want in a relationship with a man – which is not necessarily what they think they can expect – is strikingly egalitarian and mutual compared with the hierarchical if complementary marriages they see around them. They draw upon the rhetoric of individualism to argue for a different conception of female personhood; they speak forcefully of a woman as a 'human being,' as a 'person.'

After Yorghos' bleak description of the antagonism between men and women and the supposedly 'natural' objectification of women, Soula responded. She argued that equality – a word they had been debating all afternoon – was not a matter of sameness, of identical physical capacities. Equality meant regarding the woman not as an object but as subject.

> But Yorghos, *this* is what we want to do. To make it so that a man doesn't look at a woman as an object no matter what place she walks into. Why should he see her as an object? We want to get to the level where the man looks at the woman as a person.

At this point, Amalia – shyly, tentatively – added her own remarkable assertion. She argued that a female person's desires and her right to act upon them in some way be allowed and be recognized as legitimate. After the men had smugly quipped to Soula that 'the woman also sees [that is, desires and objectifies] the man,' Amalia countered:

> You know what happens? Everybody says, it's men who tease girls, and boys who tease girls, but if a girl likes someone, for her to approach him first, he'll

think she's 'easy'. If she's known as easy, that's it, she's had it. And yet that guy, he might not ever make the first move.

Soula and Amalia reject the equation of female moral goodness with passivity even as they feel it impinge upon them. In embracing an alternative view of the female person, they redefine her power, her interests, her desires, and the meanings of her sexuality and her actions in the world. They enact their own independence by coming to the *kafeteria*, and then (provoked by me, the anthropologist) they use it as a forum to articulate and explore what 'woman as person' means. However weak and inchoate, their voices draw out and give tongue to the contradictions that the other voices only directly express.

Ambiguities of resistance

Important social meanings of gender and sexual difference emerge in the discourse surrounding everyday sociability and are reproduced through the practices it entails. Pleasurable and trivial, these practices articulate, mostly nonverbally, particular dominant notions about the female person, her sexuality, power, and moral capacities, which help to organize how she is perceived as a social actor. The speakers articulate verbally the implicit meanings that inform these practices.

In describing the objects and sites of consumption, Sohoians portray males and females as acting out 'natural' preferences for the sweet or the pungent and salty. Sohoians' use of gender as an adjective for objects in the material world (as in calling certain drinks 'manly' and 'womanly') further links these supposed preferences to constitutional differences. Consuming and enjoying sweets, a woman shows herself to be socialized as well as sociable. Acceding to the terms of this language of pleasure is not merely a performance of gender; it is a moral act, as well. Insofar as Sohoian explanations blur the natural with the moral, moreover, they veil the ways power and interests are at play in the very definitions of what males and females are and what they desire.

The emergence of a new leisure space, however, has provided a discursive space in which some townspeople are beginning to contest hegemonic ideas about women's nature and women's place. Sophisticated, European, and modern in its symbolic nuances, catering to a new kind of person as it engenders, in Williams' (1977: 128–35) striking phrase, a new 'structure of feeling,' the *kafeteria* confounds neat gender boundaries. As it conceptually bumps against seemingly rigid categories of gendered space, shock waves rumble through the everyday world.

The entrance by young women into previously male-controlled public leisure spaces is undeniably a potent symbolic act of protest against locally configured patriarchal restrictions. And yet it does not make sense to see the *kafeteria* as heralding a new era of liberated pleasures for women. Such a conclusion could only rest on the assumption that gender inequalities reside uniquely in societies with traditional forms of gender segregation. It would also imply that by adopting Western – what scholars and Sohoians alike have often called 'modern' – ways, the position of women is automatically improved.

The implications of such acts of resistance are more ambiguous. Though the *kafeteria* is a site where the traditional restrictions of the dominant local ideology of gender are being contested, it is hardly a revolutionary institution. On the contrary, and with no small irony, the recent appearance of *kafeteries* in Sohos exemplifies the hegemonic penetration of one Macedonian community by urban Greek and European institutions, symbols and forms of sociability that are displacing their indigenous counterparts. The *kafeteria* offers a new model of human 'being,' one stressing leisure, luxury, and males' and females' ostensibly equal opportunities to consume. In such a context, the subtle manifestations of gender inequality associated with the consumer society the *kafeteria* represents are easily obscured. The struggles of Sohoian girls and women to imagine and put into practice new definitions of female personhood will inevitably reflect, as they engage with, the contradictory dimensions of their everyday reality, with its competing discourses about gender and desire.

References

Connolly, W. (1983) *The Terms of Political Discourse*, Princeton NJ: Princeton Univeristy Press.

Irigaray, L. (1974) *Speculum de L'autre femme*, Paris: Minuit.

Williams, R. (1977) *Marxism and Literature*, Oxford: Oxford University Press.

Chapter 3

Relationships and meanings

Novelists, dramatists, filmmakers and songwriters, amongst others, share an interest in human relationships. And, of course, Western society as a whole is obsessed by 'relationships' as a quick glance at any glossy magazine will show. As Dorinne Kondo's account of a Japanese grandmother's recollections of marriage reminds us, the subtleties of relations between people are also the raw material out of which ethnography is woven:

> He was a real 'Meiji man', a tyrant, she claims. . . . Still she fulfilled her duties as a wife beautifully. . . . 'Every morning', she said, 'I would see him off at the door, help him on with his shoes, and bow down to him to say, "*Itte Irrasshaimase*" [God speed]'. In other words, she was the exemplary housewife. But as soon as he stepped out of the door, she would hiss, *sotto voce*, '*Kuso jiji!*' (Shitty old man!)
>
> (Kondo 1990: 133)

And yet, despite engaging examples such as this, students quite often express frustration with the cold and distant way in which professional anthropologists write about human relations. 'How can something as interesting as other peoples' lives become so uninteresting when anthropologists write about it?' is a commonly voiced complaint. This stems from the fact that anthropologists frequently discuss relationships in a highly abstract way. Consider the following description of some key relationships in the BaSotho social world:

> [W]hen the sister's son wishes to obtain a wife, he must go to his mother's brother to help him to find the necessary cattle and his uncle may give him some of the *ditsoa* cattle received at the marriage of his sister, or may even give him some of the *ditsoa* cattle from his own herd, trusting to being repaid from the *ditsoa* cattle to be received in the future from the marriage of a niece.
>
> (Radcliffe-Brown 1979: 26)

It is very easy, when we begin to read anthropology and encounter passages like this, to become lost in the welter of complicated relationships and local ideas so different to any we are familiar with. In addition, having watched films and read novels, our expectation is that we should gain some emotional or intuitive connection to the people involved: Who is this sister's son? What kind of character does he have? What does he feel about having to take cattle from his uncle? While ethnographies sometimes give us that kind of personal insight (the passage from Kondo above is a good example), very often they present us with knowledge more removed, less personal and immediate, than we might expect. And even the more person-alized and engaging accounts are often used to argue points that seem abstract or disconnected from everyday life. Learning to read ethnography involves gaining familiarity with abstract ways of thinking about relation-ships and what these modes of thought imply.

In this chapter we will look at (1) how ethnographers write about rela-tionships in terms of wider patterns or frameworks; (2) how the picture of relationships is built up and integrated within an ethnography; and (3) how the abstract pattern of relationships becomes a basis for comparison. And, because ethnographies are written from a very particular perspective, with a set of conventions and a specific audience in mind, we will also explore (4) the distance/difference between the ethnographer's analysis and lived experience.

How ethnographers write about relationships

In Chapter 2 we showed how ethnographers differentiate the specific social capacities of particular actors as part of a process of contextualisation in order to build up the picture of a life world. So, for instance Barth highlights the special role of the netboss within the Norwegian fishing vessel to demon-strate dynamic features of that social context. Now, an important further anthropological insight, one that is often difficult to grasp at first glance, is that any social role or social capacity is inherently relational in character. When they talk of social capacities as 'relational', anthropologists mean that these capacities or forms of **agency** cannot exist outside a framework of rela-tionships. For example, the role of the netboss cannot exist except *in relation to* the role of skipper and the role of the crew. The special capacities or agency of the netboss mean nothing outside the pattern of those relation-ships. Take the netboss out of that context and the individual in question ceases, actively at least, to *be* a netboss and instead takes on a new role, different capacities – a husband, a voter, a television viewer. It is part of the work of ethnography to elaborate the relational patterns regarding which kinds of **personhood** like the netboss can be interpreted or explained.

An essential premise of ethnography is that social life is relational, then. In the womb, from birth, and onwards, we are engaged in relationships which shape or influence our ability to act, relationships that form the groundwork for our current and future capacities. As social beings or social persons, we can be understood, from one anthropological angle at least, as adding up to the sum of our relationships. And herein lies an important difference between the ethnographer and the novelist. Whereas a novelist will typically focus our attention on an individual, their struggles and motivations, a similar starting point will take the ethnographer in an abstract direction. From the immediate features of a life or lives, an anthropologist will extract key elements and use them to understand and generalise social aspects of seemingly individual capacities and motivations. In the example that follows, anthropologist Pierre Bourdieu (1984) intends us to ignore the particularities of a group of people in a French café and instead consider how their interactions – their relationships with each other – have created a certain kind of relational situation:

> The café is not a place a man goes to for a drink but a place he goes in order to drink in company, where he can establish relationships of familiarity based on the suspension of the censorships, conventions and proprieties that prevail among strangers. . . . In the café free rein is given to the typically popular art of the joke – the art of seeing everything as a joke . . . also the art of making or playing jokes, often at the expense of the 'fat man'. He is always good for a laugh, because in the popular code, his fatness is more a picturesque peculiarity than a defect, and because the good nature he is presumed to have predisposes him to take it in good heart and see the funny side.
>
> (Bourdieu 1984: 183)

Bourdieu tells us that the café scene, in key ways, is the opposite of the life outside. The café is a place to create 'relationships of familiarity' between strangers, friendly connections not hemmed in by rules of politeness. One way of making these relations and showing them positively is through joking, especially 'the art of seeing everything as a joke'. The 'fat man' takes on an interesting role amidst this pattern as the focus for the individual humour of members of the group. His fatness achieves a special meaning in the café situation which it does not have elsewhere. This is because of the way relations in the café work in combination with a 'popular code' that says that fatness in the café is 'picturesque' not a 'defect'. That is, the kinds of relationship in which people are involved transform the meaning of statements and behaviours.

In this passage Bourdieu asks us to think beyond our initial reactions to a typical café scene ('what funny characters', 'what a bunch of bores'). Once more, unlike that of the novelist, Bourdieu's analysis focuses on the fat man or his jocular friends not as individuals but as particular kinds of agents in a pattern of interaction. The personhood of the 'fat man' is meaningful within this pattern but not outside it. Take him out of the relational framework of the café and his personhood changes. Indeed, all ethnographies are concerned with identifying elements of regularity in relationships, often by focusing on one kind of role framework that is explained in detail. Let us examine a classic example from 1927 – Bronislaw Malinowski's *Sex and Repression in Savage Society*. In the Trobriand islands, he tells us, the marriage relationship does not mean what it means to the typical Western European:

> To begin with, the husband is not regarded as the father of the children in the sense in which we use this word; physiologically he has nothing to do with their birth. ... Children in native belief, are inserted into the mother's womb as tiny spirits, generally by the agency of the spirit of a deceased kinswoman of the mother.
>
> (Malinowski 1927: 11)

Because Trobriand children are only physically and spiritually related to their mother and her people, being a father in the Trobriands is an entirely different role from being a father in, say, a middle-class family in England or France:

> The father is thus a beloved, benevolent friend, but not a recognized kinsman of the children. He is a stranger, having authority through his personal relations with the child, but not through his sociological position in the lineage.
>
> (Malinowski 1927: 10)

A Trobriand child has a friendly and loving relationship with her father, but is not physically or spiritually related to him. Instead, she is related to her mother and her mother's ancestors, and occupies a 'sociological position' in their lineage: it is from them that she inherits her formal position in society, including social, political and religious roles, and also property. So, what Malinowski is explaining to us is that the cultural meaning of one kind of Trobriand relationship, 'fatherhood', is best understood if we know how Trobrianders organise and think about other social relationships, especially lineage membership and inheritance. In particular, we need to know that Trobrianders think that some of our most important physical, spiritual and social attributes, the characteristics that make us who we are, are inherited through our mother and her line of maternal ancestors (her **matrilineage**) only.

What Bourdieu and Malinowski present us with is a kind of map of ways of relating in the French bar or the Trobriand village, which we can use to judge certain kinds of experiences of social life in France and New Guinea. So, underlying their ethnographic sketches of relationships in

France and in the Trobriands, are Bourdieu's and Malinowski's under-standings of wider patterns made up of different kinds of relationships between people. In both cases, the authors are telling us, in order to under-stand a specific relationship we have to have a picture of the wider organisation of relationships and vice-versa.

Recently, anthropologists have pointed to a **holographic** quality of how ethnographers, such as Malinowski, very often present relational patterns in their analyses and how these are then deployed in wider anthropological conversations (Strathern 1991; Rumsey 2004). If you cut a photograph into segments you will end up with parts of a whole image. A curious feature of a hologram is that, in contrast, if you cut it into pieces, the smaller sections will provide the same image as the larger one, but at a lower level of definition. The pattern of essential relationships in the smaller microcosm is the same as in the more detailed macrocosm. In Malinowski's picture of the father-child relationship we can see the micro-cosmic version of Trobriand society more broadly. When Trobriand society as a whole is discussed, we discover that this central relationship lies at the heart of the fuller discussion. Bourdieu's analysis depends on a somewhat different framework. The bar is 'the opposite' of life outside. It is a system within a system – dependent on the wider one, but distinctive in its patterning.

Summary points

1   Ethnographies seek to uncover the relational basis for central roles and social capacities.
2   Particular relationships are emphasised in order to indicate wider patterns.
3   By abstracting and highlighting relationships as the basis of wider patterns, ethnographers try to map out distinctive social worlds.

Building the picture of relationships according to key metaphors

We have seen here and in the last chapter that, for ethnographers, recog-nising and explaining the genuine diversity of human social experience paradoxically requires a particular kind of contextualising and formalising of social life as experienced. Some relationships, and some dimensions of those relationships, are emphasised at the expense of others. Indeed to attempt to account for every relationship would simply result in a compendium or a list (a list with no end or beginning). In turn, ethno-graphic analysis of relationships typically works in tandem with the exploration of key ideas, images and metaphors used by members of the group in question. Bourdieu's description of the bar presents us with a significant metaphor of this kind, the lovable fat man; the Baloma spirit that impregnates Trobriand women, another. These are, the ethnographer suggests, the crucial metaphors, ideas or images that give meaning to people's participation in these specific relational patterns.

As we have seen then, ethnographers tend to work with an abstracted and hence simplified image of a core nexus of relationships, what we call a relational pattern. This they distinguish from, and compare to, statements people make about their concrete experiences of relationships. In her ethnography of an English village, Elmdon, Marilyn Strathern (1981) shows how one of the most important metaphors defining Elmdon social life is the idea of the 'real Elmdoners'. The 'real Elmdoners' are, according to the villagers, those who belong to a limited number of families whose historical ties of blood are considered to lie at the 'core' of village life. They are contrasted with incomers to the village ('Londoners', 'weekenders' or 'strangers') whose claims to belong are not as 'real' because they lack these long-term ties of kinship thought of as ties of blood. Hence the title of her ethnography, *Kinship at the Core*. By exploring this image of a key relationship that differentiates the 'real Elmdoners' and the incomers Strathern creates a sense of the organisation of village relationships as a whole even though she cannot and does not aim to show in her ethnography all the relations of village life simultaneously at work.

Strathern argues that the villagers' description of certain families as being, historically, 'real' Elmdoners is built on a set of claims through which they explain the way they organise their present day social relationships. For this reason,

> it would be our mistake to take statements about antiquity in a literal way and not see them for what they are, a set of ideas. These ideas compromise a belief (certain families are connected with Elmdon), a classification (their members are real Elmdon people) and an interpretation of kinship (they are interrelated). The idiom is a historical one, and renders a present situation as the product of past events.
>
> (Strathern 1981: 16)

In this paragraph Strathern introduces three ideas. The claim made by villagers that there are 'real Elmdoners' who are inherently different to the others is based on (1) a way of *classifying* the world into two kinds of villager; (2) a *belief* that this way of classifying the world is justified by history; and (3) an *interpretation* of reality which holds that there is an authenticity to relationships formed through family, which in turn reinforces the historical worldview. Needless to say, this unpacking of what it means for the villagers to say that there are 'real' villagers (and others who are not) provides an interpretation of Elmdon relationships quite different to any the villagers themselves would put forward.

In fact, when we look at Elmdon through this analytical lens, Elmdoners' statements about who is a villager come to resemble quite closely Trobriand islanders' statements about what it means to be a father. Just as newcomers to Elmdon are not 'real villagers', because they have no authentic kinship links to the village, so Trobriand fathers have no physiological link to their children even though they are fathers in other senses. In the Elmdon case, Strathern is able to draw on parish records which suggest that certain families who are thought to be 'core' families arrived in the village after other families who do not have this distinction. This reinforces her argument that statements about 'real Elmdoners' cannot be taken at face value. Instead, they have to be understood with regard to the way social relationships, including relationships to do with class, status and privilege, are organised in Elmdon in the present. In the Trobriand example, Malinowski makes a strong case for connecting the Trobriand beliefs about procreation (Trobriand fathers have nothing to do physiologically with the birth of their children) to the way they organise economic and political relationships (people inherit only from maternal relatives and belong to their lineage). Only when we model the logic of Trobriand social relationships can we understand why, in Trobriand expressions of reality, the father has no biological role in the conception of his child. Beyond showing that there is a pattern to relationships, ethnographers aim also show that there is a logic to them too: that is to say, the way certain kinds of relationships are organised has consequences for the way other kinds of relationships work out. Showing, and giving insight into, aspects of this relational logic is a key task of ethnography. However, ethnographers do not always make it explicit that this is what they are trying to achieve.

What we discover in both cases is that local ideas about what is, or is not, seen to be 'real' can be shown fairly convincingly to agree with certain fundamental social relationships. In both cases, the ethnographer shows this by distinguishing between social relations and what people say about those relations. Instead of treating the statements of Trobrianders or Elmdoners 'in a literal way', Strathern and Malinowski separate the framework of relations in the abstract (as elucidated by the anthropologist) from the ways people talk concretely about relationships and positions. They then embark on a further process of integration.

This abstract picturing of relationships as forming a pattern or framework serves two purposes. It makes the diversity and complexity of lived experience intellectually manageable. The framework then acts as a **heuristic** device, a simplified model which should not be confused with lived reality itself but which helps us to understand it (we explore aspects of heuristic modelling in Chapter 5). This model provides a critical framework for ideas that might otherwise seem either absurd or which we might simply take for granted as literally true. So although Trobriand statements about paternity could seem to us to be plainly wrong, once we consider them with regard to core Trobriand relationships, these ideas are presented to the readers of the ethnography in terms of a relational logic. By contrast, we might treat Elmdon villagers' claims about 'real' inhabitants as literally true, not recognising the metaphor at their heart. Because their ideas are relatively familiar to us, we can easily lose sight of the fact that they are just as much predicated on a set of social relations as are the Trobrianders'. The creation of a social or cultural framework to explain crucial statements about reality or interpret behaviour is a primary element of the ethnographer's equipment.

Summary points

1   The ethnographer aims to grasp the key metaphors that give meaning to specific social relationships.
2   By analysing in combination relationships and key metaphors, ethnographers build up the sense of a relational logic particular to these people's lives.
3   This logic provides the basis for new ways of thinking about concepts, (such as paternity), or contexts (such as the village of Elmdon).

Abstracting relational pattern as a basis for comparison

In Chapter 1 we showed how comparison, both implicit and explicit, lies at the heart of the ethnographic enterprise. In this section we build on this notion as well as on the discussion of relational patterns above. Because the ethnography allows us to think about relationships in terms of their patterned qualities, it becomes a powerful tool for comparing human ways-of-being, and hence for generating and revising the concepts that enable comparison across distinct contexts. Exploring relational patterns and logics so as to examine our Western or anthropological ideas has been essential to ethnographic writing from its inception, as the following comments of W. H. R. Rivers from 1914 suggest. By concentrating on a particular relationship (between parents and children) on the island of Mota in Melanesia, Rivers throws Western ways of thinking about family relationships into stark relief:

> The practice of adopting the children of others is very frequent in the Banks islands and is accompanied by many interesting features. Of these features the most important is that a man who fulfils certain conditions may take the child of another in spite of the unwillingness of the parents to part with their offspring. The true parents may be unable to keep their own child if others want it and it is interesting in this connection that the word for adoption, ramo, seems to have primarily the meaning of 'snatch.' . . .

In . . . [Mota] island a newly born infant becomes the child of the man who pays the chief helper or midwife at the birth. The sister of the father settles who shall be the midwife, so that the father usually has priority of information on this point and as he will usually be on the spot . . . but if he has not the necessary money or if he is away, it may happen, and frequently does happen, that another may step in before him and become the 'father' of the child.

(Rivers 1914: 50)

Rivers showed that Mota adoption practices had major consequences for the way early twentieth-century anthropologists should analyse kinship relations, and in particular for their tendency to think of blood relationships or consanguinity as the defining feature of kinship connections. Just like Malinowski and Strathern in the sections above, he asked his readers to step outside their own taken-for-granted ways of thinking about relationships and to allow room for other possibilities so that new kinds of judgment about human social experience could be made. His analysis is important and interesting because he revealed that Mota islanders and Westerners shared the idea of kinship relatedness but not the essential meanings of this relatedness. Westerners found it difficult to account for adoption within their definition of kinship, whereas on Mota adoption was at the heart of the conceptualisation and practice of kinship (albeit that adoption for the Motese was synonymous with 'snatching' a child). Therefore the anthropological concept of kinship, as a term used to account for both Western and Mota island patterns, had to be redefined:

[L]et us now consider what we mean by kin and kinship. The first point to consider is whether these terms can be defined by means of blood-relationship or consanguinity. Among ourselves this usage would work perfectly well until we come to the practice of adoption, when it would break down; so, adoption being far more prevalent in many societies than among ourselves, this mode of defining kinship must be put on one side. In parts of Melanesia, for instance, the family to which a child belongs is not determined by the physiological act of birth, but depends on the performance of some social act; in one island the man who pays the midwife becomes the father of the child.

(Rivers 1924: 52)

Rivers assembled certain interactions on Mota in a pattern of kinship relationships and then drew together corresponding features of Western thinking about family relations. Next he compared the two logics of relatedness and revised the meaning of an anthropological concept, kinship, which at the time was being vigorously debated within the discipline. Again, Rivers' example exemplifies the **holographic** approach we indicated earlier. Notice once more how a minor example (adoption practices on a geographically microscopic island) becomes a relational pattern. This pattern can be demonstrated in terms of increased or reduced levels of contextual detail. It can then be used to challenge the way we use ideas in our discipline. By showing up features of a logic of relationships, ethnographers are able to redefine concepts and create the ground on which new ways of thinking about lived experience can emerge.

Yet another dimension of analysis is opened up if we examine the place the anthropologist himself occupies within the relational logic. Since he is present in the lived milieus he examines (and his presence shapes how social relationships happen and how they are understood by himself and by others) adding the ethnographer **reflexively** into the pattern can have significant effects on the judgments made in the ethnography. In *The Man Who Could Turn Into an Elephant*, Michael Jackson (1989) presents some aspects of the relational logic behind shape-shifting amongst the Kuranko of Sierra Leone through the lens of his relationship with Mohammed, an informant. He starts by telling us that the Kuranko belief that people can turn themselves into animals has its roots in the way they think about being a person, *morgoye*.

> The concept of morgoye, personhood, reflects the . . . priority of social relationships over individual identity. . . . [M]orgoye does not suggest notions of personal identity, distinctive individual character, or autonomous moral being . . .
> Being is not necessarily limited to human being. Thus, morgoye, though a quality of social being, is not necessarily or merely found in relationships between persons. Put another way, the field of social relationship may include ancestors, fetishes, bush spirits, a divine creator, and totemic animals as well as persons. Morgoye . . . may therefore be found in relations between people and ancestors, people and Allah, people and bush spirits, people and totemic animals, and so on.
>
> (Jackson 1989: 106)

To explain certain features of the Kuranko relational logic Jackson considers the relations Kuranko refer to when they talk about being a person. For a Kuranko, assessing who you are as a person means assessing the relationships you are involved in. And the field of Kuranko relationships includes a range of connections relatively unfamiliar to us. According to the Kuranko, in particular circumstances the relationship between a Kuranko person and his totemic animal can give rise to a transformation of the person, so that a man can turn into an elephant. However, having established that it is their view of personhood that allows the possibility of shape-shifting, Jackson also emphasises that the individual experiences of Kuranko people cannot be reduced to a Kuranko 'conventional wisdom'.

Instead, he tells us that 'lived experience is irreducible; no matter how fervently or uncritically Kuranko espouse conventional beliefs in shape-shifting, it is evident that different individuals construe the beliefs in different ways' (1989: 108).

Jackson next creates another level of analysis. He tells us that

> The manner in which understanding is constituted intersubjectively can be studied ethnographically by observing indigenous interaction, but it can also be studied reflexively by focusing on the ethnographic encounter itself. In this context the limits of understanding are often set by the human limitations of the ethnographer and defined as much by his or her social relationships in the field or within the anthropological profession as by the methodology used and the theory espoused.
>
> (Jackson 1989: 111)

In other words, Jackson argues that our sensitivity to social organisation and local ideas can be increased by analysing the anthropologist's own personal relationships in the field. He explains how, at one stage of his life, his informant Mohammed was keen to reveal to Jackson aspects of his ability to shape-shift into elephant form. Six years later, Mohammed is no longer interested in talking about these issues, the balance of his own interests within Kuranko society having changed. Jackson in turn connects Mohammed's personal evolution with his own and with the way in which their relationship has moved on. Jackson compares a simplified and abstract picture of Kuranko ideas about shape-shifting with the richness of experience as it is lived, and does it by setting his own personal relationship with a particular man against the abstract delineation of Kuranko conventional wisdom.

Jackson's reflexive exploration of his relationship with Mohammed allows him to mediate between depicting Kuranko society in relatively abstract, formalised terms, and a much more contingent view of human relations as made up of subjectively understood incidents and accidents. Put another way, Jackson shows that the ethnographer's knowledge about, and abstract patterning of, relationships is dependent on the relationships that exist between himself and the people he studies.

Summary points

1   Distinguishing arenas, modes, or levels of analysis is essential to establishing ethnographic knowledge.
2   Different arenas of analysis – focusing on relational logic, on cultural metaphor and worldview, or on reflexive dimensions, for instance – produce specific kinds of ethnographic knowledge.

3   Ethnography creates new insights by establishing new frameworks for knowledge, by re-mixing established arenas or levels, or by contrasting and comparing modes of ethnographic knowledge.

The difference between the ethnographer's analysis and reality

At this point we need to examine more closely the abstract nature of the patterns anthropologists build and against which they interpret and explain statements and behaviours. Clearly these frameworks exist primarily as images or sets of images in the mind of the ethnographer: they represent the bringing together of a series of judgments the ethnographer has made about the reality she has encountered. They are also arrived at through the application of concepts (such as 'lineage', 'sociological position', 'social relation', 'classification', 'belief', 'kinship') that have been developed through time within our discipline. As we have explained above and in Chapter 1, these concepts are the product of anthropologists working in conversation with each other and debating ideas whose meaning they share to a lesser or greater extent. Although of course, as in any intellectual enterprise, concepts and accounts are regularly challenged and fall into disuse or disrepute within specialised debates (see Chapter 8).

There are those who argue that everyday life has no pattern and hence ethnographic writing imposes a completely extraneous framework onto pattern-less social reality. This is not a completely naive objection, but it is naive nonetheless: anyone who truthfully believes that their social relationships are utterly pattern-free should, from a reasoned point of view, live in the utmost fear of what is going to happen to them next. In daily life relationships fulfil or challenge our expectations because we recognise regularity in them: common things are common, rare things rarely happen. Economist Amartya Sen (1976), for example, has shown that in drastic situations, such as famines, people will pursue standard notions of obligation and entitlement in relationships, often with disastrous results. In that sense a social relationship is always more a prediction than an actuality, more imaginary than real (Weber 1962).

In his ethnography, *Travesti*, Don Kulick (1998) investigates the lives of homosexually oriented men who alter their bodies to approximate to an ideal of femininity in Salvador city, Brazil. Malinowski would perhaps have laid emphasis on how *travestis* occupy a particular 'sociological position' in a society where being a man and being a women is organised in particular ways. We take up this difference of emphasis between American **cultural anthropology** and British and French **social anthropology** in Chapter 8. However, here Kulick analyses the relational patterns involved in being a *travesti* as demonstrating an 'unexpressed' cultural logic:

The ethnographic puzzle, as I see it, is to attend to the contextually situated interactions and attempt to make explicit the unexpressed logic that undergirds those interactions – the logic that makes it possible for people to act in certain taken-for-granted ways and say things to others and expect understanding. My goal in this book is to attempt this kind of analysis for travestis by focusing on their bodily and social practices and the words they use to talk about their lives. Rather than speak for the travestis, I try here as far as possible, to let travestis speak for themselves. So while the interpretations in this book are all mine, many of the words, in what follows, belong to them.

(Kulick 1998: 17–18)

Kulick separates the meanings and metaphors used by *travestis* from his own pattern analysis. Recognition of a set of patterns in his material leads him, in turn, to the identification of an 'undergirding' cultural logic. He sees it as his responsibility both to allow *travestis* to 'speak for themselves' and to put forward an analysis which is his own explication of the cultural logic and which is different from what *travestis* and other Brazilians say. In their ways of talking and behaving *travestis*, suggests Kulick, reflect a larger set of concerns about relations between men and women existing in Brazilian culture. However, rather than being simply an inversion of the dominant model of maleness, as they are often represented by Brazilians, the *travesti* condenses 'general ideas, representations, and practices of male and female' (1998: 9). It is this analysis of an underlying logic that makes it possible to understand how the *travesti* world view presents itself to a wider culture in such a way that the things *travestis* say and do have meaning for others.

Clearly, writers of ethnography impose their own patterns onto reality, but that does not mean that social life is itself without pattern. The social relationships you will read about are the meeting point between (1) people's ideas about how social life does or should develop, as told to and interpreted by the anthropologist; (2) the many examples of face-to-face social interaction anthropologists observe and participate in whilst in the field; and (3) their specialised ideas established historically in the dialogue we call anthropology.

Summary points

1   The relational logic presented in an ethnography is built on the ethnographer's work of recognising pattern in his ethnographic material.
2   The fact that people act on the basis that relationships are predictable and patterned provides a groundwork for the ethnographer's analysis of the relational logic.

3   Ethnographic analysis of social patterns is the connecting point between selectively explored aspects of relationships and anthropologically debated concepts.

Concluding remarks

At its best, ethnography can evoke a world of experience as engaging and as aesthetically complex as a good novel or even a film or a song. But we have suggested in this chapter that the main work of the ethnography has an added emphasis. Ethnography, in very varied ways, tries to approach the logic of social life from a perspective as close as possible to the way in which the people concerned themselves live it. In so doing, it transforms everyday relationships into social relations. This intellectual transformation depends on the fact that all human relationships contain within themselves elements of wider patterns: 'fatherhood' carries within itself a range of expectations deriving from a broader set of interrelationships. Relationships themselves also generate further patterns – once someone becomes a father, this creates new outspreading links between persons and new expectations.

Ethnography is inevitably selective about the kinds of relationship and key metaphors or ideas it distinguishes as relevant. Here it is the judgment of the ethnographer that counts and their work of highlighting, simplifying and abstracting. By focusing on local ideas to guide analysis, and by examining the interplay between these ideas and social interactions, the ethnographer attempts to build a picture of interaction that stresses the logical characteristics of social life in that context. We have seen here that ethnographic knowledge is established through the creation of levels of analysis which are the product of these processes of filtering and organising. The separation of levels of analysis – by emphasising a reflexive viewpoint the ethnographic material, for instance – enables the creation of new kinds of ethnographic knowledge and the development of new concepts. This, of course, says nothing about the *degree* of simplification, abstraction or **reification** that the lived situation undergoes in the ethnographer's written analysis, nor the *background* to the choices of focus and emphasis made by the ethnographer. These are issues that we explore in more detail in the latter part of this book.

Chapter 3 – activities

In this brief ethnographic outline of inter-village warfare in Papua New Guinea, Fortune explains features of the relational pattern of inter-village social life in order to establish aspects of the relational logic of warfare in this locality. He combines evocative description of the general situation with a more simplified and abstract delineation of the types of relationships involved. In particular, he shows that relationships centred on women are valued in a distinct way to those centred around men. These different evaluations are one determinant of the causes of war for people in this locality. Read the excerpt and respond to the following questions:

1   Give an example of the distinct ideas, images and metaphors orienting the way people think about male and female relationships in Fortune's account.
2   Which kinds of relationship count when war alliances are formed?
3   Which social relationships are considered 'neutral' in war? How does the principle of neutrality function?
4   Explore processes of ethnographic scene-setting or evocation in Fortune's article, as opposed to processes of simplification and abstraction.
5   How does a study of inter-clan relationships shed light on the issues of international law that Fortune raises in his final paragraph?

Fortune, R. (1947) 'The Rules of Relationship Behaviour in One Kind of Primitive Society', Man 47: 108–10.

The variety of central New Guinea warfare described here was observed in an area between longitudes 145° 30' and 146° east of Greenwich, at and about 6° 15' south latitude, in the year 1935. The tribesmen who maintained the wars in description had no name for their linguistic unit or tribe, and are accordingly distinguished here by their area of residence and not by name. They dwell on a part of an undulating plateau about six thousand feet above sea level, treeless except along river sides, and covered with grass which reaches about eight feet in height in the valleys, and about two or three feet on the hills.

Description of the warfare

The warfare observed took place between the independent and sovereign villages of Finintigu, Fukaminofi, Kumuina, Jehovi, Compari, Ikanofi and others situated near the Kamamentina river head-waters, between Ramu and Benabena airfields. It normally broke out, in each case observed, a few days after the natural death of an adult male in a village.

It may be observed that, when a woman died naturally in this area, other women present in the village began wailing. Men and women of other villages in the neighbourhood, hearing the keening for the dead, came in long lines over the hills and up and down the valleys, to take part in the wake. The host of the place that had lost the woman slaughtered many pigs to feast these visitors. When a man died naturally, however, an entirely different sequence took place. The women of the village where the death took place remained mute, while the men of the same place carried the corpse and hid it in the long grass outside the village. The men then held a divinatory ritual in the course of which they implored the earth-bound shade of the dead to give them a sign to indicate the identity of their enemies. At the same time they sent out reconnaissance parties with the mission of detecting a payment due at this time from those who desired this natural death to those who had been ready to procure it by evil magic, or soul-stealing, undertaken for a promise to pay; and sometimes the parties out on reconnaissance were successful in detecting such payments. In an instance noted the magicians and their village, having lost one man killed in ambush, were afraid and fled without accepting battle, shouting as they ran that they had indeed performed the magic for which they had been held to account, but that the accounts were square, since the life they had already taken by magic balanced the life lost in the ambush. Their imputed clients were of a different clan and village; two of their young men were ambushed and killed instantly, and a third died of his wound; they stood their ground and fought very gallantly in an unequal affair that culminated to their disadvantage.

After the ambushes which opened a war had taken place the aggressors notified their own women that they might now keen over their own man who had died a natural death a few days earlier; in this manner mobilization occurred somewhat dramatically, with women in one village wailing over a man dead in the course of nature, and in another village (or more often two others) in the neighbourhood, over men killed with arrows.

In this case, some of the aggressors maintained a stand upon a hill-top which overlooked the scene resulting from their earlier ambush and there maintained a derisive chorus of a shouted 'Oh! Ho! Oh! Ho! Oh! Ho!' above the wailing of the mourners of the slain. Below, the men of the village which had suffered in the ambush buried their dead with military honours. In the course of the funerals they paraded in column in the plaza of the village with a high-stepping knee action, and with their long-bows held vertically and centrally up and down the body; as they presented arms in this manner, they returned the shout 'Oh! Ho! Oh! Ho! Oh! Ho!' in reply to the similar shout of the aggressors, but, unlike them, did not maintain it for more than a few minutes.

War-parties of men from surrounding villages within a radius of a few square miles soon began to come into the villages of both principals in the issue that had been raised. Those bound for the village of the aggressors might be distinguished by the fact that they came with battle-dress of cassowary plumes worn in the hair; those bound for the village or villages who had suffered an ambush came without offensive battle-dress of cassowary plumes, but with clay daubed over the torso instead. When these latter entered the village they had come to help, their hosts immediately brought them warm water and washed the clay from their bodies for them. Thus each principal in the war received its allies with ceremony, and prepared a feast of pork and sweet potatoes and green beans for all comers to its aid before the serious fighting began. The women of each principal party secured their domestic pigs to poles, and slung their bags of shell-money on the poles in such a way that every two women might carry pigs and money in subsequent movements.

If the weather was fine and the grass dry, the attack opened with one party firing the grass downwind upon its opponents, following through the smoke and deploying

opposite the enemy fire at thirty to fifty yards range. The village huts of both principals were usually reached and burned on the first or second day. If it was wet it was
naturally more difficult to mount an offensive than in the dry season when the grass
might be burned. The war continued until one party was decisively routed. The
victors returned from the pursuit calling the number of their kills and the number of
pigs and bags of shell-money secured in plunder. Their women and children received
them back with a lyrical song, and soon afterwards men, women, and children of the
victors systematically plundered the gardens of their routed and conquered
enemies.

Relationship Behaviour in War

The villages of the upper Kamamentina river valley which act as independent
sovereigns in war are peopled by the men of parallel lineages on their fathers' sides,
and in the male line of descent, together with their families. A few elderly widows
who were born in the village may also be resident. Intermarriage between the sons
and daughters of families of the same village is prohibited and regarded as inces-
tuous. The daughters of the families of a village are normally betrothed to young
men of all villages in all directions within a five-or-six-mile radius from their home.
As any single village is connected with every other village in its neighbourhood by
the marriages of at least a few of its daughters, there are always some women
whose brothers and fathers are members of one principal party to a war, while their
husbands and fathers-in-law are members of the other principal party to the war.
These women are permitted neutral rights and have an acknowledged right to
immune passage between the lines. In case they are behind their brothers' lines
towards the climax of a war in which their brothers' party have the ascendancy, they
are expected to walk over to their husbands' lines to do their duty in carrying
domestic pigs and shell-money in the rout which may be expected soon to follow.

In one case I observed an instance of a woman taking such action towards dusk.
As it happened, she was probably killed in the sequel, for next morning early, when I
saw the victors returning from the pursuit, the principals were heatedly engaged in
informing the men of a village allied to their own that they would be the next
enemy on their list; the accused allies went off home immediately without waiting
for, or demanding, their share of the plunder, and when I enquired what the matter
in dispute was, I was informed that the men of the allied village had shot down a
married daughter of a family of their principal in the confusion and darkness.

In another case I saw women in the relationship under discussion come centrally
between the lines, emerging there with two seriously wounded men of one line
under their wing. The arrow-fire ceased immediately. They turned across the centre
of no-man's-land to the side lines and there left the wounded men with a large body
of friendly passives who were keeping an interested eye upon the development of
the war, and who sent the wounded men under escort to their own homes. They
also escorted four or five combatant members of their own village into the war
every morning, and out of the war every evening. They went to their own village

every evening to sleep in their own houses, while the burned-out and homeless principals and some others of their allies lay down to snatch no more than a few hours sleep where their lines were drawn. The women who had escorted the wounded men to safe keeping across the centre of the narrow no-man's-land returned by the same route to the lines from which they first emerged. They had the right to pass into the opposition lines if they so desired, but in the case in mention they were probably well aware that they had been partisan, and that if they went over they might be scolded for it.

A man was certainly expected to serve his village in action against his sister's husband or against his wife's brother. I observed one case of a newly wed lad of our acquaintance taking the field against his bride's folk a few days after his wedding. I also overheard two or three instances of men shouting that they had just made their sisters war-widows, or their wives brotherless. I never met a man abstaining from action with his village because his village was opposed to the village of his brothers-in-law. On the other hand I frequently met a man abstaining from action with his co-villagers in battle because they were fighting against the clan of which his mother was born, or against the clan into which his paternal aunt was married. In respect to brothers-in-law, we may say that they are not permitted neutral rights when their respective villages are in conflict.

A man is expected to aid his maternal uncle's son or his paternal aunt's son in war when he can. In order to bring aid such a man must command the agreement of the men's council of his village, who are responsible; if he secures it he may also secure the fighting alliance of all his co-villagers for the aid of his kinsmen through his mother or through his paternal aunt. In the above-mentioned instance of the body of friendly passives, for example, the combatant persons escorted into and out of the war daily by the passives were maternal uncles' sons and paternal aunts' sons of some members of one of the principal parties involved. (Incidentally, the caution of the passives in committing themselves no further than they did may possibly be explained by the circumstance that the principals to whom they gave limited aid were outnumbered ten to one. In the sequel, however, the passives had to take action to protect their own comparatively few combatant members; they fought a rearguard action when other resistance had collapsed, and gave the entire defeated party shelter in their own territory, at some distance from that of the victors.) The relationship between a man and his mother's brother's son – reciprocally viewed as that of a man and his father's sister's son – is the unique relationship upon which alliances in war are made to hinge in this area, if we except alliances made between villages simply for payment. When a man's village goes in battle against the village of his maternal uncle's son or of his paternal aunt's son, the relative, who is an ally in war or else nothing, becomes neutral. The rule here is reciprocal, so that when a man withdraws from one side his maternal uncle's son or his paternal aunt's son also withdraws from the other. The individual persons who were frequently met abstaining from action with their co-villagers in battle, when their co-villagers were in action against a mother's village of birth or a paternal aunt's village of marriage, were not generally withdrawn from action. In fact I noticed one such person particularly when he was in action on one occasion, and far removed from it on another, since it had then gone against his mother's village of birth.

The natives of this area maintain the custom whereby a brother or a father's brother's son becomes the husband of a brother's or a cousin's widow. It is of some interest to note that when the men of one party to a war make a sister of one or more of their number into a war-widow, they need not then attempt to alienate the widow from their enemy. I observed three cases bearing on this point. In two instances the sister and widow was sent across the lines to mourn for her husband whom her kinsmen had killed, and to remarry his surviving brother or cousin after a decent interval. In one instance the sister and widow was retained by her kinsmen and given in remarriage to an ally of the day instead of to the enemy of that time.

Conclusion

These, then, are the rules of relationship behaviour derived from events observed in one variety of primitive warfare. They include provisions special to the constitution of clans and to New Guinea society, as contrasted, for example, with the constitution of nations and with European society. They do not, incidentally, include any provision for the capture or for the proper treatment of prisoners of war. However, differences in type admitted, these rules are related in a general way to those which the French call *le droit des gens*, and which Bentham called international law. Inter-clan law, the subject of our present paper, is impartial enough, but severely limited in scope: the type of justice associated with international war is, in contrast, not equally impartial and not equally limited.

Chapter 4

Narrating the immediate

In 1974, Renato and Michelle Rosaldo returned to the Philippines, where four years earlier they had been carrying out fieldwork among the Ilongot, forest-dwelling shifting cultivators and headhunters. Their Ilongot friends were very keen to listen to the tapes of headhunting songs that the couple had recorded in the late 1960s. And yet,

> 'Insan – one of our most loyal friends, and an insistent pleader for the old recording – snapped brusquely at me to turn the tape off just moments after I had turned it on. No eyes explained themselves as I obeyed – and found myself confused, annoyed, perplexed, and even angry. . . . (L)ater in the day, when guests had gone and we were alone with people we considered our true friends and 'kin', I asked 'Insan to recall the morning's drama. I found I had spent the day with feelings of indignant hurt – and so demanded an account of his abrupt command. . . . I saw that 'Insan's eyes were red. Tukbaw, Renato's Ilongot 'brother', then broke into what was brittle silence, saying he could make things clear. He told us that it hurt to listen to a head-hunting celebration when people knew there would never be another. As he put it: 'The song pulls at us, drags our hearts, makes us think of our dead uncle'. And again: 'It would be different if I had accepted God, but I still am an Ilongot at heart; and when I hear the song, my heart aches as it does when I must look at unfinished bachelors whom I know I will never lead to take a head'. Then Wagat, Tukbaw's wife, said with her eyes that all my questions gave her pain, and told me: 'Leave off now, isn't that enough? Even I, a woman, cannot stand the way it feels inside my heart!'
>
> (M. Rosaldo 1980: 33)

'Indignant hurt', 'my heart aches', 'cannot stand' . . . Rosaldo's description, and her book as a whole, revolves around what is most immediate to any of us, our emotions and feelings. It is easy to imagine the two anthropologists awkwardly facing their friends/informants, unsure of their footing and what they have done to generate the anger of people they consider their 'kin'. It is also easy to picture 'Insan, Wagat and Tukbaw and their distress. What is harder is to empathise with is these Ilongots' regret at the demise of headhunting. And indeed, this short paragraph condenses the tension between familiarity and unfamiliarity that lies at the heart of the anthropological enterprise of translation and interpretation – a tension that Vincent Crapanzano has presented as a paradox. The ethnographer, he tells us, 'must render the foreign familiar and preserve its foreignness at one and the same time' (1986: 52); he 'has to make sense of the foreign' (*ibid.*) whilst not compromising its unfamiliarity. According to Crapanzano, anthropologists manage this by producing ethnographic *descriptions* that emphasise how different from us our informants are, and *interpretations* or analyses in terms that make sense of these acts both to us and to our readers. So for example, in the pages that follow the passage above, Rosaldo presents us with Ilongot sadness at the demise of headhunting, and accounts for it by reference to anthropological concepts of 'person', 'self' and 'society'.

Rosaldo's account and Crapanzano's insight point to the central but ambiguous role that familiarity plays in ethnographic writing. The notion of familiarity merges intimacy and understanding: it stands both for closeness in personal relationships and for thorough knowledge of something or someone. In anthropology this connection is taken for granted: what we know, we know because we were there. And yet, although familiarity and intimacy are the bases of all ethnographic knowledge, they do not imply total transparency, complete understanding of the people we are trying to comprehend and interpret for others. Hence Rosaldo also talks about her inability to understand the feelings and motivations of her 'kin', and about how this inability prompts her to dig deeper and question her own assumptions concerning the Ilongot, anthropology, and what the claim of knowing other people really means. And in fact anthropological narratives of intimacy often emphasise not just the similarities or the differences between the author/audience and the subjects of study, as Crapanzano indicates, but the very limits of our ability to know and represent others. So in the conclusion to her book Rosaldo tells us that '(i)nterpretation never really "gets inside" the native's "head"' (1980: 233).

In spite of these various caveats and reservations, it is fair to say that descriptions of familiarity and intimacy are the backbone of ethnographic writing. Ethnographers often write, as Rosaldo does above, about their own experiences of close interaction with a group of people, and about the insights this closeness generates. At other times the author herself is absent from the account, but nonetheless she pictures the minutiae of everyday life in such a way that her intimacy with the people she studies is clearly shown. In either case, it is this close contact that is seen to validate ethnographic descriptions and interpretations. As we will discuss at length in

Chapter 7, ethnography as a genre and as a epistemological enterprise
relies on the assumption that it is 'being there' (Geertz 1988) that enables
the anthropologist to turn her own experiences and recollections into
analytical descriptions of particular social worlds.

In this chapter we subsume familiarity and intimacy (between ethnographer and subjects but also among subjects themselves as described by the
anthropologist) under the notion of *immediacy*, the quality or condition of
being immediate, in direct relation or connexion with something or somebody else. Whereas intimacy and familiarity suggest to us ease in the
company of others and enjoyment of conviviality, as well as empathy and
knowledge, immediacy encompasses also discomfort, puzzlement and
confusion, annoyance, resentment, ignorance and conflict. So when
Rosaldo reveals to us her bewilderment ('What were they saying? Once
again, I was distressed by the great gap between my superficial understanding of their words and the significance their simplest phrases seemed
to carry' [1980: 33]), she too is narrating the immediate.

Accounts of the immediate are omnipresent in ethnographic writing and
include first-person narratives like the one above, and others where the
author removes herself from her text; descriptions of daily life, of cyclic
rituals, and of one-off events; transcripts of diaries or fieldnotes; transcripts of conversations with or among informants; and life-histories. In
spite of this wide variety of stylistic devices and of the broad diversity of
theoretical standpoints around which they are oriented, these accounts
share a focus on the nitty-gritty of human existence and a close attention
to detail in the way social life is portrayed. And, as we argue in this
chapter, underlying these diverse narratives is a common concern with
exploring the relationship between what is specific and occasional in
human relationships, and what is general and shared communally, between
the one-off and the pattern of social and cultural life. This concern, as we
have already discussed and will continue emphasising in Chapter 5, is one
of the core organisational themes that define anthropology as a particular
mode of questioning, knowing and representing the world.

Indeed, it is important to realise that narratives of the immediate in
ethnographic writing are underpinned by the will to create an anthropologically meaningful account of a life world. Moreover, these narratives are
positioned within specific fields of anthropological debate as well as within
the history of the discipline more broadly. Whereas Crapanzano argues
that these accounts provide the starting point for the ethnographer's interpretations and abstractions, we would say that the two are in fact
inseparable. Neither takes precedence or 'happens before' the other. That
is, through descriptions of the immediate writers attempt both to convey
the feel of life among a particular group and to address questions about
culture and society that have emerged out of anthropology's trajectory and
not only out of the history and concerns of their informants. And the

anthropologist's very experience in the field is shaped by their knowledge of the discipline. João de Pina-Cabral has argued that the ethnographer matches what he observes in the field 'against the accumulated knowledge of his discipline, and not against the worldview of the social group with which he most fully associates himself' (1992: 6).

Insofar as narratives of the immediate emerge out of and are shaped by anthropological enquiries and approaches they are not 'immediate' at all, but indeed 'mediated' by these and other concerns. It can be argued that, because these accounts are framed by the discipline and in fact wholly directed at making points of anthropological significance, they distance the reader from the everyday life they purport to describe. It might even be reasonable to see these narratives as smokescreens that separate us, both writers and readers, from experience. These descriptions of people and events work as the meeting point between the author's experiences and recollections, her interpretations of these events, and her orientation towards her discipline. And of course the reader approaches these accounts through the lens of her own experiences and recollections, as well as anthropological intuitions, standpoints and opinions.

Below we start by identifying two of the most widespread styles of narrating the immediate, focusing on the role that these types of account play in particular kinds of ethnographic texts. We concentrate on what an author's way of narrating the immediate reveals about her understanding of anthropology as a way of knowing the world: that is, on how the immediate is mediated by a particular writer's ideas about the nature of anthropological knowledge. Whereas some ethnographers use narratives of the immediate to support **positivistic** and/or **normative** explanations of society and culture, others concentrate on the partial and provisional character of ethnographic interpretations. We close the chapter by exploring the role that the immediate plays in the construction of anthropological arguments, examining in detail the layering and intertwining of ethnographic description and theoretical construct.

Summary points

1 Ethnographic writing has to sustain the tension between familiarity and unfamiliarity, between demonstrating the distinctiveness of people and events and translating them in terms that make sense to readers.
2 Narratives of the immediate are omnipresent in ethnographic writing, including a wide array of stylistic devices and strategies, but always emphasising the nitty-gritty of everyday life.
3 Narratives of the immediate emerge out of the author's engagement with anthropology, and as such are 'mediated'. They also mediate between experience, recollection, and argument.

Transience and recurrence

> 'Why do church bells ring so often?' I asked Nailza de Arruda soon after I had moved into a corner of her tiny mud-walled hut near the top of the Alto de Cruzeiro. It was the dry and blazing hot summer of 1964, the months following the military coup, and save for the rusty, clanging bells of Nossa Senhora das Dores Church, an eerie quiet had settled over the town. Beneath this quiet, however, were chaos and panic.
>
> 'It's nothing', replied Nailza, 'just another little angel gone to heaven.' Nailza had sent more than her share of little angels to heaven, and sometimes at night I could hear her engaged in a muffled, yet passionate, discourse with one of them: two-year-old Joana. Joana's photograph, taken as she lay eyes opened and propped up in her tiny cardboard coffin, hung on the wall next to the photo of Nailza and Ze Antonio taken on the day the couple had eloped a few years before . . .
>
> Nailza could barely remember the names of the other infants and babies who came and went in close succession. Some had died unnamed and had been hastily baptized in their coffins. Few lived more than a month or two. Only Joana, properly baptized in church at the close of her first year and placed under the protection of the powerful saint, Joan of Arc, had been expected to live. And Nailza had dangerously allowed herself to love the little girl. In addressing the dead child, Nailza's voice would range from tearful imploring to angry recrimination: 'Why did you leave me? Was your patron saint so greedy that she could not allow me one child on this earth?'
>
> (Scheper-Hughes 1992: 268–9; original italics)

This text, an excerpt from Nancy Scheper-Hughes ethnography of motherly love and motherly neglect among Brazilian slum dwellers, brims with immediacy. Like Rosaldo, Scheper-Hughes puts herself, and hence vicariously us also, at the centre of her account. Her question, 'Why do church bells ring so often?', is one that we can imagine ourselves asking, just as we can envisage lying awake at night waiting for Nailza to begin her sorrowful litany. Again like Rosaldo at the start of this chapter, Scheper-Hughes lays out her informants' feelings and her own, and calls also for our own emotional engagement and thus for our interest and curiosity. With just one word, 'Forebodings', the title of the section brings informants, writer and readers together: whose forebodings? Hers? Theirs? Ours? The three, however, are disjoined later on when the writer describes herself 'failing to understand the meaning of the social drama being played out before me for the first of many times that year' (1992: 271).

Scheper-Hughes draws on a series of key details to individualise the lives of the people in the passage and convey the uniqueness of their lives: the heat, the political instability after the coup, Nailza's discourse and her love for just one of her many deceased babies, the picture of the two-year-old in her coffin. The excerpt is followed by an equally immediate description of Scheper-Hughes' awakening to the ubiquity of infant death in Alto Do Cruzeiro: carrying a dead child in her arms, the apathy of the mother, the indifferent wake and procession to the cemetery. This emphasis on the idiosyncracy of each person and event opens the way for the question around which the chapter and the whole ethnography revolves: 'What had made death so small, of such little account on the Alto Do Cruzeiro?' (1992: 272–80).

Like all writers of ethnography, Scheper-Hughes grounds her analysis of a widespread social phenomenon (one that she would observe 'many times' during her research) on the individuality of persons and the evanescence of occurrences. After all, it is fieldwork, a unique collection of interactions and relationships, that is the source of anthropological knowledge. But, unlike many other ethnographers, Scheper-Hughes goes out of her way to make explicit and visible in her writing this connection between a specific set of social relations in the field (such her own with Nailza) and her representation of the social and cultural context within which these relationships developed. So her book revolves around a succession of descriptions of *protagonistic* and *transient* immediacy very much like the one above, in which both herself and other named individuals occupy a central role. These are then used to reflect on motherhood among Brazilian slum dwellers and also among the middle classes and in the discourses of Western academics. And so to a most immediate question – 'What finally can be said of these Alto women?'(Scheper-Hughes 1992: 400) – Scheper-Hughes responds with a challenge to grand theory:

> Contemporary theories of maternal sentiment – of mother love as we know and understand it – are the product of a very specific historical context. . . . My argument is a materialist one: mother love as defined in the psychological, social-historical, and sociological literatures is far from universal or innate and represents instead an ideological symbolic representation grounded in the basic material conditions that define women's reproductive lives. The journalist who reviewed my research . . . in a feature article entitled 'Anthropologist Calls Mother Love a Bourgeois Myth' may have overstated my case. But in effect I suppose it is close enough to what I am saying.
>
> (Scheper-Hughes 1992: 401)

Scheper-Hughes' way of narrating the immediate contrasts strongly with that of Ruth Benedict's in *The Crysanthemum and the Sword*, an ethnography of the 'rules and values of Japanese culture' (1989 [1946]: 6) that she was commissioned to write during the Second World War to help further America's victory. Although Benedict's aim was to understand Japanese 'habits of thought and emotions' (*ibid.*: 4), she was unable to carry out conventional fieldwork in Japan and had instead to rely on written material and, in particular, on interviews with Japanese detainees in American camps. And, although Benedict was attempting 'the study of culture at a distance' (Vogel 1989: ix) she nonetheless produced an ethnography that relies heavily on the immediate. But, by contrast with *Death Without Weeping*, the immediacy we glimpse in the *Chrysanthemum and the Sword* is not protagonistic and transient but *recurrent* and *undifferentiated* – that is, she gives us a **normative** account. It is recurrent in that it is the regular and repetitive aspects of daily life that are emphasised, and it is undifferentiated in that no individuals, neither the people she interviewed nor even Benedict herself, are present. And, because the author has stepped out of the text, the relationship to which Crapanzano pointed, between a concrete series of events and relationships and the series of conclusions premised upon them, is downplayed.

Describing how Japanese babies are treated after birth, Benedict tells us that:

> For three days after birth the baby is not fed, for the Japanese wait until the true milk comes. After this the baby may have the breast at any time either for food or comfort. The mother enjoys nursing too. The Japanese are convinced that nursing is one of women's greatest physiological pleasures and the baby easily learns to share her pleasure. The breast is not only nourishment: it is delight and comfort. For months the baby lies on his little bed or is held in his mother's arms. It is only after the baby has been taken to the local shrine and presented there at the age of about thirty days that his life is thought to be firmly anchored in his body so that it is safe to carry him around freely in public. After he is a month old, he is carried in his mother's back. A double sash holds him under his arms and under his behind and is passed around the mother's shoulders and tied in front at the waist. In cold weather the mother's padded jacket is worn right over the baby. The older children of the family, both boys and girls, carry the baby, too, even at play when they are running for base or playing hop-scotch.
>
> (Benedict 1989 [1946]: 257)

This passage tells in detail of the intimacy of Japanese everyday life (the pleasure of breast-feeding for mothers and babies, the games of older children, the way a mother shelters her baby from the cold and so on) but we are left to conjecture whether the author had or not any close familiarity with it. Most importantly, unlike in Scheper-Hughes' depiction of Alto de Cruzeiro (where one-off events take place at a definite point in time) in this and similar passages Benedict presents us with an out-of-time, *ongoing* immediacy. This is because her aim is to convey, in a **normative** manner, the recurrence and typicality of events. She achieves it by using the present tense together with broad categories like 'women', 'babies' and 'the Japanese' as tools to aid generalisation – a widespread strategy commonly referred to in anthropology as 'the **ethnographic present**'. And so, as we read today a passage first published in 1946, we gain the impression that many (or perhaps all) Japanese women have treated, treat and will treat their babies like this, feed and dress them in just this way. That is, we are led into a timeless now where the idiosyncracy of individuals becomes irrelevant and we are provided with a sense, not only of the feel of everyday life among Japanese people, but of its continuity and of the enduring validity of the ethnographer's observations and interpretations.

These two styles of narrating the immediate (one transient and protagonistic, the other recurrent and undifferentiated) are ubiquitous in ethnographic writing. But, if you read Scheper-Hughes' and Benedict's excerpts carefully, you will see that each style is premised on a different understanding of the kind of knowledge anthropology should and does deliver. In Scheper-Hughes' case, we are expected to learn about a small hamlet, the Alto de Cruzeiro, at a particular point in time. And it is clear that what we know, we know through the eyes of Scheper-Hughes. Her own experiences and those of the Alto women are used to challenge universalising theories about motherhood that, Scheper-Hughes tells us, are ethnocentric and grounded in the history of the Western family, in Western population dynamics, and in Western thought. That is, we are led to a view of anthropological knowledge – and of academic knowledge at large – as bound by the context of its production. By contrast, although Benedict acknowledges and is aware of culture change and variation, she is also searching for the most resilient and widely shared patterns of Japanese culture. She explicitly looks for features that are general and enduring (that 'what makes Japan a nation of Japanese' [1989 (1946): 14]), and uses them to define millions of people. She also removes herself from the text, and hence downplays her role in shaping the conclusions that she is presenting. Underlying Benedict's excerpt is therefore a view of anthropological knowledge as transcending the immediate context of its production and as existing out of time.

And yet, in spite of their very different premises and orientations, you will find that these two styles typically coexist within single ethnographic texts. This is because they complement each other and together embody anthropology's distinct aim to elucidate at once the specific and the general and indeed the one by way of the other. So for example the ethnographic present creeps even into the work of anthropologists that go out of their way to contextualise and personalise their descriptions and frame them firmly within a point in time. Just a few pages on from her account of Nailza's sorrows, Scheper-Hughes tells us that,

Throughout Northeast Brazil, whenever one asks a poor woman how many children she has in her family, she invariably replies with the formula, 'Z children, y living'. Sometimes she may say, 'Y living, z angels'. Women themselves, unlike the local and state bureaucrats, keep close track of their reproductive issue, counting the living along with the dead, stillborn, and miscarried. Each little angel is proudly tabulated, a flower in the mother's crown of thorns, each the sign of special graces and indulgences accumulated in the afterlife.

(Scheper-Hughes 1992: 286)

Each anthropologist seeks to strike her own balance between fore-grounding the recurrent and shared dimensions of life among a particular group of people and nodding to the fact that, really, at the root of all ethnographic knowledge is an unrepeatable set of past events. Below we explore in detail how writers move between these two poles, both of which are essential to the ethnographic enterprise, in order to construct arguments and abstractions – that is, to say something anthropologically meaningful about human life.

Summary points

1   Protagonistic and transient narratives of the immediate emphasise authorship and the context-dependent nature of anthropological knowledge.
2   Recurrent and undifferentiated narratives tend to downplay author-ship and to present anthropological knowledge as existing out of time.
3   Although they stand on very different epistemological premises, both styles tend to co-exist within ethnographies.

Narratives of the immediate and the construction of anthropological arguments

We started this chapter by emphasising how accounts of the immediate in ethnography are interlinked with the ethnographer's theoretical aims. As we further explore in Chapter 8, it is the theorising and positioning of events within the field of anthropological debate that gives ethnography direction and distinguishes it from other ways of reflecting on human experience. Thus narratives that highlight the complexity and detail of lived experience are used in the construction of every kind of anthropolog-ical abstraction, argument and explanation. They form the building blocks from which conclusions about the quality of social life among a particular group or groups are built and they are shaped by the ethnographer to illus-trate, support and in fact lead to these conclusions. That is, in these narratives the immediate is presented to the reader at once as the raw material that is to be understood and analysed, and as evidence of the appropriateness of an author's particular interpretations and standpoint. There is constant feedback and intertwining between recalled experience and interpretation, between narrative of the immediate and abstraction. This intertwining is what gives descriptions of life among a particular group a distinctively anthropological flavour.

Let us consider first how two events witnessed and remembered by an anthropologist are absorbed into a descriptive analysis of daily life that foregrounds social dimensions and cultural meanings. The events – two male initiations – are analysed by Raymond Firth in his classic ethnography *We The Tikopia* (1983) [1936]. From his own observations of these two rituals, and from the Tikopia's accounts and descriptions of these and others, Firth tells us, he has extracted the basic common features that he thinks are shared by all Tikopia initiations. That is, he has arrived at an ethnographic abstraction or concept, 'Tikopia initiation':

> Initiation in Tikopia consists in essentials of an operation akin to circumcision; it is practiced upon young males, a few only at a time, and is accompanied by the distribution of huge quantities of food and gifts, regulated upon the basis of kinship to the initiates. A similar ritual, but on the economic side only, is sometimes performed for girls.
>
> (Firth 1983 [1936]: 382)

This distillation of the core characteristics of male initiation in Tikopia is paralleled and supported by a similar category in Tikopia thought:

> In native belief, then, the ceremonies of initiation are the continued reproduction of a model supplied in the dim past by a supernatural person, who, amid his other activities, is still proud enough of his creation to approve of its perpetuation and reward its perpetuators accordingly.
>
> (Firth 1983 [1936]: 390)

Having established firmly the distinctiveness of the concept 'initiation' in Tikopia practice and in Tikopia belief, Firth backtracks to elaborate and support his analysis of this kind of practice through intimate and careful ethnographic description over several pages:

> The lads are now carried out for the operation. They are seized by *tuatina* (matrilateral male relatives) and taken this time in the man's arms. For the moment there is general confusion, from which the rising wail of the dirge breaks out with renewed force. Outside there is a rush of children to see what is happening, and a hurly-burly in which orders are shouted back and forth and people swirl around the

immediate performers, who have to push their way through the crowd. At both the ceremonies I witnessed I was left to fend for myself at this moment, and had great difficulty in making observations and taking photographs. The press of men, usually so ready to make way, ignored me in the concentration of their interest on the lads (*v.* Plate XI). Some coconut leaves are laid out and on them sit *tuatina*, one to each initiate, to hold the boy in his arms. These are the *tanata me*, 'the men on whom the boys sleep', and they are important. The operation is then performed as described. In every case I observed the hand of the operator was trembling, and it was quite evident that there was considerable emotional stress in the men immediately concerned. At the moment the cut is made the man who is supporting the boy covers the lad's eyes with this hand.

(Firth 1983 [1936]: 408, our brackets)

This paragraph relies heavily on the immediate: 'the hand of the operator was trembling . . . the man who is supporting the boys covers the lad's eyes with this hand'. But note how in his narrative Firth continuously travels between anecdote and generalisation, marking the transition between the two with a change of tense: from the ethnographic present ('coconut leaves are laid . . . ') to the concrete recollection from the past ('I was left to fend for myself . . . '). This change of tense signals to the reader that there is a distance between the concrete events Firth participated in and his abstraction 'initiation' (drawn, as we have said, from his own observations, but also from the Tikopia's understandings and their expectations of what an initiation should look like). That is, whilst field experience should provide the basis for analysis, and whilst analysis should build on field experience, the two are not identical. And yet it is clear from Firth's paragraph that the relationship between anecdote and abstraction in ethnographic writing is circular. Not only can they not be separated, but they support and mutually constitute each other. Firth's analytical construct ('Tikopia initiation'), emerges as an abstraction from his singular experiences and memories, but relies on his intensely evocative description (of the shaking hand of the operator, the men surrounding him, his own uncertainty). Simultaneously, the concept 'Tikopia initiation' frames his evocations, shaping and charging them with anthropological significance.

This mutual shaping is evidenced also in Lila Abu-Lughod's (1986) ethnography of the Egyptian Awlad 'Ali Bedouins, which is peppered with anecdotes that depict events and individual lives. Abu-Lughod frames these anecdotes with more abundant and longer narratives in the ethnographic present, anonymous and non-personalised but nonetheless very detailed and intimate. Most importantly, she combines these two styles of narrating the immediate to construct a conceptual support and provide a structure for her account of Bedouin life. This structure revolves around the notion that there is a discrepancy between the 'Bedouin poetic discourse and the discourse of ordinary social life' (1986: 32), between the sentiments Bedouin men and women express in short lyric poems (called *ghinnawas*) and the ideas and moral evaluations they put forward in the contexts of everyday life. In these ordinary contexts Bedouins emphasise hierarchies and inequalities between men, who are seen as autonomous and independent, and women, who are seen as dependent on men. In their poems, on the other hand, the Bedouins challenge and undermine these shared public understandings.

Abu-Lughod employs several lengthy, detailed examples in order to show how the dominant values play out in everyday life. One of these examples is the story of Rashid, a man in his forties who took as his second wife a much younger woman. She was unhappy in the marriage, and abandoned him shortly after the wedding, thus insulting Rashid and his kin:

> These men (Rashid's agnates) all thought it best that Rashid divorce her for insulting them: she had compromised Rashid's pride, which reflected on them as kinsmen; they wanted to turn the tables and make her family look bad. They preferred to leave the bride at her home and, as an insult, not even demand the return of the bridewealth, to which they would have been entitled because she wished the divorce. But Rashid wanted her back, so a few days later his elder brother went to negotiate the bride's return, furious for having to endure the humiliation of begging.
>
> He was not the only angry one. One of Rashid's cousins later commented, 'Rashid is an idiot. You don't go chasing a woman when she leaves!' . . . Rashid's mother, an outspoken old woman, ranted, 'He's an idiot [*habal*] I never heard of such a fool. The woman goes and throws herself at the Mrabtin. If you are a man you don't throw yourself after her, for God's sake. Idiot! I've never seen such a thing. What you do is leave the girl there – don't even tell her family she has run away. Let them hear in the marketplace that their daughter is in the house of strangers. . . . He's no man!'
>
> (Abu-Lughod 1986: 95–6)

Abu-Lughod provides a very detailed, step-by-step account of the events surrounding the desertion of Rashid's wife. She also deploys the exact words of Rashid's family to great effect: the reader is placed face to face with them so that, for example, we can clearly visualise Rashid's mother, her gestures and grimaces, her appalled disgust at her own child. The author tells her readers about the Awlad 'Ali and their morality through lively descriptions of individuals' experiences, explaining how they draw on this morality to make sense of and represent their own actions and those of others. In other words, Abu-Lughod uses anecdotes to build up a sense of, a *feel* for, the morality of the Awlad 'Ali that enables us to engage with her material at an emotive, imaginative level. This emotive, imaginative engagement is essential in furthering also a cognitive or intellectual engagement and in convincing us of the validity of the writer's abstractions and interpretations.

Thus, one of the key roles that the immediate plays in ethnographic writing is to help validate the author's standpoint, and this is the case even when authors use the recurrent, depersonalised style of narration that we have analysed in the preceding section: think back to Benedict's excerpt on Japanese mothers and babies, her statement that mothers enjoy nursing their babies, that '(t)he breast is not only nourishment: it is delight and comfort' (Benedict 1989: 257). Reading Benedict, we not only imagine the little baby nestled against his mother's breast under the warmth of her padded jacket, but we remember, if fleetingly, how it feels to delight in being warm and comfortable – we empathise. In other occasions, as with the excerpt from Michelle Rosaldo with which we opened this chapter, we are confronted with much more alien practices and ways of life – head-hunting in this case – and empathy may be more difficult, but our feelings are made to do hard work nonetheless. Our intellectual interest is aroused because our emotions are challenged.

An emotionally and imaginatively compelling description, then, furthers and facilitates a convincing interpretation – which, in anthropology, always is built around modelling and abstracting. In *Veiled Sentiments* this connection between powerful narrative of the immediate and persuasive theoretical construct becomes strikingly visible when Abu-Lughod explains how the Awlad 'Ali challenge the dominant gender ideology that dictates the autonomy of men and the dependence of women. First we are told about a private conversation with Rashid, where the ethnographer asks him about his feelings towards his wife and he responds with a poem: 'Cooking with a liquid of tears / at a funeral done for the beloved . . . / Her bad deeds were wrongs that hurt / yet I won't repay them, still dear the beloved' (1986: 189). Then Abu-Lughod explains:

> The poems revealed sentiments of grief and pain caused by the loss. . . . When I shared these poems with some of my women confidantes, they were touched. Yet these were the same women who had condemned Rashid as foolish or unmanly when he had earlier betrayed sadness over his bride's departure and expressed his desire to have her back. Their different attitudes towards statements made in poetry and those in ordinary interaction suggest that poetic revelations are judged by different criteria than are nonpoetic expressions.
>
> (Abu-Lughod 1986: 189)

In less than eighty words the ethnographer moves from Rashid's intimate acknowledgement of his grief and sense of loss, to the women's evaluation of this recognition, and to her own conclusion that two competing discourses on gender relations and on feelings co-exist.

Summary points

1 Narratives of the immediate function as the building blocks of anthropological arguments.
2 Description and interpretation and analysis cannot be separated in ethnographic writing.
3 Narratives that engage the imagination and emotions of the readers help advance an author's argument.

Concluding remarks

> Even eight-year-old children are familiar with the bewildering maze of streams and eddies through the swamp to the west and north of the village. I have been along these waterways dozens of times, and no matter how I concentrate I often find that I am at a loss not only about the path back to the village but even whether the village is upstream or down. The forests are equally disconcerting, since they permit no long view of the surroundings and the trails are often so overgrown they appear nonexistent. The Mehinacu, however, never lose their way.
>
> (Gregor 1980: 43)

Like Thomas Gregor, becoming acutely aware of his foreignness when trying and failing to find his way back to a small village in the middle of the Amazon forest, all anthropologists are confronted with the distance between the world of their informants and their own comprehension of it. At the core of this limited and peripheral understanding are one-off experiences, singular events, and encounters with individuals that together build up a feel for what life among a particular group is like. This is what in this chapter we have called an experience of immediacy, encompassing both puzzlement and knowledge, rejection and acceptance, empathy and confusion.

In ethnographic writing these experiences of immediacy are transformed into narratives of the immediate, where authors attempt to convey the texture of everyday life. The aim of these narratives, however, is not solely evocative or reflexive, but analytical, and they always revolve around a concern with elucidating a pattern, with extracting the wider social and cultural meaning of even the most irrelevant of events. Thus, narratives of the immediate are made to do hard work furthering an author's theoretical standpoint within ethnographies that always aim to be authoritative abstractions. In the two chapters that follow we explore further the authoritativeness of ethnography and its ultimate aim of producing texts that always address the discipline, both drawing from and adding to its reservoir of concepts and debates.

Chapter 4 – activities

In this excerpt from the classic *Tristes Tropiques*, first published in French in the mid-1950s, Claude Lévi-Strauss analyses the role of chiefs among the Nambikwara of the Brazilian Amazon. While you read, look for passages that reveal Lévi-Strauss' closeness with the Nambikwara, his knowledge of their everyday life and of their concerns and perspectives. Consider in what ways these narratives are integrated within an anthropological argument and respond to the following:

1　What are the key stylistic devices that Lévi-Strauss uses to give the reader a feel for the quality of life among the Nambikwara?
2　At what points does Lévi-Strauss use the ethnographic present and at what points does he use the past tense, and what does he achieve with each style of narration?
3　What similarities and differences might we draw between the narrative style of Lévi-Strauss and those of Benedict and Abu-Lughod in the chapter above?
4　Give examples of the way Lévi-Strauss interweaves narrative of the immediate and theoretical argument.
5　Summarise Lévi-Strauss' conclusions, and evaluate whether they are adequately supported by the ethnographic material he provides.

Lévi-Strauss, C. (1984) [1955] Tristes Tropiques, Harmondsworth: Penguin, 400–9

In 1938, the post of Vilhena, which lies on the highest point of the plateau beyond Campos Novos, consisted of a few huts in the middle of an open space a few hundred metres square, which had been intended, by the builders of the railway line, as the site of the future Chicago of the Mato Grosso. I understand that it is now a military airfield; in my time, the population was composed of only two families, who had received no supplies for eight years and who, as I have already explained, had managed to maintain themselves in a state of biological balance with a herd of deer, which provided them with a carefully husbanded supply of meat.

At Vilhena, I made the acquaintance of two new native groups, one of which comprised eighteen people, who spoke a dialect akin to those with which I was beginning to be familiar, whereas the other, which had a total of thirty-four members, used an unknown language that I was unable subsequently to identify. Each group was led by a chief; in the first group his function seemed to be purely secular, whereas the leader of the larger group eventually turned out to be some kind of shaman. His group was called Sabané; the others were known as Tarundé.

Apart from the difference of speech, it was impossible to distinguish one group from the other: they were alike both in appearance and culture. That had already been the case with the Campos Novos Indians, but the two Vilhena groups, instead of displaying hostility to each other, were on friendly terms. Although they had separate camp fires, they travelled together, camped side by side and seemed to have thrown their lot with each other. It was a surprising association, given the fact that the two groups did not speak the same language and the chiefs could only communicate with each other through the one or two individuals in each group who acted as interpreters.

Their coming together must have been quite recent. I have already explained that, between 1907 and 1930, the epidemics brought in by white men had decimated the Indian population. As a result, several groups were so reduced in numbers that it was becoming impossible for them to pursue an independent existence. At Campos Novos, I had been able to observe the antagonisms within Nambikwara society and had seen the disruptive forces at work. At Vilhena, on the contrary, I was able to witness an attempt at reconstruction. There could be no doubt that the natives with whom I was camping had worked out a plan. All the adult males in either group addressed the women in the other group as 'sisters', and the women used the term 'brothers' in speaking to the men in the opposite group. The men in both groups, in speaking to each other, used a form of address which, in their respective languages, means 'cross-cousin' and corresponds to the relationship through marriage that we would translate as 'brother-in-law'. Given the rules governing marriage among the Nambikwara, the modes of address meant that all the children in either group were 'potential spouses' of the children of the other group. It followed that as a result of inter-marriage, the two groups could be expected to have merged by the next generation.

But there were still obstacles in the way of this great plan. A third group, hostile to the Tarundé, was moving around in the area; on certain days their camp fires were visible and the Tarundé were prepared for any eventuality. As I had a little knowledge of the Tarundé dialect, but not of the Sabané one, I felt closer to the first group; the other group, with whom I could not communicate, was also more suspicious of me. I am therefore not in a position to explain its point of view. All I can say is that the Tarundé were not absolutely sure that their friends had agreed without reservations to the principle of union. They were afraid of the third group, but still more so of the possibility that the Sabané might suddenly decide to change sides.

It was not long before a curious incident was to show how well founded were their fears. One day when the men went hunting, the Sabané chief did not come back at the usual time. No one had seen him during the day. Night fell, and at about nine or ten o'clock in the evening the whole camp was in a state of consternation, particularly the family of the missing man, whose two wives and child were huddled together in a close embrace and weeping in advance for the death of their husband and father. At that point, I decided to take a few natives and make an exploratory tour of the vicinity. Before we had gone even two hundred metres, we discovered the lost chief crouching on the ground and shivering in the darkness; he was completely naked, that is, he had neither necklaces, bracelets, earrings nor belt, and by the light of my torch, we could catch a glimpse of his tragic expression and drawn features. He let himself be helped back to the camp, where he sat down without uttering a word and in a most convincing attitude of dejection.

His account of what had happened was extorted from him by an anxious audience. He explained that he had been carried off by the thunder, which the Nambikwara call *amon* (there had been a storm – heralding the beginning of the rainy season – that same day); the thunder had borne him through the air to a point which he named, twenty-five kilometres away from the encampment (Rio Ananaz), had stripped him of all his adornments, then brought him back in the same way and set him down at the spot where we had found him. The incident was discussed until everybody fell asleep, and the following morning the Sabané chief had recovered not only his usual good humour but also all his adornments too: no one showed any surprise at this, and he offered no explanation. During the next few days, a very different version of the episode began to be repeated among the Tarundé. They maintained that the chief, under pretence of communing with the other world, had begun negotiations with the group of Indians who were camping in the neighbourhood. These insinuations never came to a head, and the official version of the affair was openly accepted. But, in private conversation, the Tarandé chief made no secret of his anxiety. As the two groups left us shortly afterwards, I never heard the end of the story.

This incident, together with my previous observations, prompted me to reflect on the nature of the Nambikwara groups and the political influence that the chiefs were able to exert within them. There can be no more fragile and ephemeral social structure than the Nambikwara group. If the chief appears too demanding, if he claims too many women for himself or if he is incapable of providing a satisfactory solution to the food problem in times of scarcity, discontent becomes manifest. Individuals or whole families will leave the group and go off to join some other with a better reputation. This second group may have a more abundant supply of food through the discovery of new hunting or collecting grounds, or it may have acquired ornaments and instruments by means of commercial exchanges with neighbouring groups, or it may have become more powerful as a result of some victorious expedition. A day will come when the chief finds himself leading a group which is too depleted to cope with the difficulties of everyday life or to protect his women from covetous strangers. This being so, he has no option but to give up his chieftainship and, along with his remaining companions, to amalgamate with some more fortunate community. It is obvious, then, that the social structure of the Nambikwara is quite fluid. The group forms and falls apart, increases or disappears. Within the space of a few months, it can undergo changes in composition, size and distribution which make it unrecognizable. Political intrigues inside the same group and clashes between neighbouring groups superimpose their pattern on these variations, and the ascendancy and downfall of both individuals and groups follow each other in an often surprising way.

What, then, are the principles governing the division into groups? From the economic point of view, the scarcity of natural resources and the large area needed for the feeding of one individual during the nomadic period make the division into small groups almost obligatory. The problem is not why the division occurs, but how. In the initial community, there are men who are recognized as leaders: it is they who form the nuclei around which the groups assemble. The size of the group and its greater or lesser degree of stability during a given period are proportionate to the ability of the particular chief to maintain his rank and improve his position. Political power does not appear to result from the needs of the community; it is the group rather which owes its form, size and even origin to the potential chief who was there before it came into being.

I was well acquainted with two such chiefs: the one at Utiarity, whose group was called Wakletoçu, and the Tarandé chief. The first was remarkably intelligent, conscious of his responsibilities, energetic and ingenious. He was a most useful informant, since he understood the problems, saw the difficulties and showed an interest in the work. However, his duties took up a good deal of his time; for days on end he would be away hunting, or checking on the state of seed-bearing trees or those with ripe fruit. Frequently too, his wives would invite him to join in amorous play and he would readily respond. ... In spite of precarious living conditions, and with the pathetically inadequate means at his disposal, he showed himself to be an efficient organizer, capable of assuming sole responsibility for the welfare of his group, who he led competently, although in a somewhat calculating way.

The Tarundé chief, who was the same age – about thirty – was just as intelligent, but in a different way. The Wakletoçu chief struck me as being a shrewd, very resourceful individual, who was always planning some political move. The Tarundé Indian was not a man of action, but rather a contemplative with a charming and poetic turn of mind and great sensitivity. ... His curiosity about European customs and about those of other tribes I had been able to study was in no way inferior to my own. Anthropological research carried out with him was never one-sided: he looked upon it as an exchange of information and he was always keen to hear anything I had to tell him. Frequently he would even ask me for drawings of feather ornaments, head-dresses or weapons that I had seen among neighbouring or distant tribes, and these he carefully preserved. ...

In Nambikwara society, political power is not hereditary. When a chief grows old or falls ill, and feels that he is no longer capable of carrying out his arduous duties, he himself chooses his successor: 'This man will be chief ... ' However, this autocratic decision is more apparent than real. I shall explain later how weak the chief's authority really is; in this instance, as in all others, the final choice appears to be preceded by a sounding of public opinion: the appointed heir is also the person most favoured by the majority. But the choice of the new chief is limited not only by the positive or negative wishes of the group; the individual concerned must also be prepared to fit in with the arrangement. It is not unusual for the offer of authority to be rejected with a vehement refusal: 'I do not want to be chief.' When this happens, a second choice has to be made. Actually, there does not seem to be any great competition for power, and the chiefs I knew were more inclined to complain about their heavy duties and many responsibilities than to regard them as a source of pride. This being so, we may well ask what privileges the chief enjoys and what are his obligations.

Around 1560, at Rouen, Montaigne met three Brazilian Indians who had been brought back by a navigator, and he asked one of them what privileges the chief (he used the term 'king') enjoyed in his country; the native, who was himself a chief, replied that 'it was to march foremost in any charge of warre'. Montaigne tells the story in a famous chapter of his *Essays*, and expresses astonishment at this proud definition. For me, it was an even greater cause of astonishment and admiration to be given exactly the same reply four centuries later. Such constancy in political philosophy is not displayed by civilized countries! Striking as the definition may be, it is less significant than the Nambikwara word for chief: Uilikandé would seem to mean 'he who unites', or 'he who joins together'. The etymology suggests that the native mind is aware of the phenomenon I have already emphasized, namely that the chief is seen as the cause of the group's desire to exist as a group, and not as the result of the need for a central authority felt by some already established group.

Personal prestige and the ability to inspire confidence are the basis of power in Nambikwara society. Both are indispensable for the man who has to act as guide during the hazardous nomadic period of the dry season. For six or seven months, the chief is entirely responsible for the leadership of his group. It is he who orga-nizes the departure, chooses the routes, decides on the camping places and the duration of each camp. He takes the decisions about all hunting, fishing, gathering and collecting expeditions, and he determines the group's policy towards neigh-bouring communities. When the chief of a group is also a village chief (the term 'village' being taken in the restricted sense of semi-permanent quarters for the rainy season), his obligations extend even further. He fixes the time and place for the sedentary period; he superintends the gardening and decides which plants are to be grown; and, more generally, he relates the group's various activities to its needs and the seasonal possibilities.

It should immediately be noted that the chief, in carrying out these numerous functions, has no clearly defined powers and does not enjoy any publicly recognized authority. Power derives from consent, and it depends on consent to maintain its legitimacy. Any reprehensible behaviour (reprehensible, that is, from the native point of view) or demonstrations of ill-will on the part of one or two malcontents can jeopardize the chief's plans and the well-being of his little community. Should this happen, the chief has no powers of coercion. He can get rid of undesirable elements only if he succeeds in getting everyone else to share his point of view. He must therefore display the skill of a politician trying to maintain an uncertain majority rather than the authority of an all-powerful ruler. Nor is it enough for him to preserve the unity of his group. Although it may live in virtual isolation during the nomadic period, it is not unaware of the existence of other communities. The chief must not only do his job well; he must try – and his group expects this – to do better than the other chiefs.

In fulfilling these obligations, his primary and principal instrument of power lies in his generosity. Generosity is an essential attribute of power among most primitive peoples, particularly in America; it plays a part, even in those rudimentary cultures where the only possessions are crude objects. Although the chief does not seem to be in a privileged position as regards material belongings, he must have at his disposal a surplus of food, weapons and ornaments which, however small, may nevertheless be of considerable value in view of the general poverty. When an individual, a family or the group as a whole feel a desire or a need for something, they turn to the chief. It follows that generosity is the main quality expected of a new chief. This is the note which is constantly struck, and the degree of consent is determined by its harmonious or discordant resonance. There can be no doubt that, in this respect, the chief's capacities are exploited to the utmost. Group chiefs were my best informants, and, realizing the difficulties of their position, I was keen to reward them generously. But I rarely saw any of my gifts remain with them for more than a day or two. By the time I took leave of a group, after living with it for a few weeks, its members had become the proud possessors of axes, knives, beads, etc. Yet, as a general rule, the chief remained just as poor as he had been when I arrived. Everything he had been given (and this amounted to considerably more than the average presents made to each individual) had already been extorted from him. This collective greed often drives the chief into a kind of despair. When this happens, his refusal to give is more or less tantamount, in the primitive democracy of the Indians, to the demand for a vote of confidence in a modern parliament. When a chief gets to the point of saying: 'I am not giving anything more! I am not going to be generous any more! Let someone else be generous instead of me!' he must indeed be sure of his power, since his reign is going through the gravest possible kind of crisis.

Chapter 5

Ethnography as argument

Gregory Bateson opens his 1936 ethnography, *Naven*, with reflections on how to transform the chaos and diversity of fieldwork experience into meaningful ethnographic writing.

> Since . . . it is impossible to present the whole of a culture simultaneously in a single flash, I must begin at some arbitrarily chosen point in the analysis; and since words must necessarily be arranged in lines, I must present the culture, which like all other cultures is really an elaborate reticulum of interlocking cause and effect, not in a network of words but with words in linear series. The order in which such a description is arranged is necessarily arbitrary and artificial, and I shall therefore choose that arrangement which will bring my methods of approach into sharpest relief. I shall first present the ceremonial behaviour, torn from its context so that it appears bizarre and nonsensical; and I shall then describe the various aspects of its cultural setting and indicate how the ceremonial can be related to the various aspects of culture.
>
> (Bateson 1958 [1936]: 3)

The relationship between lived experience and an ethnography as a sustained piece of writing is a highly arbitrary one, argues Bateson. Specifically, writing is sequential (propositions, ideas and examples follow one after another in a printed line) but every moment of social life, as it is lived, is multi-stranded and multi-dimensional. In order to bring the reader to an understanding of what the ethnographer has undergone during fieldwork, fieldwork as lived experience must be converted into evidence. That is to say, ethnography as fieldwork must be transformed into the grounds on which an ethnographer makes certain general claims and, regarding which, a reader will either accept or reject those claims. Evidence must then be organised according to a set of propositions that give it relevance and meaning. The distinctiveness of ethnography – as opposed, say, to archival research – comes from this work of transforming immediate personal, lived experiences of an alien setting into a line of reasoning on a page.

A fundamental aim of ethnographic writing, then, is to convince the reader that a particular life world can be understood in terms of the specific propositions put forward by the ethnographer. Another way of encapsulating this is to say that an ethnography is not lived experience itself (we have already seen in Chapter 4 how this is mediated), nor is it intended as merely one person's interpretation of lived experience. More purposively and challengingly, ethnographic writing argues for a particular way of understanding certain lived experiences: ethnography is argument. And, beyond the key ethnographic techniques (comparison, contextualisation, relational analysis) it is the argument of an ethnography, the claims it makes, that will bring it to the notice of readers and will form the primary basis on which it is judged.

This chapter is about how argument acts to give coherence and solidity to ethnography. We begin by exploring the tensions that exist between the need to provide a framework of argument and the requirement to do justice to lived experience. In order to persuade, ethnographic material has to be reshaped as evidence for the argument in hand. This reshaping will inevitably cut across the ways in which the people concerned themselves describe reality. The awareness of this conflict is a characteristic of ethnography as a kind of academic knowledge and represents one of its most valuable contributions. In the second section below, we show some of the devices ethnographers use to give their ethnography a persuasive shape. In their writing, ethnographers aim to focus the attention of the reader on the relationship between evidence and core propositions, providing evidence appropriate to the claims made. In order to orientate ourselves through the reading of an ethnography, we as readers need to recognise the way arguments and evidence are being formulated in combination.

Ethnographic argument does not take place in a vacuum, though, but rather in a long-term conversation. To convince others of their propositions, ethnographers must draw on and adapt conventions and concepts already available to, and understood by, their audience. Ethnographies respond to debates that have preceded them in other texts, as well as in the academic discussions that are going on when the text is being written. Reference to these debates helps readers to navigate new ways of combining evidence and argument. Ethnographic argument is, therefore, typically positioned in relation to what has been argued already. It is the argumentative challenge that an ethnography poses which is most likely to ensure its enduring significance in anthropology as a discipline.

Summary points

1   There is a difference between ethnography as a text and ethnographic experience.

2   Beyond a work of description or personal interpretation, an ethnography is a concerted attempt to convince readers of certain claims using the evidence of fieldwork. Ethnography is argument.
3   To learn to read ethnography is to understand the way ethnographic arguments are constructed within a context of anthropological debate.

The tension between ethnographic argument and ethnographic experience

We explained in Chapter 2 that ethnographers need to integrate ethnographic material while acknowledging diversity in the attempt to address particular ethnographic questions. Here we revisit this issue, this time with regard to how ethnographic material is organised into a concerted argument, and the conflicts that ensue. Establishing a convincing balance between integration and diversity is crucial to the persuasiveness of ethnography as argument. Christine Hugh-Jones' (1979) ethnography, *From the Milk River*, reminds us of the difficulties of providing a core set of propositions about social reality when the basic material of ethnography – what people say and do – is so intractable as evidence.

> The character of Vaupés social structure is such that no model can come close to the 'facts' as revealed by field research. The anthropologist's social structure must be pieced together from a muddling mass of statements that the Indians make about kinship connections, group names, ancestral derivations, linguistic affiliations, geographical sites and so on . . .
>
> To make the presentation as clear as possible, the model is described first and the extent to which it is an accurate reflection of social groupings is discussed afterwards. This treatment of the larger structural units is followed by an account of the local longhouse communities and how these are reproduced over time. Before proceeding to the model some preliminary points must be made about the relation of Pira-parana Indians to other Vaupés Indians; the use of technical terms for social-structural units; and the relation of these units to patterns of language affiliation. Let me say at the outset that I am well aware that much of the material in the remainder of this Chapter is not easy to understand, but I do not believe it can be simplified without distorting the data.
>
> (Hugh-Jones 1979: 13–14)

We immediately notice the strain between the model as a potential distortion and 'facts' that are, in themselves, a seemingly 'muddling mass'. Hugh-Jones refuses to give up on the complexity of the material and decides to show the reader first her model, then how the simplified version cannot do full justice to Vaupés social reality. The initial modelling offers a route into the more complex evidence. By presenting the ethnography at these two levels, the ethnographer underlines the divergence between, on the one hand, providing the reader with a sense of scale – some kind of map with which to judge the territory in question – and, on the other, a fuller awareness of the multifaceted actuality concerned. She makes this divergence a central element of the argument itself.

Throughout *From the Milk River* we can find reminders like the one above that lived reality is more complicated than the ethnographer's model suggests alongside highly schematised renderings of Vaupés culture. The below diagram (Figure 1) of how metaphors of birth are interconnected in a total system shows this tendency towards high level abstraction.

The use of diagrams similar to this is widespread in ethnographic writing. Here information is presented in the most condensed and abstract way possible and the reader should not confuse this schema with the fieldwork experience that it is meant to represent. Models and schemas have a **heuristic** value in approximating to, without being the same as, the ways in which people live or talk about their lives. As the book develops, Hugh-Jones will elaborate a central claim that at the core of Vaupés culture there exists an analogy between bodily and social processes – society like the body ingests, excretes, gestates. The justification for using abstract models is that by removing excess information the model, however approximate, will bring us closer to this core set of Vaupés cultural principles. The

PROCESS	STARTING POINT	BOUNDARY	PATH	BOUNDARY	END	MOVEMENT
1 BIRTH *movement of child*	WOMB (foetus)	CERVIX	VAGINA	ENTRANCE TO VAGINA	OUTSIDE WORLD (new-born child)	UP→DOWN
2 BRINGING-IN OF CHILD *movement of child*	MANIOC GARDEN (natural child)	GARDEN BOUNDARY	GARDEN PATH	SIDE DOOR OF COMPARTMENT	FAMILY COMPARTMENT (social child)	WEST→EAST
3 CREATION OF DESCENT GROUPS *movement of anacondas/ ancestors*	HOUSE BEYOND WATER DOOR	WATER DOOR	MILK RIVER	PORT (river→land)	ORIGINAL HOUSE SITES	EAST→WEST
4 GROWTH OF *KANA PLANT*	UNDERGROUND ROOT	EARTH SURFACE	STEM	STEM/FRUIT	FRUIT	DOWN→UP
5 NOURISHMENT OF CHILD	PLACENTA IN WOMB	JOIN WITH CORD	UMBILICAL CORD / CORD SEVERED	JOIN WITH CHILD	CHILD	—
6 METAPHORICAL GROWTH OF CHILD FROM EARTH	PLACENTA IN GROUND	EARTH SURFACE		BELLY BUTTON	SEVERED CHILD	DOWN→UP

Figure 1 Metaphors of birth
Source: Hugh-Jones 1979: 127.

model makes a claim to be weighed against the more complex evidence, at the same time focusing our understanding of that evidence.

If, in Hugh-Jones' statement, the question is one of complex data versus more simplified and abstract explanatory models, the issue runs deeper than this. Peter Lawrence (1984), in trying to demonstrate the structure of Garia society explains how a model of Garia relationships from a Western point of view cuts across and potentially negates the way these Papua New Guineans themselves think about the world. Europeans distinguish the 'natural' and the 'supernatural', often with a geographical separation in mind – 'down' on earth, 'up' in heaven. Human society as a rationally conceived entity is separate from any notion of a supernatural realm. According to this view, society can be modelled because ultimately the ethnographer can point to real people doing real things in the real world. However, the Papua New Guinean Garia see human activity as blended with what Europeans call supernatural activity. This means that any attempt to model social relationships and then separately to examine cosmological or religious ideas is artificial or arbitrary from a Garia perspective.

> Traditionally, the people regard their cosmos as a finite terrestrial envi-
> ronment containing two realms, one inhabited by human beings, and
> the other by gods and spirits. They make no ontological distinction
> between these two realms: they place them both firmly on earth, and
> do not equate them respectively with what Europeans call the natural
> and the supernatural or transcendental . . .
>
>   I am concerned with the pattern, maintenance and restoration of
> order in the total cosmos. Ideally, because the Garia do not conceive of
> its human and superhuman realms as spatially intrinsically separate, I
> should examine in turn each . . . [ethnographic issue] simultaneously
> in both realms. Yet this is methodologically cumbersome: inevitable
> cross-referencing leads to continuous and tedious repetition. Like
> McSwain, who faced the same difficulty, I follow anthropological
> convention and, even though it is artificial in this instance, present the
> two realms as if they were discrete. . . . My analysis, therefore, is an
> attempt to provide answers to two sets of questions: First, what is the
> structure of Garia society. . . . Second, what is the conceived structure
> of the realm of the deities and the spirits of the dead?
>
>   (Lawrence 1984: 5)

Lawrence is forced to bow to 'anthropological convention' in separating social from cosmological issues, because otherwise his ethnography would become 'cumbersome' as an explanation, and perhaps be incomprehensible to people not versed in the scales and complexities of Garia thinking. He cites another anthropologist as a precedent for his own decision. His overall argument results in an 'as if' presentation of the Garia because to organise it otherwise would create an unbridgeable gulf to analysis and understanding. Lawrence is not alone. Since all ethnography meets this basic problem in different forms, all ethnography is presentation 'as if' in this sense.

The objection may recur, why reshape complex lived experience? Why develop models and arguments that simplify and reorganise this complexity? Why not simply describe fieldwork experience as it happened? Bateson's discussion above presents us with a first response: the act of writing forces the telling of ethnographic experience into a particular shape. The very fact that, when we read, we read lines of text influences us to treat what we are reading as a continuous, organised flow. And when we read ethnography, as when we read other texts, our schooling has trained us to look for the core claims 'contained' in the text – both the arguments that the ethnographer explicitly intends and, perhaps, arguments that result from their unconsidered assumptions about the world. Second, as we have discussed in Chapter 4, the narration of lived experience inevitably distances us from, and reorders that experience: we find ourselves treating this narration as potential evidence for what is being argued, or not. And third, as Lawrence points out, there is a conflict between readers' ways of thinking and those of the people written about. As a result, to know anything about the Garia inevitably involves careful reformulation of what the Garia say and do in terms other than those the Garia themselves use.

The constant awareness of the difficulty in bridging different life worlds – of the people who are written about and of those who are written for – is one of the most important and enduring contributions of ethnography to intellectual activity generally. Ethnography is a curiously double-edged sword: the difficulty of doing justice to lived social experience is ever present, but the need to organise ethnographic material convincingly is also pressing. What holds an ethnography together is not its various ethnographic examples or the interpretations of particular aspects of social life. What gives an ethnography its coherence is the degree to which its central argument or arguments give organisation and meaning to this information. The next section examines the way models and concepts are deployed to develop ethnographic evidence into a concerted argument.

Summary points

1   Ethnographic arguments rely on models and schemas to present simplified claims with regard to more complex evidence.
2   Ethnographic models result in an 'as if' picture of social reality being created.

3   It is the central argument, or arguments, of an ethnography that gives overall coherence to the accumulated models and narrative evidence.

The co-shaping of evidence and argument

'Evidence', like 'fact', is a high-sounding word. And, unsurprisingly, the degree to which fieldwork experiences and the narratives that emerge from them can be considered as evidence is one of the areas of greatest contention in anthropology. We return to these debates in the conclusion of this book. Here though, we suggest that argument and evidence are twinned in ethnographic writing. The more an ethnography strives toward a coherent argument, the more its ethnographic material must be presented as evidence for that argument. This cuts across differences of style and school – **post-modern, structuralist, interactionist, functionalist,** and so on (see Chapter 8). The issue in this section is the differing ways in which evidence and argument are brought together in ethnographies. We compare a flexible style of presenting evidence/argument with a significantly more structured one.

In the last chapter we examined how narratives of the immediate form the building blocks from which ethnographic analysis is built. We explained that, while it is ethnographic narrative that gives the ethnography its flavour and much of its force as thought-provocation, narration is always subordinated to the work of convincing the reader of certain core arguments. Here we explore further how the kind of argument pursued in the ethnography will shape the kind of evidence presented and vice-versa. The following segment of ethnographic reportage and argument is extracted from the middle of Phillippe Bourgois' (1995) *In Search of Respect: selling crack In El Barrio.*

> The contemporary street sensitivity to being dissed immediately emerges in these memories of office humiliation. The machismo of street culture exacerbates the sense of insult experienced by men because the majority of office supervisors at the entry level are women. Hence the constant references to bosses and supervisors being 'bitches' or 'ho's' (whores), and the frequent judgemental descriptions of their bodies. . . . For Example . . . [Caesar] launched into a tirade of male outrage at having been forced, in the legal labour market, to break the street taboo against public male subordination to a woman.
>
> Caesar: I had a few jobs like that where you gotta take a lot of shit from fat, ugly bitches and be a wimp.
>
> My worst was at Sudler & Hennessey – the advertising agency that works with pharmaceutical shit. I didn't like it but I kept on working, because 'Fuck it!' you don't want to fuck up the relationship. So you just be a punk.

Oh my God! I hated that head supervisor. She was a bitch . . .

Ultimately the gender disses respond to economic inequality and power hierarchies. The crack dealers' experience of powerlessness is usually expressed in a racist and sexist idiom.

(Bourgois 1995: 146–7)

Bourgois' book is a study of drug dealers in New York. It represents a sustained case for understanding crack dealing as 'a symptom – and a vivid symbol – of [the] deeper dynamics of social marginalization and alienation' of people living in El Barrio, New York (1995: 3). The book is primarily made up of long transcriptions of taped conversations with the dealers themselves, including the one quoted here, followed by sections of analysis. Throughout the book, Bourgois continuously refocuses our attention on his central claim. Every vivid transcription is used to give another accent on his concern with how people living in a deprived subsector of American society give meaning to their experience of marginalisation.

In the excerpt above Bourgois is working with, on the one hand, specific conversations, and on the other, broad generalising and contextualising statements ('the majority of office supervisors . . . ', or, 'ultimately, the gender disses respond to . . . '). He emphasises the crack dealers' distinctive cultural worldview by demonstrating their use of the language of 'street machismo'. Bourgois does not analyse this linguistic performance in great detail: in sustaining his argument a primary necessity is that our attention should not be diverted. Instead, he simply reinforces the point that this 'sexist and racist idiom' is part of the armoury that these men use to give positive meaning to their social positioning in a situation over which they in fact have no control. '[Y]ou don't want to fuck up the relationship. So you just be a punk': phrasings that would ordinarily be lost in the noise of city life, take on a new meaning and relevance as evidence for the central proposition of the book.

Bourgois' text is relatively easy to understand because case studies and analysis are combined loosely but effectively according to a clear polemical proposal. This overarching proposition is well served by the open-ended use of tape transcriptions, each of which evidences in miniature broader claims about marginality and resistance. In other ethnographies though, the presentation is much more abstract since several strands of modelling or argument are being presented in any given example. What we will also meet in almost all ethnographies is specialised terminology or jargon, as well as frequent reference to other anthropological authors who have discussed similar issues to the ones in hand. These are all part of the way anthropologists – alongside showing their intellectual authority (see Chapters 6 and 7) – marshal different levels of argumentation and intertwine argument with evidence.

This excerpt from David Parkin's *Palms, Wine and Witnesses* (1972) shows a denser argumentative style at work than that of Bourgois. Parkin's is also a book in which evidence and propositions are much more closely interwoven. *Palms, Wine and Witnesses* is a study of how and why the Giriama of Kenya have begun to change from a traditional society led by elders to a more cash-oriented one, with increasing amounts of wealth concentrated in relatively few hands. The agents of this change, Parkin argues, are young Giriama entrepreneurs who have seen the potential for deploying particular customs to create economic opportunities for themselves according to a novel framework of cultural values. Hence, throughout the book, Parkin compares two models of Giriama society – the traditional society and, by contrast, the society that is coming into being, a market-influenced one. In his ethnographic narration, he continuously highlights these two sides. Below, he deploys the example of a funeral ceremony amongst the Giriama to integrate certain key themes essential to his overall argument about Giriama society.

> Funerals among Giriama have two broad aspects. One is the familiar one of bringing people together who in other contexts are opposed and, through the use of symbolic motifs, of obliging them – at least ostensibly – to reconcile their differences. I say 'ostensibly' because, during the course of the funeral, many participants use the occasion to assess the standing of their rivals or of possible supporters, and to advertise their own. A second aspect of the funeral, therefore, is that it provides an opportunity for men to display their worthiness as possible supporters of accumulators or as buyers or mortgagees of palms and land. In other words, the occasion is an opportunity for the organization of social credit, played out under an umbrella of communal amity.
>
> (Parkin 1972: 77)

Parkin's is a highly structured use of narrative as evidence. It is not primarily important for the moment who the specific 'people' involved are likely to be, or what the 'motifs' they use are, or what the 'differences' consist in. Instead, we are being asked to direct our attention towards specific features relevant to the model that he has developed at the beginning of his ethnography. From reading the introduction we know that Parkin aims to show how an emerging entrepreneurial grouping is manipulating traditional gerontocratic Giriama values for its own ends. Hence, despite the customary symbolism of reconcilement, we are now provided with initial evidence that the funeral can be conceptualised in different, economic, terms – it is a venue for garnering and gauging support for enterprises concerning palms and land, sources of wealth and status.

Summary points

1 Types of evidence and modes of argument work together in the process of providing the reader with an understanding of a social context.
2 The ethnographer will strive to orient the reader's attention towards specific features of the evidence using recognised concepts or jargon.
3 The combination of models organised in an argument provide complex insights which could not have been gained by reading a string of in-depth descriptions of fieldwork experiences.

Ethnographic arguments are relational

As readers of ethnography we are expected to understand a range of concepts or, more rudely, jargon terms – 'marginalization' or 'communal amity', for instance. This can represent one of the most frustrating hurdles to understanding ethnography. It is easy to decry jargon, but behind its use is the fact that ethnographers' arguments and use of concepts are set up *vis-à-vis* the specialist arguments and concepts of other anthropologists. We need to understand how ethnographers shape their ethnographic evidence in response to the evidence and arguments of other ethnographers. In other words, to use another jargon word, we must consider ethnographic arguments in **relational** terms: in terms, that is, of how ethnographers form intellectual relationships with other ethnographers in their debates over shared ethnographic concepts.

Here we need to return to issues that we discussed from a different perspective at the beginning of this book. The currency of particular ethnographic concepts derives from their usefulness in encapsulating fundamental debates. Continuing the intellectual dialogue around a particular issue will in all likelihood require reference to these recognised core ideas. As we explained in Chapter 1, on comparison, key concepts like these may originate in the work of just one author, are then taken up and revised by others, and become important points of reference for an entire group of researchers. As the basis either for agreement or disagreement, key concepts are the shared ground regarding which anthropologists organise their own ethnographic material. In this section we look at arguments developed, initially in the anthropology of the Caribbean, around the concept of **matrifocality**. We use this example to show how ethnography-as-argument can only be appreciated within a larger relational web of anthropological debate. We will also show how, as broader anthropological assumptions change, a shift can occur in the basic meaning of a concept, from, for instance, representing a radical challenge to taking on a conservative significance.

We will first examine how Raymond Smith coined matrifocality in order to organise his analysis of Guianese society. Then we will look at four authors, writing between the 1950s and the 1980s, all of whom have created further arguments on the basis of criticisms of R. T. Smith's concept. In the first example, disputing R. T. Smith's analysis leads M. G. Smith to create yet another term, **patrifocality**. Writing in the 1980s, Olwig questions matrifocality in feminist terms. Blackwood takes this a step further in her work on a different region. We will examine each ethnographic argument in turn, showing the process of debate and conceptual rethinking and, eventually, redefinition. Each of the ethnographers responds to earlier theoretical arguments, using these to weave their own analysis and narrative into the larger web of ideas.

> It is part of the mythology of the West Indies that the lower-class Negro is immoral and promiscuous, and that his family life is 'loose' and 'disorganised', and unless it is clearly recognized that such myths are an integral part of the system of relationships between various groups, reflecting value judgements inherent in their status rankings, then serious bias may be introduced into objective study.
>
> (R. T. Smith 1956: 259)

R. T. Smith's 1956 ethnography, *The Negro Family in British Guiana*, is a study of kinship in a Caribbean colony. He aims to show that lower-class family life has a systematic pattern and – contrary to the contemporary (1950s) stereotype put forward by colonial officials and middle-class Guianese – is not 'disorganised' or 'promiscuous'. The stereotype picture emphasises the fragility of the relationship between a woman and the father of her children and the apparent lack of respect for marriage. Searching for organising principles – for the system behind the 'myths' of familial chaos – Smith instead highlights the way in which women as 'mothers' have a central role in organising family relationships. Men, by contrast, are marginal or often not present at all. His evidence and arguments were taken up in order to criticise the contemporary assumption that, in all societies, the nuclear triad of father, mother, child lies at the heart of family organisation.

R. T. Smith's book builds an extended model of how kinship relationships work in this context, presenting extensive evidence of the kinds of activity going on in the household and the way different members of the household take on distinct family roles. He shows, in particular, that the status 'mother' subsumes a range of capacities, including aspects of economic and political leadership, not included in being a mother in, say, West Africa (much of Smith's analysis is based on implicit and explicit comparisons, particularly with African societies). He comes up with a concept-term for this, matrifocality:

> The household group tends to be matri-focal in the sense that a woman in the status of 'mother' is usually the *de facto* leader of the

group, and conversely the husband-father, although *de jure* head of the household group (if present), is usually marginal to the complex of internal relationships of the group. By 'marginal' we mean that he associates relatively infrequently with the other members of the group, and is on the fringe of the effective ties which bind the group together.

(R. T. Smith 1956: 223)

Once a concept has been introduced, it will be sustained in as much as it becomes part of a relational web of conversation and argument between anthropologists. The concept takes its meaning from, and continues to have significance because of, this relational nexus. Numerous anthropologists took up features of R. T. Smith's work and deployed them in their own ethnographies. Michael G. Smith disassembled the basic premises of R. T. Smith's ethnographic argument in his own 1962 analysis of kinship in a West Indian island, Carriacou. In effect, R. T. Smith's ethnography is built on a model of the household as the place where family life happens: he had treated family and household as aspects of each other. But it is common in the West Indies for a man to be the father of children by different mothers living in several different households. In Carriacou, alongside the children they had through marriage and who lived together with him, a man also very often had children with partners who lived elsewhere. How should we conceptualise these 'extraresidential' linkages made between households by a man in his role as father?

The Carriacou mating system defines the extraresidential union and marriage as alternatives for females only. Marriage is obligatory for men, and the extraresidential relation is normally complementary for men. ... This family system depends on the fact that most men will play both sets of paternal roles simultaneously. It is therefore patrifocal. The patrifocality or matrifocality of a family structure cannot be defined by reference to the domestic organisation only, since, as we have already seen, the family structure includes relations between households as well as within them and is not limited to the level of domestic family relations alone. The marginality of the extraresidential mate in Carriacou at the domestic level is a structural axiom of this patrifocal mating system. Carriacou folk are well aware of this.

(M. G. Smith 1962: 246)

M. G. Smith here organises his own ethnographic argument by inverting the terms of R. T. Smith's analysis. His concept, patrifocality, is a logical extension and reversal of the model underlying matrifocality. Instead of examining what is going on inside the household, he emphasises the links between households. As a result, rather than foregrounding the marginality of men in the household his analysis highlights the focal role of men in linking households. Perhaps ironically, M. G. Smith's criticisms of R. T. Smith's concept, amongst others, had the effect of making matrifocality a stable reference point for anthropologists working on Caribbean family life.

The success of an ethnographic concept in becoming the shared focus of debate correlates with the leaving behind of most of the complex evidence and modelling from which the concept initially emerged. Beyond criticising the precise terms that R. T. Smith originally used, in the following excerpt Olwig is challenging a general climate of debate in the 1980s. She criticises a range of assumptions present in the diverse work of the, by now very numerous, anthropologists writing and talking about the Caribbean region and about matrifocal kinship.

> The research on the West Indian family reveals some of the biases which social scientists hold concerning the male and female roles which are reflected in the family system. Thus, having discovered that women have a dominating role, interest has focused on the question of why men are weak in the family, how this is deleterious, and what can be done about it. There has been a great deal of discussion of whether it is the men's poor economic and social condition, the African past, or the background of slavery which has led to this situation. . . . With few exceptions . . . there has been correspondingly little discussion of what women have done to become so independent of the men except to imply that this was a consequence of male weakness. I shall there-fore attempt to compensate for this with and through an examination of the economic and social conditions which may have enabled the West Indian women to gain such comparative independence.
>
> (Olwig 1981: 60)

In his Guiana ethnography, R. T. Smith had made relatively cautious statements about male marginality – '[b]y "marginal" we mean that he [the husband-father] associates relatively infrequently with the other members of the group, and is on the fringe of the effective ties which bind the group together'. However, by the time Olwig wrote her essay, matrifocality now carried with it an additional swathe of implications (as a result of twenty-five years of debate). It is these implications alongside the original formulation that Olwig is now combating. Relatively detached from its author's intentions, the ethnographic concept of matrifocality has come to circulate in a much larger network of intellectual relationships.

Almost fifty years after the publication of *The Negro Family*, in an essay on 'matrifocal follies', applying a feminist critique to research on Minangkabau in Indonesia, Blackwood makes the following comment.

> Matrifocality seems to be irrevocably associated with the absence of men . . . the one who should be the primary earner, the one in control

and in charge – in fact the Patriarchal Man. Although ostensibly about women, the concept of 'matrifocal households' is an ongoing conversation about the 'missing' man.

(Blackwood 2005: 8)

Here we might note how a concept originally developed as part of a strong critique of the idea that families without a father are dysfunctional, has come to signify the opposite. Continuing use of the term 'matrifocality', for Blackwood, has become evidence of the refusal by anthropologists to come to terms with 'the absent man' without whom the family is deficient. In Chapter 7 we will see how the larger political context in which ethnography is written can influence this kind of shift in anthropological assumptions.

An ethnography is never a free-standing intellectual entity. The reason we have given an extended treatment to one anthropological concept in this section is to show processes of argument between ethnographies and how individual ethnographies are positioned in relation to these arguments. The book in which R. T. Smith originally proposed the term matrifocality was an ethnographic response to debates coming out of, in particular, the anthropology of West Africa. The authors who then took up the term, either critically or supportively, used R. T. Smith's propositions as a foundation for their own entry into a specialised conversation focused, initially, on Caribbean anthropology. Matrifocality, and other ethnographic concepts, endure, then, because of their continuing significance in the formation of these conversational relationships between anthropologists.

Over time an ethnographic text can become iconic of the central arguments or concepts for which it is recognised by anthropological readers. In the process, as we saw in Chapter 1, these concepts can float free of the ethnographic modelling and evidence that gave rise to them and be used in quite different contexts of argument. And here is one of the major difficulties in learning to read ethnography. There is an expectation that readers will have knowledge of the intellectual pathway an idea has taken before it is used in this particular instance. In addition, and this is perhaps the more complex element, we are expected to appreciate the relational character of the debate about certain ideas – the way in which concepts and arguments always arise *vis-à-vis* other concepts and arguments. These issues will be explored in more depth later in this book.

Summary points

1   We need to understand the ethnography as relational; as a work of evidence and argument organised *vis-à-vis* the work of other ethnographers.
2   Shared ethnographic concepts become the bridging point between ethnographers and their evidence and arguments.

3   In the process of debate between researchers, a concept may change its basic significance, e.g. from having a radical to having a conservative value.

Concluding remarks

The argument of an ethnography can be viewed as the culmination of the techniques we examined in the first chapters of this book. But ethnography as argument steps beyond these techniques in the way it deliberately positions ethnographic knowledge with regard to the wider conversation of, and about, anthropology. By and large, ethnographies are remembered for the central propositions they assert as well as for the way these have been judged, accepted, challenged and reformulated by other anthropologists. Ethnographers will seek to position their ethnographies in a larger conversation. For their part, readers seek stable points of reference in ethnographic writing in order to find relevance in what they are reading. Without this work of argumentative positioning – including the use of well known academic precedents and shared concept terms – the significance of the narratives, ideas and models presented in an ethnography would be lost on the reader. At the same time, this form of presentation usually demands a great deal of prior knowledge on the reader's part – one of the most difficult hurdles in reading ethnography effectively.

We have seen that argument, as the bringing together of models and evidence, entails relinquishing the fullest range of ways of talking about social experience. Instead, typically, ethnographic argument involves the deployment of a more delimited framework of concepts and evidence in order to give answers to specific questions within specialised debates. While here we have emphasised the persuasiveness of ethnographic arguments as a central issue, in practice other qualities such as suggestiveness and insightfulness also are key in how ethnographic arguments are judged. An argument may persuade with its combination of relevant evidence and coherent modelling, but it may fail to provide much insight – perhaps because the questions researchers are interested in asking have changed. A relatively unpersuasive, even incoherent, argument may be highly suggestive for further research. We have also left aside in this chapter the role of rhetoric as opposed to reasoning in increasing the persuasiveness of ethnographic arguments. We will pursue these issues in Chapter 8 and in our conclusion.

Chapter 5 – activities

Edmund Leach's *Political Systems of Highland Burma* is a classic study of Kachin political ideas as these affect lived social reality. Here we have included Raymond Firth's 'Foreword' to the 1954 edition of *Political*

Systems, followed by Leach's 'Introductory Note to the 1964 Reprint'. The book centres on the distinction between two polar ideals in Kachin life, *Gumsa*, a hierarchical view of how social relations should operate, and *Gumlao*, an egalitarian viewpoint. Kachin politics exists in a further complex relationship with the Shan states that border Kachin territory. One way of understanding Kachin history and society, argues Leach, is to look at how individuals manipulate the distinction between these two ideals for political ends. Leach's book, as an argument, is positioned against contemporary anthropological theories. Read the excerpt and respond to the following questions:

1   What features of Leach as an anthropologist does Firth highlight in his foreword?
2   What is the contribution of Leach's book in Firth's view? What criticisms does Firth make of his argument?
3   What kind of theoretical approach is Leach arguing against in his introductory note?
4   How does Leach go about positioning his own argument *vis-à-vis* those of his contemporaries?
5   What overall purpose does this 1964 note on a book published in 1954 serve?

Raymond Firth (1964) [1954] 'Foreword' to Political Systems of Highland Burma: a study of Kachin social structure, by Edmund Leach, London: Athlone, v–viii

To have been asked by Dr. Leach to write a foreword to this book is a tribute to an old friendship and academic association.

It is generally expected of a foreword that it will introduce the book either to a wider public than knows its author, or that it will make manifest some hidden virtue which the book contains. Neither of these objectives is sought here. The author is already known not only to his British colleagues but also internationally, as a leading social anthropologist. He is also by the force and clarity of his thought fully capable of presenting the merits of his own work. What then can this foreword do? By our ordinary conventions the writer of a foreword is presumably restrained from reviewing the book when it appears. He cannot compensate by reviewing it in his introduction. But what he may do is to give some notice in advance of some of the themes which he sees as being of major significance in any discussion of its merits.

'Dynamic' is an overworked word. But if one says that the primary feature in Dr. Leach's analysis is its attempt to provide the elements of a dynamic theory for social anthropology, the point will be generally understood. What is meant is an analysis of forces in movement or principles in action. Much of social anthropology nowadays is concerned with institutions in change. But the treatment is usually mainly descriptive, or where it becomes abstract the concepts are apt to become over-elaborate, highly artificial, and out of relation to the real world of observed human actions in specific societies. What Dr. Leach is attempting to do is to handle dynamic theory at a higher level of abstraction than has been done heretofore in social anthropology while still using the materials from empirical social observation among named groups.

He works forcibly and elegantly. To do this he makes certain assumptions. These involve the notion of descriptions of social systems as models of a social reality. There is a growing tendency in social anthropology, and rather a slipshod one, to call any set of assumptions or abstractions used as a basis for discussion, a model. At times the notion serves as an excuse for an evasion of reality, by emphasising the personal character of the construct. But with the author a model is clearly a representation of a structure with the parts articulated or related in such manner that manipulation of them is possible for the illustration of further relations. Dr. Leach has already demonstrated his skill in such manipulation in his article on Jinghpaw Kinship Terminology, which he described as 'an experiment in ethnographic algebra'. The essential feature of this analysis was the demonstration that by taking a limited set of assumptions about kinship structure, and by relating them in operation in the simplest possible manner, a behaviour scheme was found adequate to provide an explanation in terms of ideal rules for the noted events in a real society.

A consequence of Dr. Leach's analysis was to stress again the distinction drawn by Malinowski and others between 'ideal' and 'real' (or 'normal') patterns of behaviour. But in Dr. Leach's hands this distinction assumes a new importance. To him it is the ideal patterns – the social relations which are regarded as 'correct' – which are expressed in the model which give the structural description of a social system. The necessary equilibrium of the model as a construct means that essentially it is debarred from providing in itself a dynamic analysis. The difficulty lies not so much in introducing time abstractly as a factor into the model as in getting into it a true expression of what is really relevant in actual conditions. Application must therefore be made to the observation of what people actually do in their normal everyday life to give a basis for a dynamic consideration, a consideration of structural change. The situation here is analogous to that in economic theory. But the social anthropologist has an advantage over the economist in that from the beginnings of the science, it has been the 'real world' that he has studied at first hand. The anthropologist is already familiar with the raw stuff of social change.

In actual life individuals are continually faced by choices between alternatives for action. When they make these choices Dr. Leach believes their decisions are made commonly to gain power – that is, access to office or to esteem which will lead to office. The development of this argument is pursued with a wealth of detail and subtlety of interpretation that must command the admiration of every careful reader. His challenges to accepted views may not please everyone, but the reader will gain much by the way from the author's direct presentation, his complete intellectual honesty, and the freshness of his approach. Some of us, for example, have not hesitated to tell our students in private that ethnographic facts may be irrelevant – that it does not matter so much if they get the facts wrong as long as they can argue the theories logically. But few of us would be prepared to say in print, as Dr. Leach has done, that he is usually bored by the facts which his anthropological colleagues present. And who of us also usually feels inclined to state so bluntly at a point in his argument that his interpretation is completely at variance with almost everything that has previously been published on the subject? This is refreshing candour; it awakes the reader's expectations and he will not be disappointed.

As yet Dr. Leach's dynamic theory is still largely a special, not a general, one. This is for two reasons. The first is that it is intended as yet primarily to refer to, and to explain, the behaviour of people in North Burma. It is true that examples from remote fields are cited. Yet while in boundary terms many 'tribes' must be ethnographic fictions, this is not so everywhere. The notions of 'becoming something else' in this situation, as Kachins become Shans, or *gumsa* people become *gumlao*, are specific ethnographic phenomena that may have only a restricted analogy. They are indeed almost an 'ideal type' of the phenomenon of becoming another social being.

Secondly, some of Dr. Leach's concepts are of a special order. I do not refer here to his redefinitions of myth and of ritual, which in their novelty offer a stimulating way of considering social relationships. Nor do I refer to his use of the terms 'social structure' and 'social organisation', for which each of us has his personal idiom. But I refer to his thesis that seeking for power is the basis of social choice. The Italian Renaissance and our own recent history have good examples to support him. And his contention is in line with many trends of modern thought. Yet the concentration of power and status on the quest for esteem as leading to office, suggests either an undue restriction of the field of motivation or a re-interpretation of the power notion in terms so wide as to include almost any social action. I would, from my own Tikopia material, give support to Dr. Leach's views both as regards the role of myth and the cardinal importance of power notions for group action. I would think that the study of other Polynesian people, such as the Samoans or the Maori, would corroborate this too. And yet one feels that there is some speciousness in such a monolithic explanation. For the operation of social affairs in Polynesian communities to seem explicable, allowance must be made empirically for notions of loyalty and obligation which cut across the narrow confines of group power interests. And in other ethnographic fields it would seem that valuations of a moral and religious order enter and jostle the power and status-seeking elements.

All this is to indicate that the stimulation of Dr. Leach's theories is wider than the ethnographic province with which he has primarily dealt. The book will appeal to those who are interested in problems of government in undeveloped territories as well as to those who wish to have a really good first-hand study of one of the more primitive types of South East-Asian society. But to me its prime importance is as a major contribution to the theory of social systems. The book is a superb piece of craftsmanship done to an exciting design; the best tribute one can pay to it is to hope that before too long the author will have the opportunity to repeat the design, with modifications to suit another material of as interesting quality.

Edmund Leach (1964) 'Introductory note to the 1964 reprint', in Political Systems of Highland Burma: a study of Kachin social structure, London: Athlone, ix–xv.

Professor Firth's generously worded foreword provided such excellent sales talk that the first edition of this book rather rapidly went out of print. This new edition is a photographically reproduced copy of the original.

Early professional comment was distinctly tepid but, in retrospect, the book's appearance seems to have marked the beginning of a trend. My own feeling at the time was that British Social Anthropology had rested too long on a crudely oversimplified set of equilibrium assumptions derived from the use of organic analogies for the structure of social systems. Even so I recognised the great power of this type of equilibrium analysis and the difficulty of evading it within the general framework of current sociological theory. My book was an attempt to find a way out of this dilemma. In brief, my argument is that although historical facts are never, in any sense, in equilibrium, we can gain genuine insights if, for the purpose of analysis, we force these facts within the constraining mould of an *as if* system of ideas, composed of concepts which are treated *as if* they were part of an equilibrium system. Furthermore I claim to demonstrate that this fictional procedure is not merely an analytical device of the social anthropologist, it also corresponds to the way the Kachins themselves apprehend their own system through the medium of the verbal categories of their own language. It is not an entirely satisfactory argument – there are many threads in the story which might have been much better expressed – but in 1964 it no longer represents a solitary point of view. Professor Gluckman, who has always been my most vigorous opponent in matters theoretical and who has consistently sustained the type of organic equilibrium theory to which I have referred, has recently admitted that for many years 'I [Gluckman] thought too much in terms of organic analysis, whereby I saw the cycle of rebellions as maintaining the system, with some implication that it strengthened the state' and two pages later he even refers with guarded approval to the argument of this book while still maintaining that I have misunderstood my colleagues and misused the English language. Gluckman asserts that the Kachin system which I describe is properly described as one of 'stable equilibrium', which seems to me true at the level of ideas but quite untrue at the level of facts, and that 'British anthropologists have always thought in terms of this kind of equilibrium', which seems to me untrue altogether. In this last connection the reader should bear in mind that comments in this book on the work of my fellow anthropologists refer to work already published in 1952. Others besides Professor Gluckman have modified their position since then.

When I wrote this book the general climate of anthropological thinking in England was that established by Radcliffe-Brown. Social systems were spoken of as if they were naturally existing real entities and the equilibrium inherent in such systems was intrinsic, a fact of Nature. In 1940 Fortes wrote:

> At every level of Tale social organisation ... the tendency towards an equilibrium is apparent. ... This does not mean that Tale society was ever stagnant. Tension is

implicit in the equilibrium ... but conflict could never develop to the point of bringing about complete disintegration. The homogeneity of the Tale culture, the undifferentiated economic system, the territorial stability of the population, the network of kinship ties, the ramifications of clanship, and especially the mystical doctrines and ritual practices determining the native conception of the common good – all these are factors, restricting conflict and promoting restoration of equilibrium.

If Professor Gluckman supposes that the Kachins have a system which is in equilibrium in any sense which is even approximately equivalent to the equilibrium here described by Fortes, he has completely misunderstood the argument of my book. I fully appreciate that a great deal of sociological analysis of the very highest quality makes it appear that social systems are naturally endowed with an equilibrium which is a demonstrable fact. It is the thesis of this book that this appearance is an illusion, and my over-all purpose in writing the book at all was to examine the nature of this particular illusion in a particular case.

The data of social anthropology are in the first instance historical incidents, intrinsically non-repetitive, but when the anthropologist insists that his concern is with 'sociology' rather than with 'history', he at once imposes upon the evidence an assumption that systemic order may be discerned among the confusions of empirical fact. Such systemic order cannot be described without introducing notions of equilibrium and to the extent the argument of this book is itself an equilibrium analysis. But it differs from most monographic studies by social anthropologists in two particular respects. Firstly, I have attempted to expand the time-span within which the equilibrium is assumed to operate to a period of about 150 years, and secondly, I have attempted to make explicit the fictional (idealist) nature of the equilibrium assumptions.

[...]

I do not believe in historical determinism in any shape or form, and those who have imagined that I here claim to discern an everlasting cyclical process in the slender facts of recorded Kachin history have quite misunderstood what I intended to say. The argument is rather that the set of verbal categories described in Chapter V form a persistent structured set and that it is always in terms of such categories as these that Kachins seek to interpret (to themselves and to others) the empirical social phenomena which they observe around them ... Kachin verbal usage allows the speaker to structure his categories in more than one way. Gumsa and gumlao use the same words to describe the categories of their own political system and that of their opponents but they make different assumptions about the relations between the categories in the two cases.

Considered as category structures the gumsa political order and the gumlao political order are alike ideal types which necessarily, at all times and in all places, correspond rather badly with the empirical facts on the ground. If this be so, it seems reasonable to enquire whether there is any analysable social process which can be attributed to the persistent discrepancy between the facts on the ground and the two polarised structures of ideal categories. The thesis of Chapters VII and

VIII is that the outcome, for any part of the Kachin region, is a long-phase political oscillation, though, since the facts at the end of the cycle are quite different from the facts at the beginning of the cycle, the 'system on the ground' is not in equilibrium in the same way as the 'system of ideas'. There are many details in this part of the book which now seem to me very unsatisfactory. It is not that the evidence is irrelevant but that I have often put the stress in the wrong place.

Over the past ten years I have come to a much clearer understanding of the distinction (often blurred in this book) between the structure which can exist within a set of verbal categories and the lack of structure which ordinarily exists within any directly observed set of empirical facts. Certainly I noted this discrepancy – a particularly clear example of what I mean is cited at pp. 279–81 – but I tended to treat it as an abnormality, whereas it is really our common experience. Events only come to be structured in so far as they are endowed with order by the imposition of verbal categories.

[. . .]

The main body of the book is concerned with the theme that empirical political behaviour among the Kachin is a compromise response to the polarised political doctrines of *gumsa* and *gumlao*. In Chapter IX, I attempted to show how these polar doctrines are actually presented to the actor through the medium of conflicting mythologies, any of which might conveniently serve as a charter for social action. Re-reading this Chapter now it seems to me 'useful but inadequate'. Professor Lévi-Strauss' numerous writings on the study of myth have all appeared since this book first went to press, and they certainly have much relevance for the understanding of Kachin tradition.

The book ends with the suggestion that this unconventional style of analysis might have relevance outside the Kachin Hills, more particularly for areas to the west where the ethnographic record is particularly lavish. This suggestion has been justified. F. K. Lehman has combined personal research with a survey of a wide range of Chin materials. The result greatly enhances our understanding of the Chins, but also, less directly, it provides a useful confirmation of the value of my Kachin interpretation, for in Lehman's hands the discrepancies of Chin ethnography fall into a pattern. Viewed over-all, Chins turn out to be even more like Kachins than most of us would have expected.

It now seems clear that, in this whole region, the concept 'tribe' is of quite negative utility from the viewpoint of social analysis. The significance of particular features of particular tribal organisations cannot be discovered by functional investigations of the more usual kind. It is rather that we come to understand the qualities of 'Tribe A' only when we measure these qualities against the antithesis in 'Tribe B' (as in the *gumsa-gumlao* case). I reaffirm my opinion that, even at this late date, the extensive ethnographic literature of the Nagas would repay study from such a dialectical 'cross-tribal' point of view.

E. R. L.
Cambridge
January 1964

Chapter 6

The setting and the audience

As I write this Introduction, President George W. Bush is on his first visit to Europe since taking office. A few days ago, speaking to European heads of state in Gothenburg, he explained why he was refusing to ratify the Kyoto agreement on climate change. People gathered on the streets of the city to protest against his policies on the environment, and against capitalism's relentless drive for economic growth against the wider interests of humanity and the natural world. Meanwhile, a television documentary gave public exposure, for the first time in Britain, to research that indicates that global warming could take place much more quickly than previously predicted . . .

Why isn't everyone an environmentalist? Why do some people care more about the future of the natural world than others? Why do some people actively protect nature while others, by indifference or intent, are prepared to see it destroyed? These questions, in some form or other, constantly puzzle those engaged in campaigning, negotiating and lobbying for a more environmentally benign society. They are also of interest to an anthropologist, for they are questions about cultural diversity. They ask why people think, feel, and act differently towards natural things. How should we set about answering these questions?

(Milton 2002: 1)

In *Loving Nature,* Kay Milton addresses an issue that is fundamental to anthropology: 'how people come to think, feel and act as they do' (2002: 2). She does this via an ethnographic analysis of the conservationist movement in the UK, individuals and organisations dedicated to the protection of biological diversity in the face of a growing sense of threat to the natural environment. From the start Milton stresses her dual position as both anthropologist and environmental activist, and explicitly grounds her investigation, not only in disciplinary debates regarding emotions, cognition and environment, but in her own participation in conservation. Anthropology can help environmentalism, she explains, by 'improving our understanding of why we are as we are' (2002: 3).

Although not all ethnographers are as explicit about their agendas and motivations as Milton, all ethnographies are written by individuals with particular interests and obsessions, likes and dislikes, backgrounds, and personal and intellectual trajectories. And, just like the people they study, writers of ethnography live within social worlds, and they partake of and help to shape determined worldviews. Writing about the early history of anthropology in the UK and the US, Henrika Kuklick tells us that nine-teenth- and early-twentieth-century anthropologists 'performed creatively within circumstantial limitations, making decisions that seemed sensible to them, using ethnography as an aid to understanding the constraints and possibilities of their lives' (1991: 4). That is, the works particular anthro-pologists write emerge within the milieu of their own histories, both before, during and after fieldwork. And, as products of human activity, ethnographies are embedded within and influenced by a period, a social setting, and an intellectual climate. Last, and as we began exploring in Chapter 5 and will develop further below, all ethnographic writing is rela-tional: in their writings authors always engage with other writers, with the discipline at large, and with the world beyond anthropology.

In this chapter we concentrate on the relationship between the ethnog-raphy and the broader context within which it is written, taking as our starting point the idea that the two, the text and its context, are in fact inseparable. Because ethnographies are written by individuals who are socially and culturally situated and engaged, the context is always part of the text's very fabric. We therefore argue that an awareness of this context will help the reader gain a greater understanding of an author's standpoint and argument. For this reason, this awareness will also lead to a better appreciation of the lives of the people an ethnographer is trying to portray.

And it is important to emphasise that the context within which an ethnography is produced is never singular. Not only do ethnographers live within at least two worlds, 'home' and 'the field', but these are themselves fragmented and multiple. At home in the UK, for example, an anthropolo-gist may at once be an academic, a migrant, a political activist, an artist, and a mother, participating in multiple spheres, all of them shaping her perception of life and her role in it, including her intellectual development and her understanding of anthropology. And her experience in the field is perforce equally manifold. See how the anthropologist Ruth Behar talks about herself in *Translated Woman: crossing the border with Esperanza's story* (1993), the life history of a Mexican peddler:

> Okay, so technically speaking, I'm not a gringa. I'm Cubana, born in Cuba, raised in a series of noisy apartments in the sad borough of Queens, New York, that smelled of my mother's sofrito. I spoke Spanish at home, learned English in school . . . I was crossing borders without knowing it long before I met Esperanza – but through

knowing her I've reflected on how I've had to cross a lot of borders to get to a position where I could cross the Mexican border to bring back her story to put into a book. We cross borders, but we don't erase them; we take our borders with us.

I have supposedly been privileged from the beginning, a Cubanita, another 'model minority', a success story, the welcome mat of the American government spread at my feet, in grateful exile from the shackles of communism in the land of freedom, always grateful, never asking for too much, thank you, thank you very much, *gracias por todo*, and sorry for any trouble . . .

I'm a Cubana but in Mexico I'm a gringa because I go to Mexico with gringa privileges, gringa money, gringa credentials, not to mention a gringo husband and a gringo car. After all, I cross the border with an American passport.

(Behar 1993: 320–1)

Behar goes out of her way to contextualise her retelling of Esperanza's story by writing at large, not only about her relationship with Esperanza, but about her own experiences as a Cuban woman in American society and academia, and by reflecting on the points of both convergence and divergence between herself and Esperanza. In Behar's writing context and content are one, and we learn as much about Behar and her border-crossing as about Esperanza, Mexico or Mexican women. Most significantly, Behar emphasises her multifaceted position, the fact that she is many things at the same time and to different people. This multiplicity and fragmentation constitute the starting point in her approach to Esperanza, to their relationship, and to anthropology at large.

Whilst, like Behar, there are other anthropologists who directly engage the context of their writings in the writings themselves, there are also many who do not or who do so less overtly. And it is important to emphasise that even authors who are explicit about the agenda they bring to their field research and to their writing are unavoidably selective in their reflexivity. They discuss some determining elements and not others, perhaps leaving aside those which to the outside observer may appear particularly significant. Behar, for example, chooses to focus on her own family history and her position as an academic, rather than on the influence of the post-modernist movement on her style and approach. And Milton dwells on her participation in environmentalism, but does not explore the impact of her earlier work on Christianity in Kenya on her current interests, methods and perspectives.

Moreover, there are influences anthropologists themselves may not be aware of, or simply take for granted. Analysing how Portuguese students of anthropology approach British kinship theory, Mary Bouquet (1993: 33) reminds us that 'British anthropological discourse, in seeking to render intelligible unknown worlds and their inhabitants to a readership assumed to be "like us", drew upon that which was already familiar'. That is, the questions put forward by anthropologists, and their approaches and concepts, borrow from the world around them and at any one time anthropologists may or may not realise this, or think it relevant. So Bouquet shows how the notion of kinship as developed in early twentieth-century British social anthropology – the idea that all societies have kinship systems that can be compared to each other – 'fitted into an English middle class way of intellectualising the world' (1993: 32). 'Kinship', in other words, was not the neutral analytical tool it was purported to be, but part and parcel of the English middle-class way of thinking. And Portuguese students found the concept correspondingly foreign.

The question, then, is how will you be able to identify at least some of the key influences that have helped mould an ethnography whether or not the author himself writes explicitly about their significance. These influences are of many different kinds, and shape ethnographic texts at multiple levels. We are talking here about dimensions as diverse as the individual circumstances and personal history of a particular anthropologist; trends in anthropological thinking; social and political movements that transcend anthropology; and widely held cultural assumptions. As a reader, you will find clues within texts themselves about these dimensions and their effects by paying attention to such things as changing stylistic conventions; the use of jargon and concepts; or, as we discussed in Chapter 5, the ways authors construct arguments relationally, by reference to the work of others. Below, however, we begin by examining the different kinds of audiences ethnographies are written for. This focus on the audience can reveal much about the intentions and perspectives of a writer, and about how she conceptualises her place and the place of her work within anthropology and the world at large. We go on to examine how the intellectual climate at the time an ethnography is written shapes its production from fieldwork onwards, and finish by considering wider social, cultural and political contexts and their impact on the production of ethnographic texts.

Summary points

1   Ethnographies are moulded by the social and cultural context within which they are produced.
2   Learning abut this context helps the reader gain a better understanding of the author's perspective, and also of the lives of the people portrayed in the ethnography.
3   Although not all ethnographers write about the context of their work, you can find clues about this context in the ethnographies themselves.

Writers and informants

> Good conversations have no ending, and often no beginning. They
> have participants and listeners, but belong to no one, nor to history.
> Inscriptions of them broaden the community of conversationalists but
> close the discussion to those without access to the written word.
>
> (Gudeman and Rivera 1990: 1)

Ethnographic texts are, as Gudeman and Rivera remind us, nodes or
moments in much broader conversations, in exchanges of ideas that
involve not only the ethnographers, but also their informants as well as
larger communities of past and present conversationalists both 'in the field'
and 'at home'. These conversations incorporate but also transcend and are
wider than anthropology. Ways of knowing and representing the world
emerge and are transformed within the framework of exchanges between
writers, the people they write about, readers, and earlier thinkers. And yet,
as Gudeman and Rivera emphasise, the act of inscription is an excluding
exercise. Producing a written text narrows the number of conversationalists and leaves aside, not only the illiterate, but those who speak another
language or who are not familiar with the conventions, jargon, and convo-
luted rhetoric of an academic discipline.

Stylistic conventions in ethnographic writing reveal much about who is
included and who is excluded from ethnographic conversations.
Ethnographies are speckled with signposts that tell the reader who the
author sees as her interlocutors, what kinds of audiences her text is written
for, and what is the genealogy of her questioning and arguments. Key
places to look for these signposts are the acknowledgements, prefaces
and introductions to monographs and edited volumes. Most often these
show that writers of ethnography separate their personal and intellectual
relationships in the field from those with other anthropologists, and so
that they see themselves as belonging to more than one community of
conversationalists. And it is at the anthropological community that ethnographic texts are primarily aimed, even when authors explicitly recognise
the contribution of their informants to the development of their work and
ideas.

This separation between informants and anthropological audiences,
between conversations in the field and conversations in the academy, is
clearly visible in Michael Herzfeld's preface to *The Poetics of Manhood*
(1985). Herzfeld thanks first the people from Glendi, the Cretan village
that is the subject of his study:

> To the Glendiots themselves, of course, my debt is enormous. Through
> their lively exegetical concerns, their imaginative interest in my work,
> their constant offers to help me in my task, and their willingness to

record on tape an enormous range of narratives and other texts, they can claim a remarkable degree of involvement in the authorship of this book.

(Herzfeld 1985: xvii)

He then goes on to thank a long list of anthropological colleagues, starting with John Campbell, the father of the Anglophone anthropology of Greece, and going on to others: 'Richard Bauman, Loring M. Danforth, Mary Douglas, James W. Fernandez, Roger Joseph, Nennie Panourgia ... all subsequently read versions of this manuscript and offered me the benefits of their critical insight' (Herzfeld 1985: xviii). Thus, although both the Glendiots and the anthropologists are credited with contributing to the ethnography as a final product, it is the latter who have read and commented on the manuscript. They are the ones who are competent in the anthropological world-view, whose command of anthropological knowledge and convention enables them to offer critical advice. The Glendiots, on the other hand, lack this competence and instead contribute by supplying the author with material – 'narratives and other texts', 'exegetical concerns' – to be analysed. Tellingly, in the context of academic writing and publishing where individual agency and creativity are considered paramount, it is as a group that the Glendiots are made to share in the ethnography's authorship. That is, it is their collective belonging to Glendi that makes them the object of Herzfeld's enquiry and that defines their position *vis-à-vis* the ethnography. The anthropologists, as individual critical readers and commentators, are by contrast Herzfeld's audience. And indeed those named in the acknowledgements stand in for the anthropological community at large who likewise will read, critique, and refer to Herzfeld's work.

The disjuncture between the roles that informants and anthropological colleagues are expected to play stems from the widespread expectation that there will be a cleft between anthropological ways of knowing and of codifying information and those of our informants. The encounter with this gap, with the ensuing need for explanation and translation, is the *raison d'être* of our discipline. See how Jean L. Briggs thanks her informants in *Never in Anger* (1970), her ethnography of the Utkuhikhalingmiut of Northern Canada:

My greatest debt is of course to the Utkuhikhalingmiut with whom I stayed, especially the members of the family who adopted me and about whom this book is written. I am sorry that they would not understand or like many of the things I have written about them; I hope, nevertheless, that what I have said will help further the image of Eskimos as 'genuine people' (their word for themselves), rather than 'stone age men' or 'happy children'.

(Briggs 1970: ix)

Paradoxically, then, it is by creating an account of the Utku that the Utku themselves are not expected to read and would not agree with or even understand that Briggs aims to challenge popular Western and academic misrepresentations of this group. And indeed, like Briggs, most authors of ethnography do not write for their informants, even though it is true that ethnographies sometimes become debated by the very people they portray (Brettell 1993; R. Rosaldo 1986). In the postscript to the second edition of *Sound and Sentiment* (1990), his ethnography of the Kaluli of the Southern Highlands of New Guinea, Steven Feld describes reading parts of the first edition to his Kaluli friends. Like Briggs, Feld stresses the distance between ethnographic and native epistemologies and portrays his conversation with the Kaluli as 'dialogic editing' in which they effectively strip the anthropology out of his accounts:

> One of the most interesting outcomes of dialogic editing with Kaluli was the way my readers essentially reconstituted versions or portions of source materials in my fieldnotes upon hearing them summarised, capsuled, or stripped of their situated details. Kaluli took my stories and resituated them as their own as they had once before. To do that they worked generalisations back to an instance, an experience, a remembered activity or action. In effect they 'turned over' my story by providing recountings of the story that more typically are left behind in my fieldnotes . . .
>
> More pointedly, the abstracting, depersonalizing, summarizing, and generalizing moments that appear in my ethnography unanchored to specific instances, attributions and intentions are the ones which Kaluli readers most often responded to with a concretizing and repersonalizing set of questions, side comments or interpretations . . . Kaluli prefer reports from direct experience. That desire to situate knowledge and experience with specific actors, agendas and instances was most on their minds in any discussion of the book.
>
> (Feld 1990: 251–2)

Thus, whereas ethnographic writing revolves around abstraction, depersonalisation, summarising and generalisation, the Kaluli emphasise the concreteness and unrepeatability of events. In their reinterpretations of Feld's analyses they challenge the most basic of his assumptions. Nonetheless, note how Feld uses the Kaluli's reactions to his writings to gain further insight into their ways of understanding, and to convey this insight to his readers. In other words, and although the Kaluli have had some mediated access to Feld's work, he does not engage them as interlocutors in his writing. Instead they remain the objects of his study and their actions and statements are, as in the first edition of the book, investigated and retold for their anthropological significance. To achieve this Feld deploys concepts and frames of reference that belong squarely within an anthropological, rather than a Kaluli, epistemology.

As we have explained throughout this book, in order to make their informants intelligible to their readers writers of ethnography approach the world and mould their accounts in uniquely anthropological ways. As Marilyn Strathern has put it, '(a)nthropological analysis achieves its proximity to and replication of its subjects' comprehensions through a form of comprehension, of knowledge, that belongs distinctively to itself' (1988: xi). This distinctive form of knowledge has parallels with and draws from but doesn't completely correspond to popular Western understandings, and its esoteric character limits its audience, leaving aside not only informants but also many 'at home'. Thus, although anthropologists have argued that growing literacy and ease in the spread of information increases the chances that both our informants and other non-specialist audiences will critically read what we write, and that this should transform the basis of ethnographic practice (Marcus 1998), the fact is that the majority of ethnographic writing, whether in articles or in monographs, is still directed primarily at fellow academics. In the previous chapter we discussed how ethnographic arguments are always constructed relationally, by reference to those put forward in other ethnographies. Below we expand our discussion by investigating the ways in which the changing expectations and assumptions held by an specialist anthropological audience shape the production of ethnographic texts.

Summary points

1   Ethnographers tend to separate their personal and intellectual relationships 'in the field' from those in the academy.
2   Ethnographic texts are built through rhetorical devices, concepts and stylistic conventions that together constitute a distinctive and exclusive form of knowledge.
3   Ethnographic texts are aimed primarily at anthropological audiences rather than at our informants or at a general readership 'at home'.

Anthropological readers and intellectual trends

As a distinctive way of knowing and representing the world, then, anthropology is constructed through conversations among writers of ethnography. As we explained in Chapter 5, in their texts anthropologists refer to the work of others not only to provide a foundation and a framing for their contentions, but also to formulate innovations and challenge taken-for-granted knowledge. This conversational framework always structures the presentation of ethnographic material and the articulation of arguments, shaping how anthropologists reflect upon and explain their field experience. And it is by paying close attention to these exchanges that readers learn about the intellectual context of a particular ethnographic text – how a writer traces links to and addresses earlier thinkers, what they consider to be the genealogy of their ideas, and how they locate themselves *vis-à-vis* disciplinary and interdisciplinary debates and currents of thought. These exchanges are often made explicit to the reader in the form of summaries and reviews, where authors outline their evaluation of the work of others whilst delineating their own position.

In the excerpt below Barbara Placido opens her study of Venezuelan spirit possession by addressing other anthropologists who, like her, have attempted to analyse possession cults. She enters the conversation by recapitulating the discussion to date:

> In most anthropological accounts, humans who become possessed by spirits are described as ill or distressed, as lacking power, control, and agency, their experience one of loss (Bourgouignon 1973; Crapanzano 1977; Lewis 1989; Obeyesekere 1981; Ong 1988). Such accounts generally assume that the mediums participate in possession so as to acquire a more powerful and authoritative voice than the one they have as humans. Spirit possession is thus described by anthropologists as a kind of ventriloquism in which the mediums use the spirits in order to speak (Nourse 1996: 425).
>
> (Placido 2001: 207).

By singling out some trends and authors as central to the analysis of spirit possession, Placido constructs her own community of conversationalists out of a field of debate whose boundaries cannot in fact be defined. Her interlocutors are these very same writers as well as other readers looking to understand spirit possession and, more broadly, the anthropological community at large. And she finds her own point of entry into the discussion by identifying an analytical void in these previous accounts and grounding her own distinctive contribution in the understandings of her informants and her observations in the field:

> What anthropological analyses leave unclear, however, is what the spirits and the possessed actually say during possession episodes. Instead, they tend to focus on the context in which spirit possession develops, on its form, and on the social, economic, or ethnic background of the participants. By contrast, mediums and believers in the Venezuelan cult of María Lionza describe their cult, their relations with the spirits, and the spirits themselves as being constituted through and by words. Words, they affirm, are what the cult is all about. This article develops out of an attempt to make sense of this

striking discrepancy between perceptions of spirit possession within the María Lionza cult and anthropological understandings of the phenomenon.

(Placido 2001: 207)

Placido is deploying ethnographic material to highlight the need for a shift in anthropological theorising. She is also using anthropological theories and theorists in order to underline the originality of her insights and ethnographic material. As a consequence, Placido's account of these other writers and their ideas is selective: her aim is not so much to produce a comprehensive summary of work to date as to provide the reader with a critical interpretation of this work that leads to an appreciation of her own argument. And, like other anthropologists using this widespread strategy and etiquette, Placido relies on her readers having some prior acquaintance with the issues and authors she is discussing.

This reliance on common knowledge of anthropology has the effect of excluding uninformed readers and of delineating an anthropological audience for ethnographic writing. It is also apparent in the excerpt below, from Malinowski's (1967) [1957] preface to Raymond Firth's *We, the Tikopia*, first published in 1936:

> A book like this is the more welcome just at this juncture when we are suffering from a surfeit of new anthropological theories. New standards are being hoisted every few months, and the reality of human life is being submitted to some queer and alarming manipulations. On the one hand, we have the application of mathematics, in fact calculus with integrals and differential equations, to facts as elusive and essentially unmathematical as belief, sentiment and social organisation. On the other hand, attempts are made to analyse cultures in terms of Schismogenesis, or to define the individual and singular 'genius' of each particular society as Apollonian, Dionysiac, or Paranoid, and the like. Under the deft touch of another writer the women of one tribe appear masculine, while in another the males develop feminine qualities almost to the verge of parturition. By contrast the present book is an unaffected piece of genuine scholarship, based on real experience of a culture and not on a few hypostasised impressions. The anthropologist who still believes that his work can be scientific can therefore breathe a sigh of relief and gratitude.

(Malinowski 1967 [1957]: vii–viii)

Naming no names but clearly expecting his audience to be familiar with the works and authors he is referring to, Malinowski produces an acerbic attack on key figures of mid-twentieth-century anthropology, including Gregory Bateson, Ruth Benedict, and Margaret Mead. He goes on to explain the distinctiveness and value of Firth's work and to locate him within the long-term development of the discipline, establishing links with founding fathers like Morgan, Bachofen and Rivers. But later on in the preface Malinowski also takes Firth to task for his approach to the study of kinship. He not only positions Firth's monograph but reviews and emphasises his own trajectory and standpoint on current debates. He thus establishes himself, the senior academic and path maker, as the ideal reader and model audience, critical but not unduly so.

Prefaces written by well established anthropologists are a common feature of ethnography, and they often replicate Malinowski's mixture of endorsement and critique. They mediate an ethnography for its audience and establish its credentials but also work to ensconce senior figures and reinforce the sense of their importance to anthropology. Book reviews in academic journals and endorsements printed at the back of some ethnographies play similar roles. Most importantly, prefaces, book reviews and endorsements evidence the conversational nature of ethnographic writing, the fact that ethnographies are moulded by personal and intellectual relationships, concerns and inclinations, out of which emerge trends within the discipline.

All ethnographies, then, are located in time. Not only are the arguments put forward by anthropologists relational, as we explained in our discussion of **matrifocality** in Chapter 5, but ethnographic writing responds to and embodies particular intellectual climates. Let us go back to Feld's Kaluli ethnography. In the introduction to *Sound and Sentiment*, first published in 1982, Feld relates his aims for his readers:

> This is an ethnographic study of sound as a cultural system, that is, as a system of symbols, among the Kaluli people of Papua New Guinea. My intention is to show how an analysis of modes and codes of sound communication leads to an understanding of the ethos and quality of life in Kaluli society.
>
> (Feld 1990: 3)

And later on he outlines his theoretical framework:

> (t)he intellectual positions I have found most helpful are the structuralism of Claude Lévi-Strauss (1966), the thick description and interpretive ethnography advocated by Clifford Geertz (1973), and the ethnography of communication paradigm proposed by Dell Hymes (1974).
>
> (Feld 1990: 14).

With these two statements, Feld firmly situates his aims, questions and approaches within a clearly defined period in the development of anthropology, the 1970s. Not only is he explicit about the influences that mould his work, but he uses concepts and terms ('cultural system', 'system of symbols', 'codes') that likewise indicate the historical specificity of his writing. Most tellingly, Feld takes a radically different tack to the Kaluli and their words in the postscript to the second edition of *Sound and Sentiment*, published eight years later at the height of the influence of the *writing culture* approach on American anthropology. Describing the response of the Kaluli when a copy of his book arrived in the village where he was living, he tells us that,

> I think of the forms of ethnographic discourse that developed in these encounters as dialogic editing, negotiations of what Kaluli and I said to, about, with, and through each other, juxtapositions of Kaluli voices and my own. This multiplicity of voices and views animates the dialogic dimension here, and unmasks editing practices to open questions about rights, authority, and the power to control which voices talk when, how much, in what order, in what language. Dialogic editing refers to the impact of Kaluli voices on what I tell you about them in my voice; how their take on my take on them requires a reframing and a refocusing of my account. This is the inevitable politics of writing culture, of producing selections and passing them off as authentic and genuine, and then confronting a recentered view of that selection process that both questions and comments upon the original frame and focus. Stated somewhat more directly, the idea here is to let some Kaluli voices get a few words in edgewise among my other readers, critics and book reviewers.
>
> (Feld 1990: 241, 244)

Feld's Postcript is a textbook example of the impact of **post-modernism** on late twentieth-century American cultural anthropology. Leaving 'systems' and 'codes' behind, Feld talks instead of 'dialogues' and 'discourses', of 'editing practices' and 'intertextual biographies' (1990: 253). Whereas the first edition of *Sound and Sentiment* was an exercise in authoritative **structuralism** and **thick description**, in the postscript Feld seems to be taking his cue from Clifford and Marcus' *Writing Culture: the poetics and politics of ethnography* (1986) and describes his own work as an exploration of 'the politics of writing culture' (1990: 244). While, in the introduction to *Writing Culture*, Clifford talks about ethnography being 'always caught up in the invention, not the representation, of cultures' (1986: 2), Feld reflects on his own experience of 'producing selections and passing them off as authentic and genuine' (1990: 244). And whilst Clifford calls for a 'cultural poetics that is an interplay of voices, of positioned utterances' (1986: 12), Feld talks about a 'multiplicity of voices and views' that 'animates the dialogic dimension' of his postcript (1990: 244). In other words, the writer here uses his account of his conversations with Kaluli in order to engage a particular trend within anthropology. Feld subordinates his Kaluli dialogues to the dialogue he establishes with other anthropological writers and anthropology emerges as a changing discipline.

Indeed, in the eight years between the two editions of *Sound and Sentiment* the anthropological canon had changed. With it changed also what was considered cutting-edge scholarship, as well as a legitimate object of anthropological enquiry and adequate anthropological approaches, methodologies and styles. And yet, we are not arguing that anthropologists passively regurgitate theories that are handed out to them. It is writers of ethnography themselves who reformulate this canon through their engagement with each other, with their informants, and with the social and political world around them. And, although links with the past are never broken, out of this engagement come the definition of novel areas of discussion, new ways of doing and writing anthropology, and new standards for the discipline. In the last section of this chapter we explore how writers of ethnography take on their social environment, and on how anthropological concerns and ethnographic conventions are transformed as a consequence.

Summary points

1   Anthropology is constructed through conversations among writers of ethnography.
2   Ethnographic writing responds to and embodies particular intellectual climates.
3   Writers of ethnography reformulate the anthropological canon through their engagement with their informants, with each other, and with the social and political world around them.

Feminist anthropology: writers of ethnography as social actors

Throughout this chapter we have argued that, just like the people they study, writers of ethnography are social actors and their texts are cultural products created at particular points in time and out of specific social and cultural milieus. These texts emerge through the participation of their authors, not only in disciplinary exchanges as we have just outlined, but also in life beyond the academy. Because anthropologists observe and examine human lives, all anthropology critically reflects on the social worlds in which ethnographers participate. But sometimes writers of ethnography are also active in political discussions, movements, and struggles, and their involvement has an impact on their writing and on their discipline more broadly. In this last section, we examine the birth and growth of feminist anthropology as a particularly telling example of a process that constantly shapes ethnographic writing: the generation of new concerns, perspectives and analytical tools as a consequence of writers' engagement with the politics of the social world of which they are a part. In order to tell this story we deploy two ethnographies, Annette Weiner's (1976) *Women of Value, Men of Renown*, and Anna Lowenhaupt Tsing's (1993) *In the Realm of the Diamond Queen*.

In her ethnography of the Trobriands, Annette Weiner (1976) argued for an anthropology that gave equal weight and attention to the activities of women and of men. She explained how, up to the mid-1970s, much anthropology had contained 'a male overload', and how 'traditional areas of investigation have too often blinded us to the complexity of female and male interaction' (Weiner 1976: 12). With few exceptions anthropologists from Malinowski onwards had either ignored or denied the significance of women's activities and women's objects. Because their assumptions about society and culture had followed 'a male-dominated path' (*ibid.*) their descriptions and analyses were inherently flawed. This was the case even in the anthropology of Melanesia – an area where, according to Weiner, women are explicitly valued and celebrated and where anthropologists like Mead, Fortune and Bateson had long before demonstrated the importance of analysing gender relations (1976: 17). And so she explains how,

> My assumption in this book is that, regardless of the variation between the economic and political roles of men and women, the part women play in society must be accorded equal time in any study concerned with the basic components of social organization.
>
> (Weiner 1976: 11)

Weiner was far from alone in wanting to correct anthropology's male bias. In the mid-1970s many other women writers of ethnography were calling for an anthropology that challenged received knowledge about the sexes and their role in society and culture – a politically engaged anthropology. They were responding and contributing to the second wave of **feminism** in the United States and Britain and saw themselves as both feminists and anthropologists. In Rosaldo and Lamphere's words (1974: 1–2), '(a)long with many women today, we are trying to understand our position and to change it. We have become increasingly aware of sexual inequalities in economic, social and political institutions and are seeking ways to fight them'. As feminists and as anthropologists, these writers looked to non-Western societies for what light they could throw on the roots and causes of sexual inequality both in the West and elsewhere: they saw understanding as a fundamental step in the path to social change and gender equality. This line of enquiry shaped Weiner's take on the Trobriands so that her analysis puts particular emphasis on Trobriand women's agency, and on the need for anthropologists to take into account specifically female forms of power when investigating the roots and forms of sexual inequality cross-culturally. Trobriand women, she argued, are not passive victims of oppression but rather actors in their own right:

> Any study that does not include the role of women – as seen by women – as part of the way the society is structured remains only a partial study of that society. Whether women are publicly valued or privately secluded, whether they control politics, a range of economic commodities, or merely magic spells, they function within that society, not as objects but as individuals with some measure of control. We cannot begin to understand either in evolutionary terms or in current and historical situations why and how women in so many cases have been relegated to secondary status until we first reckon with the power women do have, even if this power appears limited and seems outside the political field.
>
> (Weiner 1976: 228–9)

Feminist writers like Weiner wanted to redirect anthropology by making anthropologists re-examine their assumptions about power, hierarchy and inequality (1976: 236), and also by arguing the necessity of taking into account gender constructs and relations when analysing any area of social life. So for example studying the Meratus Dayak of the Indonesian rainforest, Anna Lowenhaupt Tsing (1993) emphasises the gendered nature of their marginality *vis-à-vis* the Indonesian state. It is by paying attention to gender that the impossibility of separating the Meratus mode of being in the world from broad regional and global frameworks becomes apparent. Not only are gender and marginality mutually constituted in Meratus, but their intertwining highlights the theoretical impossibility of opposing local relations and dynamics to so-called external influences. There isn't a social and cultural core upon which external influences impact:

> By putting gender at the centre of my analysis, I create a continually oppositional dialogue with more familiar ethnographic genres which segregate an endogenous cultural logic from regional-to-global influences. Generally, studies of gender and wider political relations hardly overlap. Histories of local-global interconnections still ignore gender; and gender tends to be studied as an 'internal' cultural issue. 'External' influences are portrayed as influencing gender – as in much of the literature on women, colonialism and development – only as foreign impositions upon once stable and self-regulating traditions. These conventions obscure the regionally ramifying debates and practices that produce both gender and politics. By transgressing conventions of segregated 'internal' and 'external' cultural analysis, this book shows

the connections between intercommunity divisions, including gender difference, and Meratus regional and national marginality. Attention to gender, as both an imaginative construct and a point of divergent positionings, brings wider cultural negotiations to the centre of local affairs.

(Tsing 1993: 9)

During the 1980s, Black feminists in the USA and elsewhere challenged the feminist assumption of a universal sisterhood of women. They argued that the subordination of white women and women of colour are different, because women of colour also experience other forms of oppression. White women, the argument went, are implicated in the oppression of people of colour. This challenge was taken up by feminist anthropologists who reconsidered the homogeneity of their concepts and categories: as feminism changed as a political movement, so did its contribution to anthropology. In Tsing's analysis, neither marginality nor gender are homogeneous conditions or experiences. Rather, when attention is paid to their mutual constitution both emerge as fragmented:

> In working with Meratus, my opening has been the mutual embeddedness of gender, ethnicity and political status. The three are mutually constituted. State politics shape ethnic and regional identity and are, in turn, informed by them. State and ethnic politics are gendered just as gender difference is created through state and ethnic discourse. Yet each of the three creates divided oppositions that destabilize the communities of interest formed by the other two. The state's concentric model of political status both orders and disturbs the dualism of gender and of ethnic differentiation. Gender difference breaks up ethnic unity and stimulates divergent attitudes towards the state. By treating women and men as individual commentators on their culture, I ask about disruptive as well as unifying features of their perspectives without assuming gender, ethnic or political homogeneities.
>
> (Tsing 1993: 33–4)

This has been another key contribution of feminism to anthropology: the realisation, grounded in ethnographic analysis, that communities are always fragmented, that positionings are always multiple, and that groups of interest whose boundaries may appear obvious at first sight are most likely not so. And after the initial engagement of some anthropologists with a particular political movement in society, feminism, this awareness has become a basic tenet of early twenty-first century anthropology, one accepted by feminists and non-feminists alike. Anthropological concerns and modes of enquiry, in other words, always develop in close relationship with changing social landscapes and political climates.

Summary points

1 Feminist writers demonstrate how the analytical tools of anthropology can be transformed through the political commitment of anthropologists.
2 As feminism went through various stages so its contribution to anthropology evolved.
3 By the early twentieth century anthropological enquiry has at its core insights generated through its engagement with feminism.

Concluding remarks

In this book we treat ethnographic texts anthropologically, as cultural products created within a particular milieu by somebody and for somebody. In this chapter our aim has been to analyse ethnography by paying attention both on its consumers and to the context of its production. By asking who ethnographic texts are for, and under what circumstances are they generated, ethnography has emerged as a way of knowing and representing the world that is conversational. Ethnography, we have argued, depends on the social relations that writers establish not only with their informants, but with each other and with other interlocutors both 'in the field' and 'at home'. These relations enter ethnographic texts in ways determined by stylistic conventions and by deep rooted assumptions about the roles that anthropologists and informants play in the creation of anthropological knowledge. This mode of knowing the world, moreover, is not isolated, but responds to and emerges within particular social, economic and political circumstances. In the next chapter we take the intertwining of text and context as our starting point, but narrow our focus, exploring how authors, whom we always see as social actors, position themselves within ethnographic texts.

Chapter 6 – activities

In this excerpt from 'The Female World of Cards and Holidays' Micaela di Leonardo analyses the work that Italian American women do to sustain kinship relations across households. Her discussion draws on and contributes to debates within feminism and feminist theory as well as within anthropology. The excerpt highlights the relationship between ethnographic writing and the social and intellectual contexts within which it is produced. Read the excerpt and respond to the following questions:

1 Who are di Leonardo's interlocutors in this piece? How does she position herself in relation to them?
2 What roles do di Leonardo's informants play in the excerpt? In what ways do they participate in the community of conversationalists that di Leonardo constructs in her article?

3   What intellectual trends is di Leonardo engaging? How is this engagement made visible in the excerpt?
4   In what ways are the concerns of feminism as a political movement made evident in the piece?
5   What concept does di Leonardo introduce to the conversation between feminism and anthropology? How does she deploy this concept and to what purposes?

Di Leonardo, M. (1987) 'The Female World of Cards and Holidays: women, families and the work of kinship', Signs 12(3): 440–53

Why is that the married women of America are supposed to write all the letters and send all the cards to their husbands' families? My old man is a much better writer than I am, yet he expects me to correspond with his whole family. If I asked him to correspond with mine, he would blow a gasket

(Letter to Ann Landers)

Women's place in man's life cycle has been that of nurturer, caretaker, and helpmate, the weaver of those networks of relationships on which she in turn relies.

(Carol Gilligan, In a Different Voice)

Feminist scholars in the past fifteen years have made great strides in formulating new understandings of the relations among gender, kinship, and the larger economy. As a result of this pioneering research, women are newly visible and audible, no longer submerged within their families. We see households as loci of political struggle, inseparable parts of the larger society and economy, rather than as havens from the heartless world of industrial capitalism. And historical and cultural variations in kinship and family forms have become clearer with the maturation of feminist historical and social-scientific scholarship.

Two theoretical trends have been key to this reinterpretation of women's work and family domain. The first is the elevation to visibility of women's nonmarket activities – housework, child care, the servicing of men, and the care of the elderly – and the definition of all these activities as *labor*, to be enumerated alongside and counted as part of overall social reproduction. The second theoretical trend is the nonpejorative focus on women's domestic or kin-centered networks. We now see them as the products of conscious strategy, as crucial to the functioning of kinship systems, as sources of women's autonomous power and possible primary sites of emotional fulfillment, and, at times, as the vehicles for actual survival and/or political resistance.

Recently, however, a division has developed between feminist interpreters of the 'labor' and the 'network' perspectives on women's lives. Those who focus on women's work tend to envision women as sentient, goal-oriented actors, while those who concern themselves with women's ties to others tend to perceive women primarily in terms of nurturance, other-orientation – altruism. . . .

I shall not here address this specific debate but, instead, shall consider its theoretical background and implications. I shall argue that we need to fuse, rather than to oppose, the domestic network and labor perspectives. In what follows, I introduce a new concept, the work of kinship, both to aid empirical feminist research on women, work, and family and to help advance feminist theory in this arena. I believe that the boundary-crossing nature of the concept helps to confound the self-interest/altruism dichotomy, forcing us from an either-or stance to a position that includes both perspectives. I hope in this way to contribute to a more critical feminist vision of women's lives and the meaning of family in the industrial West.

In my recent field research among Italian-Americans in Northern California, I found myself considering the relations between women's kinship and economic lives. As an anthropologist, I was concerned with people's kin lives beyond conventional American nuclear family or household boundaries. To this end, I collected individual and family life histories, asking about all kin and close friends and their activities. I was also very interested in women's labor. As I sat with women and listened to their accounts of their past and present lives, I began to realize that they were involved in three types of work: housework and child care, work in the labor market, and the work of kinship.

By kin work I refer to the conception, maintenance, and ritual celebration of cross-household kin ties, including visits, letters, telephone calls, presents, and cards to kin; the organization of holiday gatherings; the creation and maintenance of quasi-kin relations; decisions to neglect or to intensify particular ties; the mental work of reflection about all these activities; and the creation and communication of altering images of family and kin vis-à-vis the images of others, both folk and mass media. Kin work is a key element that has been missing in the synthesis of the 'household labor' and 'domestic network' perspectives. In our emphasis on individual women's responsibilities within households and on the job, we reflect the common picture of households as nuclear units, tied perhaps to the larger social and economic system, but not to *each other*. We miss the point of telephone and soft drink advertising, of women's magazines' holiday issues, of commentators' confused nostalgia for the mythical American extended family: it is kinship contact *across households*, as much as women's work within them, that fulfils our cultural expectation of satisfying family life.

Maintaining these contacts, this sense of family, takes time, intention, and skill. We tend to think of human social and kin networks as the epiphenomena of production and reproduction: the social traces created by our material lives. Or, in the neoclassical tradition, we see them as part of leisure activities, outside an economic purview except insofar as they involve consumption behavior. But the creation and maintenance of kin and quasi-kin networks in advanced industrial societies is *work*; and, moreover, it is largely women's work.

The kin-work lens brought into focus new perspectives on my informants' family lives. First, life histories revealed that often the very existence of kin contact and holiday celebration depended on the presence of an adult woman in the household.

When couples divorced or mothers died, the work of kinship was left undone; when women entered into sanctioned sexual or marital relationships with men in these situations, they reconstituted the men's kinships networks and organized gatherings and holiday celebrations. Middle-aged businessman Al Bertini, for example, recalled the death of his mother in his early adolescence: 'I think that's probably one of the biggest losses in losing a family – yeah, I remember as a child when my Mom was alive … the holidays were treated with enthusiasm and love … after she died the attempt was there but it just didn't materialize.' Later in life, when Al Bertini and his wife separated, his own and his son Jim's participation in extended-family contact decreased rapidly. But when Jim began a relationship with Jane Bateman, she and he moved in with Al, and Jim and Jane began to invite his kin over for holidays. Jane single-handedly planned and cooked the holiday feasts.

Kin work, then, is like housework and child care: men in the aggregate do not do it. It differs from these forms of labor in that it is harder for men to substitute hired labor to accomplish these tasks in the absence of kinswomen. Second, I found that women, as the workers in this arena, generally had much greater kin knowledge than did their husbands, often including more accurate and extensive knowledge of their husbands' families. This was true both of middle-aged and younger couples and surfaced as a phenomenon in my interviews in the form of humorous arguments and in wives' detailed additions to husbands' narratives. Nick Meraviglia, a middle-aged professional, discussed his Italian antecedents in the presence of his wife, Pina:

> Nick: My grandfather was a very outspoken man, and it was reported he took off for the hills when he found out that Mussolini was in power.
> Pina: And he was a very tall man; he used to have to bow his head to get inside doors.
> Nick: No, that was my uncle.
> Pina: Your grandfather too, I've heard your mother say.
> Nick: My mother has a sister and a brother.
> Pina: Two sisters!
> Nick: You're right!
> Pina: Maria and Angelina.

Women were also much more willing to discuss family feuds and crises and their own roles in them; men tended to repeat formulaic statements asserting family unity and respectability. (This was much less true for younger men). Joe and Cetta Loughinotti's statements illustrate these tendencies. Joe responded to my question about kin relations: 'We all get along. As a rule, relatives, you got nothing but trouble.' Cetta, instead, discussed her relations with each of her grown children, their wives, her in-laws, and her own blood kin in detail. She did not hide the fact that relations were strained in several cases; she was eager to discuss the evolution of problems and to seek my opinions of her actions. Similarly, Pina Meraviglia told the following story of her fight with one of her brothers with hysterical laughter: 'There was some biting and hair pulling and choking … it was terrible! I shouldn't even tell you ... ' Nick, meanwhile, was concerned about maintaining an image of family unity and respectability.

Also, men waxed fluent while women were quite inarticulate in discussing their past and present occupations. When asked about their work lives, Joe Longhinotti and Nick Meraviglia, union baker and professional, respectively, gave detailed narratives of their work careers. Cetta Longhinotti and Pina Meraviglia, clerical and former clerical, respectively, offered only short descriptions focusing on factors of ambience, such as the 'lovely things' sold by Cetta's firm.

These patterns are not repeated in the younger generation, especially among younger women, such as Jane Bateman, who have managed to acquire training and jobs with some prospect of mobility. These younger women, though, have *added* a professional and detailed interest in their jobs to a felt responsibility for the work of kinship.

Although men rarely took on any kin-work tasks, family histories and accounts of contemporary life revealed that kinswomen often negotiated among themselves, alternating hosting, food-preparation, and gift-buying responsibilities – or sometimes ceding entire task clusters to one woman. Taking on or ceding tasks was clearly related to acquiring or divesting oneself of power within kin networks, but women varied in their interpretation of the meaning of this power. Cetta Longhinotti, for example, relied on the 'family Christmas dinner' as a symbol of her central kinship role and was involved in painful negotiations with her daughter-in-law over the issue: 'Last year she insisted – this is touchy. She doesn't want to spend the holiday dinner together. So last year we went there. But I still had my dinner the next day ... I made a big dinner on Christmas Day, regardless of who's coming – candles on the table, the whole routine. I decorate the house myself too ... well, I just feel that the time will come when maybe I won't feel like cooking a big dinner – she should take advantage of the fact that I feel like doing it now.' Pina Meraviglia, in contrast, was saddened by the centripetal force of the developmental cycle but was unworried about the power dynamics involved in her negotiations with daughters- and mother-in-law over holiday celebrations.

Kin work is not just a matter of power among women but also of the mediation of power represented by household units. Women often choose to minimize status claims in their kin work and to include numbers of households under the rubric of family. Cetta Longhinotti's sister Anna, for example, is married to a professional man whose parents have considerable economic resources, while Joe and Cetta have low incomes and no other well-off kin. Cetta and Anna remain close, talk on the phone several times a week, and assist their adult children, divided by distance and economic status, in remaining united as cousins.

Finally, women perceived housework, child care, market labor, the care of the elderly, and the work of the kinship as competing responsibilities. Kin work was a unique category, however, because it was unlabeled and because women felt they could either cede some tasks to kinswomen and/or could cut them back severely. Women variously cited the pressures of market labor, the needs of the elderly, and their own desires for freedom and job enrichment as reasons for cutting back Christmas card lists, organized holiday gatherings, multifamily dinners, letters, visits, and phone calls. They expressed guilt and defensiveness about this cutback process and, particularly, about their failures to keep families close through constant contact and about their failures to create perfect holiday celebrations....

[...]

Recognizing that kin work is gender rather than class based allows us to see women's kin networks among all groups, not just among working-class and impoverished women in industrialized societies. This recognition in turn clarifies our understanding of the privileges and limits of women's varying access to economic resources. Affluent women can 'buy out' of housework, child care – and even some kin-work responsibilities. But they, like all women, are ultimately responsible, and subject to both guilt and blame, as the administrators of home, children, and kin-network. Even the wealthiest women must negotiate the timing and venue of holidays and other family rituals with their kinswomen. It may be that kin work is the core women's work category in which all women cooperate, while women's perceptions of the appropriateness of cooperation for housework, child care, and the care of the elderly varies by race, class, region, and generation.

[...]

... (T)he question remains, Why do women do kin work? However material factors may shape activities, they do not determine how individuals may perceive them. And in considering issues of motivation, of intention, of the cultural construction of kin work, we return to the altruism versus self-interest dichotomy in recent feminist theory. Consider the epigraphs to this article. Are women kin workers the nurturant weavers of the Gilligan quotation or victims, like the fed-up woman who writes to complain to Ann Landers? That is, are we to see kin work as yet another example of 'women's culture' that takes the care of others as its primary desideratum? Or are we to see kin work as another way in which men, the economy, and the state extract labor from women without a fair return? And how do women themselves see their kin work and its place in their lives?

As I have indicated above, I believe that it is the creation of the self-interest/ altruism dichotomy that is itself the problem here. My women informants, like most American women, accepted their primary responsibility for housework and the care of dependent children. Despite two major waves of feminist activism in this century, the gendering of certain categories of unpaid labor is still largely unaltered. These work responsibilities clearly interfere with some women's labor force commitments at certain life-cycle stages; but, more important, women are simply discriminated against in the labor market and rarely are able to achieve wage and status parity with men of the same age, race, class, and educational background.

Thus for my women informants, as for most American women, the domestic domain is not only an arena in which much unpaid labor must be undertaken but also a realm in which one may attempt to gain human satisfactions – and power – not available in the labor market. Anthropologists Jane Collier and Louise Lamphere have written compellingly on the ways in which varying kinship and economic structures may shape women's competition or cooperation with one another in domestic domains. Feminists considering Western women and families have looked at the issue of power primarily in terms of husband-wife relations or psychological relations between parents and children. If we adopt Collier and Lamphere's broader canvas though, we see that kin work is not only women's labor from which men and children benefit but also labor that women undertake in order to create obligations in men and children and to gain power over one another. Thus Cetta Longhinotti's struggle with her daughter-in-law over the venue of Christmas dinner is not just about a competition over altruism, it is also about the creation of future obligations. And thus Cetta's and Anna's sponsorship of their children's friend-ship with each other is both an act of nurturance and a cooperative means of gaining power over those children.

[. . .]

The concept of kin work helps to bring into focus a heretofore unacknowledged array of tasks that is culturally assigned to women in industrialized societies. At the same time, this concept, embodying notions of both love and work and crossing the boundaries of households, helps us to reflect on current feminist debates on women's work, family, and community. We newly see both the interrelations of these phenomena and women's roles in creating and maintaining those interrelations. Revealing the actual labor embodied in what we culturally conceive as love and considering the political uses of this labor helps to deconstruct the self-interest/altruism dichotomy and to connect more closely women's domestic and labor-force lives.

The true value of the concept, however, remains to be tested through further historical and contemporary research on gender, kinship, and labor. We need to assess the suggestion that gendered kin work emerges in concert with the capitalist development process; to probe the historical record for women's and men's varying and changing conceptions of it; and to research the current range of its cultural constructions and material realities. We know that household boundaries are more porous than we had thought – but they are undoubtedly differentially porous, and this is what we need to specify. We need, in particular, to assess the relations of changing labor processes, residential patterns, and the use of technology to changing kin work.

Altering the values attached to this particular set of women's tasks will be as difficult as are the housework, child-care, and occupational-segregation struggles. But just as feminist research in these latter areas is complementary and cumulative, so researching kin work should help us to piece together the home, work, and public-life landscape – to see the female world of cards and holidays as it is constructed and lived within the changing political economy. How female that world is to remain, and what it would look like if it were not sex-segregated, are questions we cannot yet answer.

Chapter 7

Positioning the author

In *Birds of My Kalam Country* Ian Saem Majnep, a Kalam from Papua New Guinea, and Ralph Bulmer, a British-trained anthropologist, use layout and font visually to flag to the reader their different contributions to the book. Before writing at length about Kalam society and ornithology, this is how they explain their collaboration and strategy:

> (t)he first sections of general discussion in each chapter . . . are edited versions of Saem's own statements, in the main freely translated from Kalam or from Pidgin. Then follows in most cases additional information drawn by Bulmer from other sources, whether from statements by other Kalam, from his own field observations or collector's records, or from the New Guinea ornithological literature.
>
> **The sections of this book which are primarily Saem's are printed in Bodoni type, as this sentence is.** Within these sections some explanatory material by Bulmer is in square brackets. Additional material by Bulmer is printed in Univers type, as the rest of this page is.
>
> (Majnep and Bulmer 1977: 12)

Thus, although Bulmer explains that his exegesis is partly based on the material supplied by Majnep and other Kalam, the two kinds of knowledge are physically separated on the page. Moreover, Majnep's and Bulmer's sections are very different stylistically. Majnep's are strongly autobiographical and read very much as transcriptions of spoken language:

> The seat of a person's *noman*, or soul, is his heart. When he stops breathing and his heart stops beating he is dead, and his soul has left him. But in sleep the soul can also leave the body. The things you see in dreams are the things your soul sees while you sleep. When a man's soul leaves him and goes off while he sleeps, we believe that it can turn into *ko* or a *jbog* or another of the lories. . . . Often while I have been in Port Moresby I have had such dreams. But if in your dream you shoot one of these birds, that is bad, it is like killing your own soul, and

you will get sick. Once in Port Moresby I dreamed that I shot two *jbog* [little Red Lories], and I was very ill when I awoke, running a high fever.

(Majnep and Bulmer 1977: 50)

By comparison with the immediacy and individuality conveyed in Majnep's sections, in Bulmer's we come across a neutral voice heavily reliant on disciplinary concepts – the voice of a-personal and transcendent anthropological erudition:

Consistent with the absence of corporate territorial groups, Kalam had not developed systems of inter-group ceremonial exchange in any way comparable in scale with those operated by the dense populations of the Central Highlands. But gifts to affines at the feasts which accompanied the dance-festivals and initiations were important, as also was individual trade and gift exchange.

(Majnep and Bulmer 1977: 33)

By distinguishing two narrators, native and anthropologist, Majnep and Bulmer emphasise at once their distinct agency *and* their shared authorship – the fact that it is from the encounter of their different understandings that their cooperation emerges. *Birds of My Kalam Country* therefore illustrates in a particularly vivid way the conversational nature of ethnography that we have emphasised in previous chapters. Ethnographic knowledge, we have argued, is always relational, the product of multiple cross-cutting conversations across diverse contexts, not only between anthropologist and informants but also between anthropologist and others in the academy and more broadly 'at home'. In this sense, we agree with James Clifford when he says that the activity of ethnography is always 'plural and beyond the control of any individual' (1983: 139).

And yet, conversations involve exchanges and hence not only depend upon but perpetuate the existence of distinct conversationalists. And, as we discussed in Chapter 6, some of these conversationalists have greater control over the ensuing representations than others. Thus, it is extremely rare for authorship and editorial control to be shared with informants as happens in *Birds of my Kalam Country*, much less relinquished by the anthropologist. Although ethnographic knowledge is conversational, authority over the final product stays firmly in the hands of the anthropologist. Indeed, in this chapter we go further and argue that ethnography, as a particular mode of knowing, depends on the creation of a singular or individual authorial self. Paradoxically, it is precisely out of a multiplicity of relationships in the field and 'at home' that ethnographic authorship emerges as individual and authoritative, rather than as shared and precarious. In ethnographic writing it is relationships between informants and anthropologist and among anthropologists that are seen to lend validity to an author's experiences, accounts and conclusions. These relationships, in other words, are seen to endow an individual with a particular kind of agency: agency to know, to represent and to argue – to write ethnography.

What we mean when we say that in ethnographic texts authorial agency emerges out of relationships in the field and at home is made clear in the excerpt below, by the French anthropologist Patrick Williams. Writing about the Mañus, nomadic Roma living in central France, Williams tells us that it is only possible to understand their way of being in the world by understanding their connections with their dead. He grounds his argument on his relationships both with the Mañus and with other anthropologists:

> We can often achieve a better perception of reality than we might have pondered for years when we come to peruse different horizons. Though I have known the Mañus from the time of my childhood, I am not sure that, had it not been for the discussion that Leonardo Piasere initiated with Judith Okely about the relations between the living and the dead among the Slovenkso Roma (Piasere 1985) and the Traveller-Gypsies (Okely 1983), I would have thought of proposing that the terms of Mañus presence in the world could be traced through the relationship of the living with the dead.
>
> (Williams 2003: 1)

As well as relating his long-term familiarity with the Mañus, Williams emphasises the intellectual origin of his project in his exchanges with Piasere and Okely. It is out of these two sets of encounters, with informants and colleagues, that his own distinctive insight into Mañus life emerges:

> What particularly struck me when I systematically researched the relationships between the living and the dead was not so much the coherence of the interpretations I could draw from them as my deeply felt loyalty to something I experienced when I was with the Mañus. There is no halfway position for observers: we have to be either completely in or irremediably out, unable to grasp anything. The position of privileged observer is totally illusory. It is not even possible to touch upon the surface of things since, as I will try to show, Mañus things do not have a surface. We either get to the bottom or nowhere at all: this is what the nature of the expression of Mañus identity requires of the ethnologist, and it is a difficult ambition to live up to.
>
> (Williams 2003: 1)

Williams claims for himself a remarkable achievement. He tell us that the Mañus will not allow half measures, that 'we have to be either completely in or irremediably out'. He then does proceed to write about the Mañus, which suggests to the reader that he *is* 'completely in'. That is, not only does Williams know the Mañus, but he knows them totally as their existential and ontological position demands. Thus,

> I propose . . . to show everything, to tell everything. I propose seeking and, I might even dare say, achieving absolute pertinence, complete coincidence. Nothing should be left out, nothing should be added: there should be no breach through which a disregard of Mañus plenitude could penetrate.
>
> (Williams 2003: 2)

The Mañus worldview is by no means universally shared, and many anthropologists would shy away from the kind of enterprise that Williams proposes, emphasising instead the unavoidably partial nature of anthropological knowledge. Nonetheless Williams' text exemplifies at once the relational nature of all ethnographic writing and how it is by emphasising this relationality that anthropologists claim a particular kind of agency – agency to know and represent. In other words, this relationality is what enables the creation of an authoritative authorial self.

Emphasising the key role of this authorial self in ethnographic writing and the control of the author over the text does not mean to say that authorial agency is always flaunted or openly displayed. On the contrary, this control is often hidden or downplayed and, to use Debbora Battaglia's terminology, agency is variously 'ambiguated' (1997: 506). Thus, ethnographic knowledge may be presented as self-evident; claims may be made that it is informants, rather than anthropologists, who really 'speak' in or through texts; and writers may present themselves as mere conduits for knowledge, facilitators or mouthpieces. Crucially, in these cases authors hide their agency just as they retain control over ethnographic texts. As a very different strategy anthropologists may emphasise their role as narrators and filters of knowledge, stressing the partial and positioned nature of their accounts. Then authorship is stressed but authority is disclaimed, and we are told that what we are reading is more like a literary narrative than like a scientific statement of fact.

In the sections below we examine how authorship and authority – what we call authorial agency – are ascribed and disclaimed, made visible and invisible in ethnographic writing, and the effects that this has both on the construction of a text and on the creation of anthropological knowledge. Following Battaglia, our interest is in

> how the notion of agency is invoked or ascribed, concealed or obfuscated, more or less strategically . . . how agency is attached or detached in social practice, how it is owned or disowned, to whom or

to what agency is referred, and what motivates agency to go around, come around, and otherwise slip around . . . such an approach will tend towards openings of discursive space in which social relationships – and more particularly here relations of power – may emerge in their mutability and displaceability. *Dis-agency*, then, might be a better term.

(Battaglia 1997: 506)

In this chapter, therefore, we explore how authorship and authority are constructed in ethnographic texts through both presences and absences. We start by analysing fieldwork accounts. Although these narratives appear to display the agency of the ethnographer, they also hide it. Our argument is that, from the classics of early twentieth-century to more recent postmodernist texts, at the core of the anthropological enterprise lies the construction of an authorial self through encounters with others. And, although this self retains ultimate control over the text, it is nonetheless variously presented as able and not able to make claims to various kinds of knowledge.

Summary points

1   All ethnographic writing is conversational or relational and yet it also revolves around individual, authoritative authorship.
2   This authorship emerges precisely out of relationships in the field and the academy.
3   In ethnographic writing the author's agency and control over the text is ambiguated: it may be hidden or displayed, claimed or disclaimed.

Stories of fieldwork

As a reader you will regularly come across accounts of fieldwork, often placed at the start or close to the beginning of ethnographies. Writers frequently emphasise the contextualising purpose of these narratives, the fact that they provide essential information regarding the ways knowledge was acquired in the field. In some cases, we are told that it is because authors want to challenge 'the conventional fictions of objectivity and omniscience that mark that ethnographic genre' that they tell us about their field research (Abu-Lughod 1986: 10). At other times they use these stories precisely to claim such objectivity: 'I believe that I have understood the chief values of the Nuer and am able to present a true outline of their social structure' (Evans-Pritchard 1969: 15). In either case, ethnographers typically describe arriving in the field, their first meetings with their informants and their initial impressions of life in an alien context. And they often emphasise the problems and difficulties they experienced in establishing contact and convincing people to cooperate in the research:

It would at any time have been difficult to do research among the Nuer, and at the period of my visit they were unusually hostile, for their recent defeat by Government forces and the measures taken to ensure their final submission had occasioned deep resentment. Nuer have often remarked to me, 'You raid us, yet you say we cannot raid the Dinka'; 'You overcame us with firearms and we had only spears. If we had had firearms we would have routed you'; and so forth. When I entered a cattle camp it was not only as a stranger but as an enemy, and they seldom tried to conceal their disgust at my presence, refusing to answer my greetings and even turning away when I addressed them.

(Evans-Pritchard 1969: 11)

Writers typically also describe experiencing a sense of disjuncture and displacement which is slowly replaced by understanding and a feeling of belonging. In the excerpt below, for example, Cecilia Busby tells vividly of her difficulties during the first half of her fieldwork in a village in Kerala:

(I)t was not physical hardship that was an issue: I was quite happy to live in one room, to draw water from the well, to use an outside latrine and wash in a bucket of water . . . What was however a greater strain than I had ever imagined, was the experience of living in a situation in which I was completely socially de-skilled. Language difficulties meant that there was no possibility of subtlety or nuance in my communications with others: everything had to be larger than life, a great joke or else a great problem. I blundered blindly through situations, sensitive to body language and tone that told me I was doing something wrong, that I was not living up to others' expectations of me, yet unable to remedy this or to explain how I felt. My sense of self, of personality, disintegrated under the onslaught of a constant reflection of self from others that was not me, but some stranger: a moody, difficult girl, well meaning but a little slow, very prone to lock herself in her room for hours, with a phenomenal need for sleep and a strange tendency to burst into tears for no very good reason.

(Busby 2000: xv–xvi)

This sense of personal disintegration – of 'being sent slowly mad' (Busby 2000: xv) – finds parallels in many accounts where anthropologists explain having to relinquish control over their lives to others, either through ignorance of the language and social norms or out of the need to fit in and be accepted and trusted. Writers describe a diminished or altered sense of self and a lack of agency – in Busby's narrative above an inability to present herself as she wishes – which sometimes has distressing emotional consequences.

In these narratives ethnographers stress their incompetence, their dependence, and their ensuing peripherality to the world of properly functioning adults. That is, they present themselves as child-like, as does Jean Briggs when she tells us that the Utku's 'unfailing anticipation of my needs (even when my needs did not coincide with theirs) was immensely warming. I felt as cared-for as a three year old, and I am sure that is precisely one facet of the light in which the Eskimos regarded me' (1970: 27). Later on she explains:

> On the whole, my helplessness seemed to be accepted as a matter of course by everybody, and it was consistently treated with tactful solicitude (*naklik*), the same solicitude that characterises Utku reactions to other helpless creatures, like puppies, children and sick people: 'Because you don't know how to do things, you are one to be taken care of (*naklik*).' If by chance I did succeed in acquiring some simple skill I was rewarded, as a child would have been, by the knowledge that the fact had been observed. 'You are beginning to be less incapable *(ayuq)*,' someone would say. It was what people said about babies when they began to smile, to speak, to grasp. Or: 'You are becoming an Eskimo,' a 'person'; the word *inuk* has both meanings.
>
> (Briggs 1970: 252)

Dependence and peripherality lie at the core of the Western understandings about children on which anthropologists draw in their fieldwork accounts: Schepher-Hughes and Sargeant (1998: 10) explain how in postindustrial consumer society children are displaced to the margins, seen as 'an economic liability and a burden'. In ethnographic writing, they tell us, childhood is represented 'as a permanent state of becoming rather than as a legitimate state of being-in-and-for-the-world', and anthropological work on children is dominated by the concepts of '"socialisation", "acculturation", "development" and "stages"' (1998: 13). It is precisely in this light that ethnographers talk about their early fieldwork experiences: not only is fieldwork a 'state of becoming', as in Briggs' excerpt above, but it is also marked by socialisation and acculturation into the host group, which take place in stages. And so writers of ethnography describe being treated as children and even spending time with them rather than with others, being burdens on the community, slowly learning how to function as adults. As children the agency of ethnographers is incomplete. And this agency that they lose is gained by their informants, who are presented as the ones in control, as in the conversation below between Evans-Pritchard and Cuol, a Nuer man:

I: Who are you?
Cuol: A man.
I: What is your name?

Cuol: Do you want to know my *name*?

I: Yes.

Cuol: Do you want to know *my* name?

I: Yes, you have come to visit me in my tent and I would like to know who you are.

Cuol: All right. I am Cuol. What is your name?

I: My name is Pritchard.

Cuol: What is your father's name?

I: My father's name is also Pritchard.

Cuol: No, that cannot be true. You cannot have the same name as your father.

I: It is the name of my lineage. What is the name of your lineage?

Cuol: Do you want to know the name of my lineage?

I: Yes.

Cuol: What will you do with it if I tell you? Will you take it to your country?

I: I don't want to do anything with it. I just want to know it since I am living at your camp.

Cuol: Oh, well we are Lou.

I: I did not ask you the name of your tribe. I know that. I am asking you the name of your lineage.

Cuol: Why do you want to know the name of my lineage?

I: I don't want to know it.

Cuol: Then why do you ask me for it? Give me some tobacco.

                (Evans-Pritchard 1969: 13, original italics)

This first stage of fieldwork and loss of agency is followed in these stories by a period of enlightenment and recovery of agency which repeatedly involves a transformation of the self, as in Okely's account below of attempting to become acceptable to English Traveller Gypsies in the early 1970s. Here deliberate deception ('I concealed some years and acted innocently') is subordinated to an overall personal transformation in which the author's agency is downplayed: an 'alternative way of being' 'comes upon' Okely and she undergoes 'unconscious' changes. Activity and passivity are both emphasised and the result is that Okely's agency is strongly ambiguated:

(I)t was important to become inconspicuous . . . I learnt as much as possible to imitate their enunciation. I threw in swear words and adopted their alternative English phrases and vocabulary . . . I made comparable adjustments in clothing: wearing long skirts, loose, high necked sweaters. My gestures and stance changed unconsciously, as the alternative way of being came upon me. A social worker accused me of 'hypocrisy' and 'deceit' in my change of appearance, as if the self is bound to a single cultural identity. The Travellers responded favourably to these adjustments to their rules and ways, recognising them as respect. On occasions, being obliged to break from the field for the London research centre or an Oxford seminar, I would switch persona, as well as clothing, in a layby en route. Such transformation in my own, the same land, was the more bizarre.

Being a single woman of an age when most Traveller women would be married with several children added to the anomaly. I concealed some years and acted innocent; an honorary virgin.

(Okely 1983: 43–4)

Eventually in fieldwork stories 'them' becomes, even if only transitorily, 'us'. Moments of heightened emotional discomfort lead in these narratives to particularly important insights, and sometimes there is a single event that catapults the writer from the margins to the centre of the community. This event allows informants to see the anthropologist in a new light, no longer as an outsider but as an adopted member of the group or at least as 'our outsider'. In Lila Abu-Lughod's description of fieldwork among Egyptian Bedouins, it is sharing the pain of an old woman over her brother's death that makes her 'fully human' in her hosts' eyes (1986: 21). This is how she describes her sense of belonging:

On entering the tent crowded with women, I knew exactly which cluster to join – the group of 'our' relatives. They welcomed me naturally and proceeded to gossip conspiratorially with me about the others present. This sense of 'us versus them', so central to their social inter-actions, had become central to me too, and I felt pleased that I belonged to an 'us' . . . Later, when we sat around the kerosene lantern, talking about the celebration we had attended, swapping bits of information we had gathered, and feeling happy because we had eaten meat, I became aware how comfortable I felt, knowing every one being discussed, offering my own tidbits and interpretations, and bearing easily the weight of a child who had fallen sleep on my lap as I sat cross-legged on the ground. It was only that night, when I dated the page in my journal, that I realized it was only a few days until Christmas. My American life seemed very far away.

(Abu-Lughod 1986: 20–1)

As in Battaglia's excerpt in the previous section, here too agency appears and disappears from sight, is lost and regained, and moves around between persons: the Bedouins have granted Abu-Lughod agency by accepting her, but she herself had to elicit this acceptance by her appropriate behaviour. And, significantly, this movement of agency from ethnographer to infor-mant and back again goes hand-in-hand with a transfer of knowledge. Richard Fardon has described how

The ethnographic and anthropological processes (from research to writing) can be seen as a succession of states of play in the allocation of different types of ignorance and knowledge; often the trajectories of informant and ethnographer intersect. Beginning in ignorance the ethnographer acquires knowledge; but as the informant divulges information so the ethnographer begins to see him as ignorant of his own society.

(Fardon 1990b: 9)

Thus in these stories the process of becoming during fieldwork is not indefinite but has a culmination: after a personal and often traumatic journey of transformation, a new self comes into view, endowed with the capacity to talk about others. In other words, through the ambiguation of agency that we have described, the ethnographer eventually emerges as able to represent. Often, as Fardon explains, the ensuing representations are presented as superior to those of our informants. Then ethnographers not only claim the insight of an insider but also the neutrality and analytical ability of an outsider, as well as the capacity to deploy specialist knowledge. Alternatively, a personal transformation is described but it is not said to yield any kind of absolute knowledge about the Other. Instead, the focus of the ethnography lies on exploring, from a deliberately emphasised position, the relationship between informant and ethnographer.

In both cases fieldwork narratives are essential to the construction of the authorial self because they enable writers to claim a dual insider/outsider status. Crucially, these written accounts form part of a much wider body of anthropological folklore which also includes verbally transmitted anecdotes and stories circulated in a wide variety of contexts, from dinner parties to conferences and classrooms. What brings these different cultural products together is the shared narrative structure – the emphasis on the arduous process of 'entering' another society and on the transition from marginal and child-like stranger to friend and even adopted member of the group – and the hold they have over the anthropological imagination. Indeed, whether or not ethnographies include a description of fieldwork, they are all premised on the assumption that the ethnographer encountered others and eventually became able to talk about them. That is, those anthropologists who write about their fieldwork experiences do a discipline-wide job of justification that permeates and legitimates also the work of others.

Summary points

1   Fieldwork stories work to ambiguate the agency of the ethnographer by presenting them as children who undergo a process of socialisation and acculturation.

2   In fieldwork stories agency and knowledge travel between informants and ethnographer. These stories culminate with the ethnographer becoming the more knowledgeable of the two.
3   Fieldwork narratives do a discipline-wide job of justification and legitimation.

Claims and the construction of authorial voices

Fieldwork narratives, then, depend on two core authorial devices: they ambiguate the agency of authors so as to endow them with the capacity to represent, and they do this by enshrining the figure of the anthropologist as both outsider and insider. But these twin strategies are not restricted to stories of fieldwork: they shape all ethnographic writing. Writers of ethnography present themselves as at once insiders and outsiders, as able and not able to make claims to various kinds of knowledge, across all sorts of ethnographic texts. In fact we argue that these categories (knowledge/ ignorance, inside/out) lie at the core of the way in which anthropology as a discipline approaches the world. It is by creatively manipulating these categories in their writing that individual anthropologists construct an authorial position for themselves, not only within a specific text but within the discipline as a whole, that they craft their own particular anthropology.

One such position that you will come across repeatedly whilst reading ethnography revolves around the construction of the author as knowledgeable specialist. Writers then tell us, 'This is so', downplaying and in fact hiding from the reader's sight any uncertainty. Authorship here relies on the establishment of authority and is built on claims to knowledge that take the form of direct assertions or presentations of information as fact, as in Phyllis Kaberry's 1939 ethnography, *Aboriginal Woman: Sacred and Profane*. Unlike the writers that we have discussed in the previous section, Kaberry does not dwell on her relationship with her informants, and does not describe her fieldwork as a process of personal transformation. But, like them, she does use the notion of 'being there' (Geertz 1988) to claim agency to know and represent. Thus, she opens her monograph by elaborating on the notion of entry into an alien world, talking about first impressions and how they might be challenged:

> At first the camp seems to offer only the grey monotony of daily existence, of a precarious livelihood that is hunted for in the hills and grubbed for in the earth ... (Later it) assumes more and more complexity, variety, and interest. After one has become familiar with the background, attention at first tends to focus on the human actors, but as time passes, the camp ceases to be just a clearing littered with material objects of the simplest type ... One becomes absorbed in the

questions of food supply, in the chatter, gossip, and quarrels, and one no longer wonders at the absence of boredom among natives of the community.

(Kaberry 1939: 7)

By writing in the present tense and using the neutral pronoun 'one' rather than the first person, Kaberry aligns reader and writer so that her first impressions become also those of her audience. Her own initial journey works as a metaphoric device to encourage us to engage imaginatively with her account, as in this description of her first sight of Aboriginal country:

As the aeroplane flies inside from Derby to the coast, following the course of the Fitzroy River, the country seems to be still untouched in spite of fifty years of European penetration. . . . Extending into the distance, it has an almost timeless quality about it, with its hills rising like islands out of the plain that resembles the floor of some sea that has never known tides or men. Below, it stretches illimitable and motionless, but for the small shadow of the aeroplane and the cattle disturbed at their feeding beneath the scrub.

(Kaberry 1939: 2)

This voyage metaphor also sets up a contrast between ignorance (not just Kaberry's but our own) and knowledge (that she is now in possession of and the rest of her book imparts). Thus, although both Kaberry and her readers start off as outsiders to Aboriginal society, their roles go on to become clearly distinct. We remain an audience to be educated; Kaberry becomes at once an insider in Aboriginal society and, through her competence as scholar and investigator, an enlightened outsider and instructor.

Kaberry blends compelling descriptions and analysis in order to make a distinctive contribution to anthropological debate, challenging what she perceives of as the misguided understandings of other ethnographers. She concentrates on the notion, widespread at the time of her writing, that it is Aboriginal men who monopolise the religious dimension of communal life. The whole of *Aboriginal Woman* revolves around the need to uncover this theory as a fallacy:

Insufficient stress has been laid on the importance of religion to women in their daily life, the benefits they derive from it. Too often we find a cursory mention of their totems, their spirit-centres, their function to incarnate the spirit-children, and the subordinate part they play in the men's initiation rites. From an analysis of the facts, it appears that there are similarities in upbringing, outlook, and environment of the men and the women. The approach to religion must be made through the range of problems which confront them both, the necessity of maintaining existence in a region that is relatively arid, and of coping with the grief, suffering, and disruption of social ties that follow upon death. . . . If this study is to have validity and reality, then women must be seen as integral units of society.

(Kaberry 1939: 190)

Kaberry's depictions of Aboriginal life, then, are geared to making a point of broad anthropological relevance. In Chapter 5 we explained that a fundamental aim of all ethnography is to convince the reader to compre- hend a life world in terms of the specific propositions put forward by a writer. Ethnography, we said, is always argument: by re-contextualising their experiences and observations within the framework of anthropolog- ical knowledge, writers imbue them with special significance. Crucially, this subordination of the story to the creation of an argument also plays the key role of enabling writers to claim a voice and a place for themselves within anthropological debate; it is therefore essential to the construction of a singular and distinctive authorial self. In *Aboriginal Woman*, this authorial self is both a raconteur and an academic specialist delivering objective anthropological knowledge of Aboriginal life. Indeed, Kaberry gives readers a clear clue as to her understanding of ethnographic writing when, in the preface to *Aboriginal Woman*, she praises Malinwoski, to whom the book is dedicated, for his ability to combine 'scientific objec- tivity and integrity to fact' with 'the imagination and sensitivity of an artist' (1939: xv).

Because all ethnographic writing re-contextualises experience, and because the new context always revolves around specialist knowledge – of anthropology, its history, its concepts and its conversations – all ethnog- raphy is based on exclusion (see Chapter 6). As such, all ethnographic writing is inherently authoritative. But, while some authors, Kaberry among them, explicitly aim to unveil for the reader the deeper meaning of informants' actions and statements – a meaning that is not visible to the actors themselves – others do the opposite, aiming to disclaim or at least challenge the possibility of final authority. The first ones are deliberately authoritative. The second group are often inadvertently so.

In the introduction to her ethnographic biography of Alourdes Margaux, or Mama Lola, a Vodou priestess from Brooklyn, Karen Brown (1991) emphasises the need for discarding a search for objectivity both in ethnographic fieldwork and in ethnographic writing. She tells us that,

Ethnographic research, whatever else it is, is a form of human rela- tionship. When the lines long-drawn in anthropology between participant observer and informant break down, then the only truth is the one in between; and anthropology becomes something closer to a social art form, open to both aesthetic and moral judgement. The situation is riskier, but it does bring intellectual labour and life into closer relation.

(Brown 1991: 12)

And so she recounts taking her dreams to Alourdes to interpret, having rituals performed for her, and finally undergoing initiation under Mama Lola's guidance. And it is precisely by becoming a participant and abandoning the quest for objectivity in research that Brown claims to deliver anthropological knowledge – knowledge that she views as artistic, aesthetic and moral rather than scientific. Brown still makes strong claims to authority, saying that she is able to bring 'intellectual labour and life into closer relationship' than those who aim for objectivity. But authority emerges here out of positionality rather than impartiality. And, rather than being presented with a transfer of agency from informant to enlightened scholar, we find that agency is described as fragmented and continually shared between Mama Lola and Brown:

> I am part of a culture that seeks to capture experience, historical and otherwise, in books. So I write a book about Mama Lola. But in doing so, I try to remember that she is part of a culture that serves Gede. Therefore I have tried to make up true stories, ones that are faithful to both Gede and Alourdes. I have tried to create her story through a chorus of voices, much as she creates herself through a chorus of moods and spirit energies. One of the voices that speaks in the book is hers, as carefully recorded and respectfully edited as I could manage. Yet another is my scholarly voice, distanced enough to discern patterns and relationships but not so distant as to create the impression of overall logical coherence. No person's life or culture is, in the final analysis, logical. A third voice is also my own, but this one risks a more intimate and whole self-revelation. The fourth voice is perhaps that of Gede – the one that tells the ancestral tales in the form of fictionalized short stories and in so doing play with truth, seeking to bring it alive for its immediate audience.
>
> (Brown 1991: 19–20)

Not only does Brown attempt to give space in the text to Mama Lola's voice, but she herself takes on several positions, speaking with different voices – analytic at times, autobiographical much more often. She traces her anthropological heritage to interpretive anthropology and feminism, and tells the reader that the book is guided by an overarching concern with explaining Haitian Vodou in connection to kinship, gender, and social change (1991: 15). She therefore links Alourdes' life and the lives of her ancestors to key developments in Haitian history. And, clearly departing from the ethnographic canon, Brown also deploys what she calls 'ethnographic invention', short fictional stories that build on Mama Lola's own tales about her family and that work to convey the feel of life in rural Haiti. Even Gede, the Vodou spirit that possesses Alourdes, is granted authorial agency here, as the originator of these stories.

Paradoxically, then, the distinctive authorial position that Brown crafts for herself relies on a challenge to the unity of the author: it is precisely through this challenge that Brown's authorial voice emerges as strikingly singular and idiosyncratic. The multiplicity of styles and voices ambiguates Brown's authorial agency by simultaneously hiding and displaying it, but ultimately Brown emerges as both an authority on Haitian Vodou and a key contributor to anthropological debates on the character of the discipline and of authorship. Brown carves a place for herself within anthropology, not just by providing a contribution to our understanding of Haitian Vodou in relation to gender and the family, but by her authorial distinctiveness. Here multiplicity and fragmentation work as a vehicle for the creation of a singular authoritative authorial voice.

There are therefore striking parallels between Kaberry's and Brown's texts. Although written at very different points in time, and embodying contrasting – even in some senses conflicting – views of ethnographic writing and of anthropology, *Aboriginal Woman* and *Mama Lola* share key features. Both authors write for specialist anthropological audiences; both structure their stories around arguments of anthropological relevance; and both claim that their insider status grants them special kinds of knowledge. In the two cases ethnographic authority and authorship emerge out relationships with others in the field, out of a personal transformation from outsider to participant, and out of participation in disciplinary conversations. Together they exemplify the key role that the creation of an singular authorial self through the ambiguation of agency plays in the constitution of anthropological knowledge.

Summary points

1   Individual anthropologists create a distinctive authorial position for themselves by manipulating the categories knowledge/ignorance and inside/out.
2   All ethnographic writing is inherently exclusivist and authoritative.
3   Some writers of ethnography are deliberately authoritative, others are inadvertently so.

Concluding remarks

Throughout this book we have emphasised the relational nature of ethnography and of ethnographic knowledge. It isn't just, as we explained in Chapter 3, that ethnographers write about relationships, but that they have to engage in relationships themselves in order to be able to write. After all, it is by participating in other people's lives that anthropologists learn about them. But also, it is through relationships 'at home' – crystallised in the form of disciplinary and inter-disciplinary conversations – that ethnographers work out how to make sense of their field experiences. In this chapter we have argued that out of specific constellations of relationships in the field and in the academy emerge writers as authors – that is, as agents with the capacity to know, represent and analyse.

Albeit relational, ethnographic authorship is singular rather than shared. Not only do writers of ethnography recognise themselves as answerable for their texts and for the knowledge these embody, their audience too expects authors to take individual responsibility. Ethnographers – even those who aim to faithfully represent the cacophony of experience, or to make space in their writings for a multiplicity of voices – very rarely share control over their writings with their informants. Whether authority and agency to know is claimed or disclaimed, flaunted or hidden, writing ethnography is always about asserting a distinct, individual, idiosyncratic perspective on social life. The ambiguation of authorial agency consistently results in the shoring up of the authoritative authorial self. This is so even in the case of writers who insist on the precarious and situated character of their knowledge but who nonetheless make strongly authoritative judgments on the discipline.

When considering the issue of ethnographic authority and authorship, then, we have to pay attention, not just to how writers conceptualise their fieldwork experience and the character of anthropological knowledge, but also to how they deploy this experience and this knowledge to engage in disciplinary debates. In the chapter that follows we take up this thread and expand it further by focusing on academic conversations and, in particular, on the various kinds of intellectual commitment embodied by ethnographies.

Chapter 7 – activities

In this excerpt from the first chapter of *An Ethnography of Cosmopolitanism*, Huon Wardle uses a variety of narrative devices to convey aesthetically and theorise the open-endedness of Caribbean social life. Wardle's aim is to communicate to the reader how Kingstonians create a sense of community and of the place of the self in the world that are premised on this open-endedness. He moves between and brings together two sets of conversations: among Kingstonians, regarding individual and communal destinies, and among anthropologists, regarding how to make sense of the apparent cacophony of Kingstonian voices. In the process he creates a distinctive authorial position for himself. Read the excerpt and respond to the following questions:

1   What voices are made present in this excerpt? How do they relate to each other?

2   In what ways does Wardle assert his authorial agency? Find relevant quotations.

3   In what ways does Wardle hide or disclaim his authorial agency? Find relevant quotations.

4   Wardle does not give us a narrative of entry into the field, but he does use narratives of the immediate extensively. What roles do these narratives play in enabling Wardle to construct a distinctive authorial position for himself?

5   How does Wardle deploy the categories knowledge/ignorance and insider/outsider?

Wardle, H. (2000) An Ethnography of Cosmopolitanism in Kingston, Jamaica, New York: Edwin Mellen

I

SEARCHING FOR COMMUNITY

FIELDWORK DIARY 8-9-1992

I step through the rank of food-stalls-on-wheels, past the grocery, past Ken's bar, between two humming buses bound for Half Way Tree (inhaling the hot stink of diesel exhaust and rotting vegetables) past the betting shop and the butcher's, following the curve of the road, crossing over to Marshy's wooden fried fish stall padlocked and empty, past Powell's shoe mending place where, as usual, Powell is at work surrounded by seated friends (Powell has still not finished my slippers – I doubt he ever will), up the road glancing in at the haberdashery and the little sewing shop and Sheryl's bar-and-eatery, leaving the hardware store on the left hand side of the street and Balive's rum bar and the upstairs saloon and the dance hall, past the bicycle shop on this side; and then the stores thin out and the valley and the mountainous edge of the city are freely visible over to the right, walking on with the Twilight Zone dance hall on the left, towards Cudjoe's tiny shoe-shop – itself a shoe-box of corrugated iron containing Cudjoe and a pile of decrepit, yet-to-be-mended, shoes.

Nan is sitting outside on a fruit box. Has he been working hard today? I ask. No, he has been waiting all day at the masonry yard for materials. I question Cudjoe as to whether Marshy is selling breakfast this morning. Cudjoe does not know, but he does not think so. Nan declares that he wants to travel up to Montego Bay this year for Christmas: I should go he says, it is very fine up there. I feel two fingers prodding the side of my head – Brother Watt 'holding me up'. He has seen Marshy putting some charcoal into his shop: Marshy returned from the country late last night, so has not prepared any food yet. I ask Watt about himself. He has not worked for over a week – 'no contacts' – and no prospect of finding a job: his phone bill was sky high so they cut it off. But Watt seems cheerful. He has brought some shoe polish for Cudjoe. Now he says he wants to buy some rum. So we go nearby to Carnie's, buy a Q [half pint], and bring Cudjoe a glass back to the shop.

[...]

Kingston may be Babylon as the Rastafarians say, a place of historic black exile, but it is also Babel in another way: home to a multitude of voices, ways of speaking and behaving, forms of subjectivity and community. The question is how to enter this environment of three quarters of a million people, where to begin to frame what goes on here from an anthropological point of view. My fieldwork diary describes various forms and stages of my own integration in the social ecology of the city. However, while I return to the diary throughout this book, an ethnography of Jamaica's capital demands a series of levels of contextualisation.

Seen from the naive bird's eye perspective provided by a map, the city presents itself as a multiple crisscross of roads circled by a horseshoe of mountains and bounded to the south by the sea. Amongst the northern foothills are the suburbs – the Gardens: Cherry Gardens, Arcadia Gardens, Constant Spring Gardens and its attendant golf course. To the south above the harbour are the slums – the Towns: Trench Town, Jones Town, Denham Town around the throbbing street market at Parade. There is a semi-completed feel to Kingston's geography – places called Half Way Tree, Three Mile, Four Mile, Six Mile.

[...]

The real essence of Kingston, though, is perhaps not streets and houses but the bus. It is the semi-regulated half-dilapidated buses carrying the thousands of Kingstonians across the city and then back again each day that provide some sort of articulation to this sprawling agglomeration. Since the 1980s, the disintegration of the bus service has also represented the most obvious sign of the state's inability to retain its leverage on the Jamaican economy and polity. An ironically polite sign on one bus expresses some of this sense of civic values gyrating out of control: PASSENGER PLEASE COOPERATE NO KNIFE, SOUL COMB NOR ICE-PICK IS ALLOWED INSIDE. The collapse of ordinary people's faith in a shared national project is played out daily on board. The buses teeter along the main thoroughfares jam-packed with sweating passengers who are cajoled and threatened into place by the driver and his team of 'ductors. Squeezed inside, hanging from an overhead railing, and braced against a metal seat, you gain the most immediate experience of the funny, noisy, generous, claustrophobic, angry and frequently violent qualities of Kingstonian social life and the way in which these urbanites give cultural expression to their experience of it.

Most unavoidably, the bus exposes its passengers to the rhythms and song lyrics of the moment with their mixed themes:

> If police have a right
> People have a right too
> If you na mess with we
> We na go mess with you....

The unwanted and unaccepted intervention of the state authorities into people's daily lives.

> There's a fire
> Burning in my soul
> And I can't out the fire
> Its burning out of control.
> One bag of food can't feed America,
> And one bag of food can't feed Jamaica,
> Two bag of food can't feed the nigger,
> And it can't support the buffalo soldier . . .

International indifference to Jamaica's economic plight.

> Grudgeful.
> Some people grudgeful
> Grudgeful 'cause me belly still full
> Grudgeful: even if I turn in
> a hole . . .

The (in this case comical) sense of individuation and lack of trust between people in the city.

> Girls, girls every day
> From London, Canada and USA.
> I got a trailer-load of girls on the wharf fi come up . . .

Cartoon machismo.

> Fireball on all the informer them
> Because one thing's for sure
> Me no want no informer friend
> Fireball on all the sodomite them
> Because one thing's for sure
> Me no keep no sodomite friend . . .

The violent frustration felt by young men in the city.

> Up on a robbery up at Papine
> Shot up a jeep and we shot it up clean
> Four tyres, shot them off clean
> Jump in a rental
> Fled the scene.

And a corresponding aesthetics of violence.

Most of the commentary in these songs comes from the perspective of male youth and it dwells on a few relatively stereotyped themes. But cultural values and meanings are significantly more heterogeneous in Kingston and more difficult to pin down than these songs would suggest. The shaky Kingstonian bus is a microcosm of people's civic existence in Jamaica, but as such it is also the venue for a strikingly varied range of expressions and cultural interpretations. The buses and bus stops serve in particular as somewhere to continue a very longstanding Kingstonian tradition of selling pamphlets, books of herbal remedies, and other self-published materials – materials that stem from and complement the emphasis on oral self-assertion so evident in Jamaican life. Many of these have a highly idiolectic flavour . . .

As we traveled together across the city, Ras Dizzy, an itinerant artist well known to academics at the University of the West Indies, gave me his own poetic encapsulation of city life. Under the title No Changes to City Peace Term, Dizzy's pamphlet charts the recent loss in Kingston of that 'goodold feeling and greets of love and understanding'. In elliptical language, he contrasts images of the island's 'human sweating columns', its 'national trade relationship' and 'internal mortagraphs' with the activities of 'Mr Bigmoney uptown' and 'Mrs. Capital Granter downtown'. The violence and contradictoriness of Jamaican political life is stirred in a melange of imagery mixing Rasta apocalypticism with experiences of the city – 'gunsmokes and running carparts', drum beats that 'wild the little sparrows':

[. . .]

I could describe many more of these literary interventions into urban life including, near a bus stop at the Heroes Circle, the 'proclamations' (including one to Mister Maza [Major] of England) written on pieces of cardboard by a man who lives in a tree there. Beyond their eclecticism these varied representations of city experience suggest not only a powerful emphasis on the individual's ability to respond creatively to her or his situation, but also a kind of unfettered sense of freedom that exists despite the degrading effects of urban life on the self. But the complexity of communication in the city also gives to these interjections the quality of singular voices in search of a community: Kingston does not provide the appearance of a unified or consensual milieu for communication between its co-inhabitants.

Riding on a Kingstonian bus, to the unengaged spectator the town presents itself as almost pure social flux: the heterogeneity of cultural expression and activity is all co-present at once in a grand cacophony. Sister Paulette, the dance-hall musicians, Ras Dizzy: all provide their own contextualisations of life here, but these jostle and compete for attention with the many alternatives available. Nonetheless, most of the time, for city dwellers the spectator's impression of mutability and uncentredness is an inverted or residual one: instead, for them, Kingstonian geography exists as definite engagements and known destinations, the achievement of which is obstructed or facilitated by other urbanites. And all these contextualisations of city life, which in total appear so diverse, have a specific value within the individual's search for satisfying forms of interaction and community with others. But to arrive closer at this point at which the flow of city life has immediate cultural meaning for its inhabitants,

I need to refine my scale of description and analysis. I have to return to the traces created by my research in Kingston – tape-recordings, diary accounts, fieldnotes – and reassemble the picture of social activity, starting now with the interactions of the people themselves, then working outwards to wider levels of cultural integration.

A change of scale

In an attempt to refigure the ethnography of the region, during the 1970s and 1980s ethnologists of the Caribbean began to attend closely to the mercurial patterns of interaction and communication that characterise West Indian cultural life. Lieber showed how ethnographic studies of the Caribbean city had over-emphasised the physical neighbourhood as the analytical unit and, as a result, failed to apprehend the ways urban geography was established and evaluated by urbanites themselves. When I move between the descriptions of events in my fieldwork diary and my more grand-scale, retrospective impressions of Kingston I recognise variant kinds of geographical-cultural understanding. Within the diary perspective, my awareness of space is dominated by the relationships formed between myself and other city dwellers: interaction, and the goals established therein, seem to shape spatial sensibility. The same, Lieber suggests, is true of the day-to-day lives of his Trinidadian street informants for whom there is a continuous search for rewarding sites of social interaction, different kinds of 'scene' for communal appreciation and appropriation. This subjective and mutual organisation of space leads to a kind of mapping very different from that provided by the traditional sociological survey, with its emphases on predictable activity taking place within preestablished geographic locales. Instead, understanding Kingstonian social life requires us to comprehend those moments of convergence when a sense of communality emerges from the diffuse patterns of urban interaction.

As on the streets of Trinidad, the frameworks giving shape to community in Kingston are frequently loose and personally oriented. Objective vehicles for consensus may be weak in the Jamaican city, but communality does come into being situationally – very often (ironically perhaps) as a result of the wider breakdown in, or absence of, social control, with its tragic consequences. Returning once more to my diary accounts gives me an impression of this emergence of communality as something both immediate and contingent. In some of these instances the sense of community is clearly fragile and fleeting, tied to temporary coalitions of interest. In other examples it has more substantial foundations in friendship and familial solidarity. The two cases that follow show some of these different qualities of community as they are directly experienced.

What becomes clear is that within people's attempt to express a sense of shared moral response, using certain images and kinds of narrative, lies their simultaneous desire to give value to varied subjective interests and understandings. In this first instance the potential for community coalesces around people's identification of themselves as sharing a neighbourhood. In the second, it derives from the common importance for members of a family of one person in that family.

FIELDWORK DIARY 21-4-1992

Sitting in Jeanette's shabby armchair in the hot afternoon annotating field notes. Racquel [Jeanette's adolescent daughter] rushes in carrying her baby brother and declaring eagerly 'me hear say them kill one woman at Tavern and rape her – me gone up the station fi look'. Then she is gone again, leaving me to hold Jeanette's baby and guard the bubbling cornmeal porridge. After a while, I turn off the kerosene stove and follow up the road carrying little Andrew. I encounter Racquel and her friend Tiffany coming back down the street, shouting at each other in excitement. Tiffany smiles when she sees me and tells me that 'crosses are go follow' baby Andrew if I take him to see the dead woman. So I hand him over and pursue the crowd round the corner into River View while the two friends scamper off together down the road laughing happily. About a hundred people from the neighbourhood have come to see the spectacle not at the police station as Racquel had thought, but in a local yard. I notice Miss Vandy with her three year old daughter making slow progress down the track.

The body is lying on the earth, to the rear of the house, covered with banana leaves. Two plain clothes police are examining the scene and large numbers of visitors are descending the slope to take a better look. In front of the gate various descriptions and theories concerning the death are being swapped. It is said that the woman is the victim of a lover's quarrel, that she was stabbed in the stomach and the heart. I suggest to Miss Vandy that she not lean too hard over the yard fence or she will get blood on her dress. I meet up with Jeanette who is talking with some of the neighbours . . .

It was only occasionally that activity on this street became coordinated beyond the level of an individual's connections with other individuals. But the death at River View focused people's identification of themselves as being locals and neighbours. While the effects of the event lasted, there emerged an intensified expression of the idea that the shared physical locality provided the parameters of a common identity – an idea which became more strongly felt as word of the murder spread and stories about the death were elaborated between people. People's identification of themselves as locals had various shadings: it appeared in stories about small acts of neighbourliness – a man living next door who had boarded up the house of the dead woman in the absence of any relatives to do the job – but also in images of concerted (violent) action against the murderer by an angry crowd (while this was much talked of, it never took place).

The swapping of stories in conversation meant that many different images of these kinds could be current at the same time. But this process of narrative elaboration, in which people's understandings of the event were synthesised with how they defined themselves, was itself made up of a complex of processes: it was characterised by the rapid take up and rejection of cultural responses, an interweaving of subjectively held and communally validated understandings, and the swift negotiation – and crystallisation – of explanations. For a while at least, people's shared relationship to the event as an event predominated over their different understandings of its underlying meaning.

[. . . .]

Concluding remarks

Travelling through New Kingston one day in 1992 I noticed, from my bus-window vantage, a smart, pinstripe-suited businessman (or perhaps a bureaucrat). He was walking with his leather briefcase towards one of the major city hotels – a fact unsurprising in itself except that, somewhat below the knee, his suit had been tie-dyed and its conservative charcoal stripes were from that point onwards transformed into luminous purple and orange. Powerfully strange in most contexts, the burlesque declaration made by this suit was finely attuned to the wider ethos of Kingston: in the Jamaican capital the weak authority of an objective institutional culture is, for the most part, a poor match for the creativity of people's subjective cultural responses to the organisation of city life.

There are an array of reasons for the weak interdependency and failure of communication between Kingston's different social sectors. These include the historical facts of slavery, the failure of colonial governments to create the grounds for political pluralism, the lack of an industrial economy and consciousness. Absence of an organic base for popular democracy has meant that, despite the brief rapprochement created by the movement towards independence, broad-based civic consensus rapidly disintegrated after 1962. The result is that, while many ordinary Jamaicans evince (on occasion) a sentimental attachment to their island, few have any deeply embedded respect for, or understanding of, the workings of Jamaica as a nation state. The destabilising effects of random violence and the de facto bankruptcy of the national economy since the mid 1980s have only added to the difficulty people face in building a shared civic life. But the picture created by these statements – of plural interests and an absence of deep-seated consensuality – requires yet more contextualisation and qualification. The perspectives presented in this chapter concerning the spontaneous creation of community will take on a higher level of focus in the final section of this book where objective and subjective cultural forms can be seen to achieve a greater level of synthesis. However, in the next chapter I examine further the social relationships lying behind the dramatic events so characteristic of Kingston street life.

Big conversations and patterns of commitment

This book is an amended version of my doctoral thesis entitled 'Male Initiation and Cosmology among the Barasana Indians of the Vaupés Area of Colombia'. The thesis submitted in 1974, was based on field-work carried out between September 1968 and December 1970 under the auspices of Cambridge University. . . . The fieldwork . . . involved myself, my wife Christine and Peter Silverwood-Cope. The project was directed by Professor Sir Edmund Leach and financed from the Social Science Research Council . . .

In 1967, when I graduated at University, Amazonia was an anthropological *terra incognita*, especially for English anthropologists with their traditional focus on Africa and Asia. One of the objectives of our research was simply to fill an important gap in ethnographic knowledge of Amazonia . . .

At this time also, the structuralist anthropology of Claude Lévi-Strauss, in particular as applied to the study of myth, had already had a major impact upon anthropological theory in England. But whilst the theoretical ideas were familiar enough, the ethnographic basis on which they were founded was not. . . . Our second objective, and one more directly related to the theme of this book, was to provide an empirical test for some of the grand generalisations that Lévi-Strauss had offered concerning the structure of South American Indian mythology and its relation to Indian thought and culture. The Vaupés, lying well outside the central Brazilian culture area that forms the focal point of Lévi-Strauss's work on Amerindian myth, appeared to be an ideal location for such a test. Lévi-Strauss himself had only given passing consideration to the myths from this area.

(Hugh-Jones 1979: xii)

In his preface to *The Palm and the Pleiades*, Stephen Hugh-Jones firmly ties the significance of his research to the ideas of a major thinker in anthropology, Claude Lévi-Strauss, the initiator of **structuralism**. Hugh-Jones' ethnography is intended as an empirical validation or falsification of

Lévi-Strauss' ideas about myth. But he makes other important statements too. The research was paid for by the British Social Science Research Council. It was undertaken in the company of his wife Christine (see Chapter 5) and another anthropologist, Peter Silverwood-Cope. And it was supervised by an august figure in British anthropology – 'Professor Sir Edmund Leach'. Hugh-Jones places emphasis on the chronology of the primary research: it was begun and ended at a certain date; its initiation coincided with the 'major impact' of Lévi-Strauss' work on British anthropology.

Perhaps the most obvious way of understanding this preface is to consider it as a justification of Hugh-Jones' allegiance to a **paradigm** or **meta-narrative**, structuralism. More subtly, and following what we have said in earlier chapters, we may recognise the importance of certain integral relationships. Relations underlined here include those with co-equals (Christine Hugh-Jones, Peter Silverwood-Cope) as well as hierarchical relationships with an academic mentor (Edmund Leach) and with, for want of a better phrase, an intellectual hero (Claude Lévi-Strauss). These relationships have their own parameters of time and space; Cambridge, Amazonia (not Africa or Asia), Britain (and implicitly France), the years 1967 to 1974.

Here, in this statement we can find the weave of intellectual engagement that characterises the ethnography as, emerging out of particular relations entered into at particular times, it becomes an authored work. In this chapter we explore the ethnography in terms of this pattern of engagement. What concerns us here is how ethnographic writing is built on assumptions about the broad intellectual state of play at the time of writing. Taking this line of approach will help us to rethink the way specific ethnographies are connected to the broader history of anthropology as a discipline. We will also shed further light on the process, explored in Chapter 7, through which the ethnographer comes to claim not only the insight of the insider but, at the same time, the analytical grounding of the outsider.

Anthropological theory is typically taught in universities as a history of theories, schools and paradigms. This type of course, often a compulsory one for higher-level undergraduates, consists of a sequence of changing intellectual frameworks and discussion of key figures. In it, students will learn how nineteenth-century **social evolutionist** anthropology, protagonised by such figures as Herbert Spencer and Lewis Henry Morgan, merged at the beginning of the twentieth century into a historical perspective that included direct observational fieldwork – the **diffusionism** of Haddon and Rivers in Britain and the **historical particularism** of Boas in America. These ideas were displaced, during the 1920s, by Malinowski's **functionalism** that espoused extended participatory fieldwork and a present-oriented, pragmatic, holistic understanding of culture. Functionalism was given theoretical sophistication by Radcliffe-Brown and re-termed **structural functionalism**. A division of interests increasingly emerged between American and European anthropology. American **cultural anthropology** emphasised the coherence of cultural meanings as a pattern and increasingly as a system. British and French **social anthropology**, by contrast, prioritised the structure and hierarchy, or system, of social relations, specifically kinship relations.

Students will go on to learn how, by the 1960s, the academic dominance of structural functionalism had begun to erode. On the one hand, theories began to give priority to individual motivation and political **interaction** as against the assumption of social equilibrium characterising structural functionalism. On the other, in Europe, figures such as Lévi-Strauss, Edmund Leach and Mary Douglas introduced a new theory, **structuralism**, that took a much broader view of society and culture than the small-scale face-to-face studies typical of the first generation ethnographers. Structuralism was, in turn, criticised for its failure to account for issues of power and exploitation, and so **Marxist** anthropology came to the fore during the 1970s. Marxism was complemented by **feminist** perspectives (see Chapter 6), which redressed the male-centred imbalance of previous ethnography.

By the 1980s, the specialist knowledge of anthropologists was itself the new battleground. These **post-modern** strands of thought, centred in the **writing culture** group, emphasised the power relations created between anthropologist and informant in the process of cultural translation. It was argued that ethnography as writing gave a fictive and primarily rhetorical coherence to culture which was absent from experience. By the mid-1990s, the evangelical fervour of post-modernism had run out of steam and was replaced by a new pragmatism that tried to amalgamate and refine the benefits of the various critiques of anthropology by experimenting with, *inter alia*, **reflexive** and **phenomenological** styles of ethnography. By the early years of the twenty-first century, new trends such as an interest in cosmopolitan standpoints had emerged, but no particular 'ism' had yet claimed the *fin de siècle* as its own.

If some nuanced variant of this schematic history is the standard fare of undergraduate anthropological training, then, as might be expected, the truth is more complex. For one thing, the 'paradigm downwards' view which emphasises the power of the big intellectual movement over individual academic activity produces a different picture from an 'ethnographer up' standpoint on the specific activities and relationships of particular anthropologists. For another, paradigms in the social sciences do not have the clear cut boundaries or marked **paradigm shifts** characteristic of the natural sciences because theories and grounding assumptions are rarely disproved in a strict sense. We return to this issue in our conclusion. There are still anthropologists who are, in effect if not in name, structural functionalists. Likewise, there are anthropologists writing now whose basic assumptions are very close those of the diffusionists of the early twentieth century. And so it goes.

The discussion in this chapter takes an 'ethnographer up' perspective, because this is the viewpoint we will encounter in ethnographies. Ethnographies are built out of a range of theoretical ideas and grounding assumptions brought together by an ethnographer to make sense of complicated experiences and information at a particular point in their intellectual career. Sometimes this process of coordination of meta-narratives and ideas, experiences and relationships will appear to be absent, in which case we will need to recover it. The excerpt from Stephen Hugh-Jones' work, above, provides us with a starting point.

As Rapport has pointed out, we should be aware of the sociological truth behind the latin tag *si bis faciunt idem, non est idem*; if two people do the same thing it is not the same thing (1994: 92). Given the very different relationships and experiences that precede the writing of a particular ethnography it is hardly likely that, for example, two structuralist ethnographies will be 'the same' as each other intellectually. From a different viewpoint, then, the particular intellectual weave of the ethnography becomes an expression of the characteristic academic personality or **personhood** of the ethnographer. This goes beyond the question of individual writing style that Geertz (1988) describes. Instead, the ethnography represents, from this perspective, a culmination of relationships lived under certain conditions and the creative synthetic response to those conditions.

The idea of ethnography as the expression of a distinctive framing of intellectual commitment captured at a particular moment, enriches the traditional view that would have us distinguish and categorise ethnographies and theories as belonging to different schools and paradigms. But since ethnographers themselves write in terms of the existence of these schools and paradigms, then we must take account of them too. We must come to understand the social processes and motives that lead an ethnographer to discuss, for instance, American cultural anthropology or British social anthropology as if these were unitary phenomena. We will begin then, by taking some classic paradigmatic statements by famous writers of ethnography, analysing these in terms of the 'ethnographer up' stance that we have proposed.

Summary points

1   Anthropological theory is characteristically taught in terms of the influence of schools and paradigms. By contrast, this chapter takes an 'ethnographer up' viewpoint.
2   Since ethnographers themselves write in terms of the existence of these schools and paradigms, then we must take account of them too.

3   A richer understanding is gained by exploring the ethnography as the expression of relationships that an ethnographer has entered into at certain times and the pattern of intellectual commitment thereby formed.

The critical thinker and the making of meta-narrative

Typically, we learn about anthropology's guiding assumptions by reading the works of anthropologists whose statements are considered to be historically pivotal. Almost by definition we can say that the most famous anthropologists are those who are most successful in giving voice to the anthropological assumptions of their times and the conflict between assumptions. Their academic viewpoint is innovative because it is they who present the most encompassing account of what the current intellectual state of play is; including and combining elements that have not previously been recognised. When we read the anthropological statements of the great historical figures we pay attention to how they changed the meta-narrative guiding the discipline at that time and how their ideas were, in turn, replaced by more sophisticated formulations.

Bronislaw Malinowski's essay 'Myth in Primitive Psychology', originally presented as the Frazer Lecture in 1925, is probably one of the most, if not the most, widely read of these defining anthropological statements. Malinowski's aim is to establish a pathbreaking set of assumptions about 'savage' society. The myths of 'primitive man' are not works of poetry or symbolic flights of fancy as nineteenth-century German scholars have assumed. Nor are they historical documents as the most famous British and American anthropologists take them to be. Malinowski will replace these images with another – the primitive as pragmatist whose myths and magical activities solve everyday dilemmas.

> In strong contrast to this theory which makes myth naturalistic, symbolic and imaginary, stands the theory which regards a sacred tale as a true historical record of the past. This view, recently supported by the so-called Historical School in Germany and America, and represented in England by Dr. Rivers, covers but part of the truth. There is no denying that history, as well as natural environment, must have left a profound impact on all important cultural achievements, hence on all myths. But to take all mythology as mere chronicle is as incorrect as to regard it as the primitive naturalist's musings. It also endows primitive man with a sort of scientific impulse and desire for knowledge. Although the savage has something of the antiquarian as well as of the naturalist in his composition, he is, above all, actively engaged in a number of practical pursuits, and has to struggle with various difficulties; all his interests are tuned up to this general pragmatic outlook.
>
> (Malinowski 1974 [1925]: 98)

Guiding assumptions are here tied to key intellectual figures, as 'Dr. Rivers' (William H. R. Rivers) is taken to be iconic of the 'historical school'. We have discussed already the process of **heuristic** simplification in the presentation of specific arguments (Chapter 5), but the simplification in the presentation of schools is even more striking in this case. Most importantly, Malinowski presents his view as a radical distinction between guiding images. His picture of the savage pragmatist leads to an entirely different understanding of myth. And, for many years, the idea that Malinowski's standpoint marked a total break from the misguided historical approach of early social anthropology was taught in universities as simple fact. And yet, increasingly, continuities between Malinowski and his predecessor Rivers are emphasised, and this parallels the degree to which Malinowski's own ideas have become part of the discipline's historical background (Hart 1998; Wardle 1999).

The iconic use of critical thinkers and associated schools can be seen again in the following statement by Clifford Geertz from his book of essays collected as *The Interpretation of Cultures* in 1973 (Geertz 1993a). Like Malinowski's essay, this book was for a long time a required text for students on many courses of anthropology. Geertz opens an essay on 'Religion as a Cultural System' with a long magisterial statement in which he dismisses the achievement of the post-Second World War (British) social anthropological 'tradition' with regard to religion. Social anthropology has become excessively narrowed intellectually and is incapable of further discoveries, he proposes. The field of ideas must be opened up to new ways of thinking. He, therefore, will focus his attention on developing an alternative viewpoint – the interpretation of religion, not in terms of social structure, but, following Parsons and Shils, as a cultural system.

> Two characteristics of anthropological work on religion accomplished since the second world war strike me as curious when such work is placed against that carried out just before and just after. One is that it has made no theoretical advances of major importance. It is living off the conceptual capital of its ancestors, adding very little, save a certain empirical enrichment, to it. The second is that it draws what concepts it does use from a very narrowly defined intellectual tradition. There is Durkheim, Weber, Freud or Malinowski, and in any particular work the approach of one or two of these transcendent figures is followed, with but a few marginal corrections necessitated by the natural tendency to excess of seminal minds or by the expanded body of reliable descriptive data. But virtually no one even thinks of looking elsewhere . . . as these men themselves looked, for analytical ideas. And it occurs to me, also, that these two curious characteristics are not unrelated. . . . Only if we abandon . . . that sweet sense of accomplishment in parading habitual skills and address ourselves to problems

sufficiently unclarified as to make discovery possible, can we hope to achieve work which will not just reincarnate that of the great men of the first quarter of this century, but match it.

The way to do this is not to abandon the established traditions of social anthropology in this field, but to widen them. . . . For my part, I shall confine my effort to developing what, following Parsons and Shils, I refer to as the cultural dimension of religious analysis. The term 'culture' has now acquired a certain aura of ill-repute in social anthropological circles because of the multiplicity of its referents and the studied vagueness with which it has all too often been invoked. (Though why it should suffer more for these reason than 'social structure' or 'personality' is something I do not entirely understand.) In any case, the culture concept to which I adhere has neither multiple referents nor, so far as I can see, any unusual ambiguity: it denotes an historically transmitted pattern of meanings embodied in symbols, a system of inherited conceptions expressed in symbolic forms by means of which men communicate, perpetuate, and develop their knowledge about and attitudes toward life.

(Geertz 1993a [1973]: 87–9)

We may notice that the 'two characteristics' of anthropological work on religion are in fact one criticism elaborated a second time for effect. Geertz argues that anthropology's 'ancestors', its 'transcendent figures', have produced a treasury of ideas that is being squandered in an intellectually narrow way. The result is study after study that invokes a critical thinker in order to present yet another, ultimately repetitive, framing of ethnographic data. The 'culture' concept may be the object of the social anthropologists' derision, but it is a principal way in which anthropological inquiry can be saved from intellectual contraction or decreasing margin of profit depending on which figure we prefer.

Here, and elsewhere in *The Interpretation of Cultures*, Geertz posits his own intellectual approach as a break with the British social anthropologists (e.g. 1993a [1973]: 142–3). Again, as with Malinowski's programmatic statement above, the argument could have been presented in different terms. Geertz could have described his project as a continuation of the American programme of cultural anthropology and a reaffirmation of his intellectual links with it. After all, the idea of culture as a 'historically transmitted pattern of meanings . . . by which men communicate' evidently reflects the anthropology of Franz Boas developed by Benedict, Mead, Kroeber and Kluckhohn to which Geertz has added Parsons and Shils.

Of course the reiteration of these intellectual and academic relationships would have had a much less radical turn than an attack on a divergent set of assumptions. Instead, Geertz underlines the cleavage between himself and the social anthropologists. In a more recent essay, which we return to at the end of this chapter, Geertz (1993a [1973]) presents his intellectual activity in a significantly more contingent way. He describes it as a result of the happenstance of being in certain academic environments with particular scholars at specific historical moments. But between the **reification** of schools and scholars, or at the opposite extreme, the description of academic activity as a purely individual and contingent exercise, there is another possibility, what we call here the 'ethnographer up' perspective. This viewpoint allows us to recognise the ways in which authors signal a pattern of intellectual commitment in their writing, and thereby capture larger flows of intellectual conversation within their ethnography. This perspective builds on the relational view of ethnography that we have developed over the last chapters. Part of the work of ethnography – of the ethnographer as author – involves substantiating how the ethnographic text not only belongs to, but also contributes to, larger meta-narratives.

What do we learn by taking this 'ethnographer up' approach to these two icons of ethnographic writing? First, ethnographers themselves have a nested view of anthropology as an intellectual practice. At the widest level is 'anthropology', the encompassing activity. Then there are schools, associated with iconic figures such as Rivers or Malinowski or Geertz. These 'ancestors' are sometimes completely identified with the school, sometimes not so completely. The idea of the 'school' itself has a disciplining role with regard to certain concepts and usages. Followers of a school may disregard a concept such as 'culture' because it is too 'vague', for instance. The 'transcendent' anthropological figures (in Geertz's own semi-serious phrasing) are those who debate at the level of grounding assumptions, challenging the assumptions of other schools. Members of schools are more likely to argue within the framework of grounding assumptions adding detail or correcting the 'tendency to excess' of 'seminal minds'. In addition, while the meta-narratives that guide the work of schools encompass very complex theorising, they can also often be reduced to simple images or metaphors – the practical-minded savage, for instance.

In the framing of a specific argument, the ethnographer will move from the general issues of allegiance to schools/iconic thinkers, to nesting much more specific detailed reference to particular concepts and arguments within this broader intellectual framework. Framing an ethnography academically, involves a signalling and combination of meta-narratives. This signalling is necessary in order to establish the relevance of specific arguments and of more particular ethnographic material for a particular audience.

Summary points

1   Core assumptions are typically tied to key intellectual figures.
2   Guiding assumptions very often take the form of quite simplified images or metaphors; Malinowski's image of the pragmatic savage, for instance.

3 In their writing ethnographers work with a nested or layered view of
the discipline, in which critical thinkers and their guiding narratives
provide the frame for the work of members of particular schools.

Signalling intellectual allegiance

One intellectually dangerous consequence of the paradigm downwards
view of ethnography is that it seems to licence us as readers to discard as
invalid any ethnography produced within the framework of an older,
perhaps now questioned, set of grounding assumptions. This view is a
mistake: its consequence is the amnesiac belief that only up-to-the-minute
ethnography has any value. But it derives, at least in part, from the way
ethnographers themselves frame their arguments in meta-narrative terms.
We have discussed in Chapter 6 how ethnographers establish their authorship by positioning their individual aims, questions and approaches within
wider debates. Establishing authorship and signalling scholarly allegiance
are two sides of a single coin. Combined, they are also a primary step
towards communicating with an appropriate audience. In the introduction
to his ethnography of Papua New Guinean exchange, Edward Schieffelin
first underlines his divergence from a sociological view of reciprocity, then
demonstrates commitment to a cultural approach:

> In this book, I shall explore this aspect of reciprocity from a cultural
> point of view. Cultural analysis refers primarily to the symbolic dimen-
> sions of human experience and the systems of symbols out of which it
> is constituted . . .
>
> Symbols are usually conceived as 'meaning' or 'standing for' some-
> thing else. At the same time, they exist in various logico-meaningful
> relationships with other symbols in a larger system. A traditional view
> holds that meanings are primarily stored in symbols and brought out
> to use when they are required. Though symbols undoubtedly have this
> storage capacity, I would like to emphasize their more creative aspect.
> Symbols do not just 'stand for' something else. They constantly and
> actively 'bring things into meaning.' This happens because symbolic
> activity brings objects and concepts into new and different kinds of
> relationships in a larger system of meaning, formulating and orga-
> nizing them in new ways according to a few simple procedures. This
> 'rendering into meaning' is the symbolic process by which human
> consciousness continually works reality into intelligible forms.
>
> (Schieffelin 1976: 2)

Very explicitly here Schieffelin vouches for his membership of a school, the
'cultural analysis point of view'. Cultural analysis is presented as clear-cut
and internally coherent. Schieffelin does not talk in terms of iconic figures

such as Geertz. Instead, he outlines the basic assumptions – that symbols form a 'system' and that cultural creativity represents how the relationships between symbols are reorganised 'according to a few simple procedures'. In retrospect, what stands out here are the metaphors on which this framing exercise depends. Apart from the repeated image of 'system' there is the metaphor of a symbol as a 'store' of meaning – 'symbols undoubtedly have this storage capacity'. However, images and metaphors like these may be far less self-evidently authoritative now than they were when the ethnography was written. So, in order to understand Schieffelin's deployment of meta-narrative we may need to do some historical reconstruction, reinstating aspects of the author's academic relationships and open-ended conversations obscured in the way the meta-narrative is here presented as definitive and final.

In the excerpt below, from *Black Gods of the Metropolis*, Arthur Fauset (1971 [1944]: 1–12) signals his intellectual allegiances, not with a paradigmatic statement like Schieffelin's, but by deploying ethnographic evidence directly against a well-recognised set of grounding assumptions. The narrative he gives us evidences strong dissent from a school of thought about New World black experience led at that time by Melville Herskovits. The Herskovitsian meta-narrative emphasised clear continuities between a coherent set of New World black cultural practices and an African past. But, in an attack on one of the cornerstones of this paradigm, Fauset undermines the idea that there is any particularly African 'bent' towards ecstatic religion which has survived into African American cultural behaviour (1971: 108): there is nothing especially 'black' about black American culture, he suggests.

> On another occasion I attended a Father Divine service in Rockland Palace when a group of young Columbia University students entered the place and were seated on the platform. They had come to observe Father Divine at first hand.
>
> It was easy to see in their faces that many of them fully anticipated an evening's entertainment consonant with popular ideas of African fetish or Haitian voodoo worship.
>
> A very quizzical look spread over the countenances of some of these when, quite early in the service, an elderly white man arose and walked to the platform, stood by the microphone, and called out to his vast audience, consisting mainly of Negroes, 'peace, Father! Peace, everyone!' . . . Now he asked everyone to join with him in a song . . . In a few seconds his song had caught on all over the huge amphitheatre. And then an amazing spectacle followed:
>
> A white woman who had been playing castanets . . . suddenly leaped to her feet and began dancing back and forth across the front of the hall.

The white cornetist . . . had to cease playing, and he joined lustily in the singing, shaking his entire body in rhythm with the song. . . . Then another white woman circled conspicuously in pinwheel fashion all over the front of the hall, while a very heavy-set . . . Jew, ran about the same place clapping his hands rhythmically, singing loudly and gaily, and contorting his face and body. . . . And finally, one of the Columbia University students, too overcome to remember where she was or what she was doing, began to sing freely and to tap the floor with her feet.

This spectacle which the Columbia students had expected to see generated by Negroes, had been inspired by an elderly white man from California . . . The spell was so tremendous that, even after the music had ceased . . . the [Jewish] gentleman . . . indulged in an orgy of jumping about, puffing, blowing, perspiring, clapping his hands, and flapping his arms in imitation of angel's wings. Here, for all the world to hear and see, they proclaimed, Father Divine is God!

(Fauset 1971: 105)

Here Fauset sets his own ethnographic experience against the guiding meta-narrative of the Herskovits school by evidencing the lack of connection between black individuals and 'black' religion. Elsewhere in the book ethnographic narration is also used to signal allegiance to the alternative sociological view of Franklin Frazier, that black culture was best understood as a response to current social conditions in America. Fauset's own pattern of intellectual commitment is woven into the way his ethnography is presented and used as evidence. It is nonetheless true that, by making his own personality so apparent in the description, Fauset makes his own membership of a particular school much less prominent.

In this sense we can see Schieffelin's and Fauset's texts as at opposite ends of a continuum. Schieffelin frames his ethnography very firmly within the parameters of an established meta-narrative, to the extent that his academic personality and the meta-narrative are presented as indistinguishable at that point in the text. Clearly the authority of this ethnography comes from its demonstration of adherence to established ideas. The weight of Fauset's arguments, by contrast, depends to a much greater extent on an assertion of the authenticity of his ethnographic voice as a reflection of his own specific experience. Fauset's career, as a teacher and in the American civil rights movement, took him out of anthropology as a professional academic conversation. This is perhaps reflected in how his intellectual commitments are framed here in more impressionistic, less theoretical terms. Ironically however, the 1971 republication of *Black Gods of the Metropolis* is introduced by John Szwed with an essay that takes a strongly pro-Herskovitsian viewpoint. Rather than dismissing ethnographies that ally themselves to now unfashionable meta-narratives, as readers we need to learn to read through these signallings of allegiance to the relations of academic commitment underlying them.

Summary points

1   Anthropologists themselves present their work in terms of schools and paradigms as a primary step towards communicating with an appropriate audience.
2   To understand an ethnographer's use of the core images or metaphors sustaining meta-narratives, we may need to reinstate aspects of that author's academic relationships, obscured in the presentation of text.
3   Different strategies regarding the deployment of meta-narrative will reflect the kind of academic personality being established in the ethnography.

The text as the weave of academic personality

Early on in his ethnography of Finnish farming life, British anthropologist Ray Abrahams comments on the dilemmas of undertaking fieldwork in the village where his father-in-law was born and on his sharp awareness of 'doing anthropology among my **affines**' (Abrahams 1991: 3).

> Some other problems of 'affinal' fieldwork were less obvious than these, and more difficult to cope with. In 1957, when I first applied to do research in eastern Africa, Audrey Richards asked me if I suffered from shyness, and I replied truthfully, though not especially helpfully, that it depended on the circumstances. Shyness turned out not to be a problem in my African research, but it did affect me during work in Finland, and I am not wholly certain why this is the case. A desire not to worry or annoy people to whom I was connected, and a fear of making a fool of myself in front of them were clearly part of the problem. But I suspect too that my special links were partly absorbed into a more general awareness of European commonalities coupled with a self-conscious feeling that I was all the time being judged by canons into which I myself had been deeply socialised.
>
> (Abrahams 1991: 5)

Abrahams goes on to note the bureaucratic backing that assured his position in his earlier African research, compared with the need to negotiate a status for himself that characterised his more equal positioning *vis-à-vis* the Finnish informants. This apparently limpid statement contains a number of subtle **reflexive** shadings. It includes reflections on a subjective emotion, 'shyness', as it affects fieldwork practice. This is an analysis of Finnish kinship that has the author's own (affinal) kin relationship with his informants at its centre. These considerations are mixed with more general sociological reasoning about 'European commonalities' and how this might affect the research of the anthropologist as someone who cannot evade his own socialisation.

The complexity here may well be enhanced if the reader needs to ask the question 'who is Audrey Richards'? Because this detail – the relationship with a major British anthropologist that Abrahams notes passingly – is rather more than just an anecdote. Of course it sets the scene; the passage of time, the growth of autobiographical experience and anthropological knowledge. However, it also roots Abrahams' account in the British school of social anthropologists of whom Audrey Richards is an avatar and Abrahams a practitioner. The importance of affinal relationships was one of the most important theoretical conversations of mid-century social anthropology (in which Audrey Richards was a key conversationalist). The minor aside about the ambivalences experienced in forming relationships can be taken as **metonymic** of a much bigger conversation. By making the reference, Abrahams signals quite clearly the audience towards whom his ethnography is directed; that is to say, readers who are party to the same conversation at differing levels of intellectual involvement (see Chapter 6).

Abrahams' comments correspond to a trend in ethnographic writing, particularly of senior scholars, in which there is a conscious attempt to interconnect autobiographical, institutional, ethnographic and grand theoretical elements, rather than separating them out for brief mention in a preface, say. In *After the Fact*, Geertz reflects on these issues in a rather different mode than the essay of his that we quoted above:

> Becoming an anthropologist is not, or anyway has not been for me, an induction into an established profession, like law, medicine, or the flying of airplanes, already there, graded and subdivided, waiting to hammer one into slot-ready shape. My wandering among programs, projects, committees, institutes, with only the odd stop-off at anthropology departments, is admittedly a bit unstandard; not a recipe everyone will find attractive. But the picture of a career less followed than assembled, put together in the course of effecting it, is not now so altogether unusual.
>
> The sequence of settings into which you are projected as you go if not forward at least onward, thoroughly uncertain of what awaits, does far more to shape the pattern of your work, to discipline it and give it form, than do theoretical arguments, methodological pronouncements, canonized texts, or even, as are these days too much with us, left and right, iron commitments to intellectual creeds. These things matter (perhaps more to some people than they do to me), but it is what you find before you – an eclectic collection of let's-get-on-with-it enthusiasts at *après guerre* Harvard; a tense, ideology ridden

society, hurtling towards violence, in post-Independence Indonesia; an equanimous community of long-distance reasoners amid the tumult of sixties Chicago; an ancient community beset by sociological blurr and cultural self-questioning in reemerged Morocco; a carefully defended island of specialist research in manicured Princeton – that most power-fully directs your intellectual trajectory. You move less between thoughts than between the occasions and predicaments that bring them to mind.

(Geertz 1995: 133–4)

We may well recognise an important difference, of rhetoric at least, in Geertz's comments here and those taken from 'Religion as a Cultural System' (above). In the first citation, Geertz holds firm to a clearly defined meta-narrative. In the comments here he places his intellectual trajectory on a much more contingent footing. As scholars build intellectual capital and academic recognition, it becomes easier for them to talk of their own achievements in terms of their own agency and the 'uncertain' factors in relation to which it was exercised. They may no longer need to phrase their intellectual activity within a shared set of assumptions because, as intellectual icons, they have come to stand for those assumptions: so, at least it seems to be in Geertz's case as presented here.

It may be much more problematic for academics earlier in their career to make these kinds of statements. On the one hand, their claims to ethnographic knowledge are made on the basis of significantly less auto-biographical experience. Their acquaintance with the long debates and nuanced conversations going on between anthropologists may be corre-spondingly abbreviated. Their network of support, including an established readership, as well as longstanding relations with senior scholars and fund-providers who support their intellectual activities, may be much more tenuous. All these factors militate towards the muting of their own intellec-tual agency and the couching of their knowledge in terms of the shared activity of a school or in accord with, or dissent regarding, the intellectual solidity of a grand narrative. If the trend in ethnographic writing is to include autobiographical contextualisation as part of a reflexive analysis, this may fall short of what Bourdieu terms 'participant objectivation' (2003). By this phrase Bourdieu means a sociologically full account of the ethnographer's own background and the way this, as a framework of relationships, may have structured the basic terms of their ethnographic inquiry.

Summary points

1   Current trends in ethnographic writing emphasise the interconnecting of autobiographical, institutional, ethnographic and grand theoretical

elements in order to give a fuller sense of intellectual context for
ethnography.

2   As scholars build intellectual capital and academic recognition, it
becomes easier for them to couch their intellectual activity in terms of
their personal autobiographical experience.

3   Lesser known/junior writers of ethnography may mute their intellectual agency, couching their knowledge in terms of membership of a
school or in allegiance or dissent from a grand narrative.

Concluding remarks

To borrow a phrase of Heidegger's . . . the self 'reflects itself to itself
from out of that to which it has given itself over.'

(Munn 1992: 15)

This comment of Nancy Munn's with regard to the fame-seeking activities
of Gawan islanders in the Massim archipelago, is pertinent also to the
work of ethnographers and their ethnographies. The academic personality
presented in the ethnography is similarly a reflection of 'that to which it
has given itself over' – relationships formed during fieldwork, relations
with particular anthropologists and their ideas, professional relationships
with specific academic institutions. This is the stuff from which academic
personality as a dimension of authorship is made, the weave of intellectual
commitment of which the ethnography is one product. The implication of
this, reiterated at several stages of this book, is that an ethnography is best
understood, less as statement of knowledge entire of itself, more as a
contribution to a continuing conversation made up of many interrelated
speakers.

There are the big conversations of well recognised conversationalists
and the smaller dialogues of the lesser known who frame what they say by
reference to the words of the better known in order to make themselves
understood. And then there are many cacophonic exchanges between
anthropologists, who having individually 'given themselves over' to particular relationships and intellectual projects, fail to understand the larger
framings of each other's utterances. In a single century social and cultural
anthropology has grown from a very limited area of academic study practised by a few well known individuals to a highly institutionalised,
professionalised arena involving thousands of salaried practitioners and
hence many thousands of intellectual, academic and practical relationships.
Hardly any surprise that there are likewise innumerable theoretical conversations and significant causes for misunderstanding.

'Paradigm' is still often used by anthropologists, after Kuhn (1962), to
describe the shared assumptions and research goals of large groups of
scholars working at a particular moment in the history of anthropology,

alongside how the structure and content of these assumptions is trans-formed in relatively radical '**paradigm shifts**'. The fact is that this way of describing anthropology as a field of intellectual activity is largely unhelpful. Anthropology has rarely been collectively coherent in this particular way, nor is it true historically that basic assumptions shift radically and deci-sively from one big collective framework to the next.

We suggested at the beginning of this chapter that, rather than paradigms or meta-narratives, at the widest level ethnographers are responding to 'big conversations'. Anthropologists are aware of dialogues going on at different scales of significance and wish to contribute to these in their own discussions with particular audiences. The broad encompassing conversa-tions and their central conversationalists provide the frame within which smaller theoretical and narrative interchanges acquire relevance. The key terms of these big conversations are reiterated in order to join in. This implies, in turn, that readers are also part of the conversation; have varying degrees of awareness of what has been said before and since an ethnography has been written; are potential contributors themselves. The reader, in order to understand an ethnography, must enter a dialogue with its author and, in so doing, joins the network of relationships that, ultimately, give ethnography meaning as a discussion of human social and cultural life.

Chapter 8 – activities

In this discussion, Keith Hart revisits his earlier (1973) ethnography of the Ghanaian 'informal economy', rephrasing it in autobiographical and polem-ical terms. He discusses both personal academic ambitions and prevailing meta-narratives, as well as key relationships with academic institutions and with key intellectual figures. He frames his ethnographic practice at a number of different levels related to his autobiographical trajectory. Read the piece and respond to the following questions:

1   What kind of audience do you think Hart is directing his writing at?
2   How does Hart link the development of his ethnographic knowledge with the trajectory of his academic career?
3   Hart often comes across as angry or frustrated in this account: with whom and why?
4   In what ways are meta-narratives and ethnography tied together here (or shown to be dissonant)?
5   What do we learn from Hart's account about the ways his own intel-lectual commitments have changed and developed through time?

Hart, K. (2006) African Enterprise and the Informal Economy: an autobiographical note,[1] *available at http://www.thememorybank.co.uk/papers/african_enterprise*

The great invention of modern anthropology was fieldwork. For the first (and last) time, a segment of the intellectual class crossed the divide between themselves and the rest of society as a means of finding out how people live. This meant that they had to join their social objects as individual subjects, thereby muddling the conventional separation of subjects ('thinkers' working for those who take the decisions that matter) from objects ('doers' or those who perform the routine work of society). One of the main tasks of social science since its inception a century ago has been to maintain this division, squeezing the individuality of the unknown urban masses into impersonal categories suitable for manipulation by those who would control them. Anthropologists too aspired to professional status within the intellectual bureaucracy; and so their twentieth century practice was riddled with contradiction and confusion as they both joined the people and made objects of them.

The typical way of handling the problem was to keep the world of 'fieldwork' separate from 'writing up' back home, a task made easier by social and geographical distance in the colonial era. Whereas extravagant claims were made for the fieldworker's subjective penetration of an exotic society (through active participation, learning the vernacular etc.), ethnographic reports were held to be strictly objective and scientific; and any comparison with realist fiction was denied, until quite recently.

The paradigm of scientific ethnography was already reeling from the blows inflicted by the end of empire and the idea of 'primitive society' as anthropology's object was already moribund, if not quite dead, when I undertook fieldwork in Accra (and elsewhere in Ghana) from 1965 to 1968. No efforts were then made at Cambridge to draw students' attention to the problem; and I was left to sort it out for myself as I went along. Aware that studying taxi drivers and pimps in a slum might not be considered anthropology proper, I chose a group of migrants, the Tallensi (Frafra), previously made famous by my head of department, Meyer Fortes (1949), in the hope that they would bestow on my work an air of classical orthodoxy.

Living in Nima, a sort of badlands on the outskirts of Accra, was something of an adventure and I was drawn into playing various social roles compatible, as I thought, with peaceful co-existence in that place. Since it was a violent and economically open society, I became by degrees a criminal entrepreneur – receiving stolen goods, money lending, illegal trading and the like. Towards the end of my stay, in order to redistribute the profits, I assumed the status of a local big man – throwing large parties, hiring many helpers, making handouts to old people, sorting out problems with the bureaucracy. Since I survived four arrests and several close shaves, I returned to write up my doctoral thesis with a feeling of considerable achievement. That was when my troubles began.

I never had any doubt that I wanted an academic job after my Ph.D. I now had to devise a form for reporting my fieldwork experiences that would be acceptable to my examiners. This meant writing myself out of the script, which did not seem all that difficult at the time. What I did not realise was that, in the guise of writing an objective report, I was deliberately embarking on unacknowledged fiction. Moreover, instead of asking myself how I learned what I did – through the reciprocal social relations I entered – I was obsessed with contributing to a body of theory in 'the literature'.

Since this was the 1960s, the prevailing orthodoxy was 'modernisation theory'. From this I took the congenial notion that development is the result of individuals struggling with traditional norms to institute modern practices. I called the men (and a few women) I was interested in 'entrepreneurs', since their economic activities impressed me most. Like a lone fieldworker inserting himself into a fast-moving society, they were individual subjects seeking to make their own way in a social setting that was in turn constraining and malleable. I stressed their individuality and the difference between the economic leaders and the rest of the migrant ethnic community. They were the stars, people whose careers changed the social map for the others. Much of my published material consisted of life histories.

For the next decade, like other ambitious young academics, I tried to turn my thesis into a book. I eventually gave up, only to return to the project – and fail again – not long ago. The reason, I told myself, was that I could not reconcile the big picture of what happened in post-war history with my own memories of fieldwork in Nima, especially since both were moving, perhaps together, perhaps not. Now I identify the problem as my failure to find an authentic voice, straddling uncomfortably the divide between subject and object, between the academy and life. I did attempt to 'come out' before, in Chicago a decade ago and once or twice since, and I was told that my confession would do irreparable harm to Anthropology Inc. Today I believe that silence is more harmful.

I was convinced that the chief deficiency of my ethnographic understanding was a weak grasp of the large forces shaping postcolonial history. Like the people I lived with, I felt that I understood well the mechanics of economic life on the streets; but, also like them, I had no idea why the world cocoa price had plummeted, precipitating shortages and an army coup, with far-reaching consequences for all Ghanaians. So I set out to penetrate the world of 'development', becoming a university lecturer, a consultant and an economic journalist. Initiation into this world came from joining an outfit at the University of East Anglia, where almost all my colleagues were development economists.

I soon learned that there was a lot of mileage to be had from assuming the role of a broker between disciplines, peddling anthropology to economists and vice-versa. But I wanted to bridge the gap between the two, to link my fieldwork to the grand abstractions of development discourse. In other words, I sought to extend my subjective experience of Africa to a more inclusive level of society, the world of states and international institutions; and that meant convincing the economists that I had something to say that they could use.

I have long wondered about the poetry that has sustained 'the informal economy' as a long-running concept in the intellectual bureaucracy. At the very least it came out of my desire to reach the 'masters of the universe' with my words and theirs to make meaningful contact with the teeming hordes outside their hotel windows. The term I chose is negative, but polite; it names the unnameable, labelling the people by an absence, their lack of 'form', as understood by the bureaucracy. In any case, at a 1971 conference on 'Urban unemployment in Africa', I argued that the Africans I knew, far from being unemployed, worked for irregular and often low returns. I combined vivid ethnographic description ('I've been there and you haven't') with some impressive-sounding economic jargon that I had worked out in conversation with my academic colleagues. I made no mention of my own economic activities.

Some members of my audience liked the idea enough to steal it; but my intellectual property rights were restored soon enough and I became known as the author of a whole new segment of the division of labour in development studies. Even more remarkable, despite the number of competing labels (second, hidden, underground, black etc), the 'informal economy' has become the term of choice in the economics and sociology of industrial countries. The poetry must be powerful indeed.

I was not overwhelmed by this success at first. Indeed I was only too aware that I had completed a thesis two years earlier using the language of entrepreneurship to analyse the same phenomena. Moreover, like many others in the early 1970s, I was undergoing a conversion to French Marxism; and the Marxists didn't like the idea of an 'informal economy' at all. I set out to resolve my difficulties, as usual, by writing a paper about it (Hart 1975).

What I was up against was the social division between the bureaucracy and the people, between a state-made elite and the city mob, between the intellectual class and those they objectify; but it came out in an even more abstract form, as the conflict between individual and society. I started from the ideological polarity of the Cold War, economic individualism versus state collectivism. I recognised that this placed liberal proponents of 'enterprise' on the side of the individual and their Marxist detractors on that of the collective. I also realised that, by switching from an emphasis on entrepreneurs as persons to the 'informal economy', I had moved from the life of the slum to the air-conditioned offices of an international elite, sacrificing individuality to an abstract category that helped bureaucrats to understand and ultimately control others.

I set out to show that the grand oppositions of western theory had their counterpart in the concrete struggles of the people I had lived with in Nima. I argued that enterprising individuals could succeed in accommodating community interests, but often did not; so that recourse to positive and negative stereotypes (accumulation of wealth as a good or bad thing) was grounded in social relations and material conditions more than in ideology. Once again I excluded myself from the analysis; and yet it seems hard at this distance to separate my own struggles with society then from those of an ethnic 'community' with whom I was becoming increasingly out of touch.

Soon afterwards, I broke with the attempt to integrate my fieldwork experience with ideas about development. It is symbolic of an escalating detachment from normal social life that the only book I wrote as a result of my African research (Hart

1982) had no people in it at all and addressed a topic, agriculture, of which I had no first-hand knowledge. Not so much a bird's-eye view as one from a Boeing 747, the book was accepted by USAID as a consultancy report and by Cambridge University Press as a monograph in social anthropology. I thus succeeded in integrating the poles of my intellectual project at the level of ideas, formally detached from the people of Nima whose living company was the real source of any original thoughts I had come to be credited with.

In this way, I recapitulated the general betrayal of anthropology's modern mission. Starting from a genuine commitment to 'go and see for myself', joining people in their everyday lives as a means of enlarging my knowledge of the world, I subsequently withdrew into academic bureaucracy and a career as an ideologue sustained by private ownership of intellectual work (see Hart 2005). For the task of ideology is to make us believe that life is the outcome of ideas, rather than the other way round. It is gratifying to be famous as the author of an idea; but I know, and so should everyone else, that the idea of an 'informal economy' was a way of turning what is defiantly external to bureaucracy into something internal to it, incorporating the autonomous life of the people into the abstracted universe of their rulers.

In a recent paper (Hart 1992), I began the process of historical reconstruction that might allow us to discover the true significance of the 'informal economy' idea. It means going back to the Nkrumah coup of 1966, which I lived through in Nima, close enough to the main action in the presidential palace. From the perspective I now have on the post-war world, Ghana was and is an integral part of global society, not the distant, exotic place I found it to be then.

In the 1960s, society was everywhere identified with the state. Despite the crude oppositions of the Cold War, national capitalism was universal; which is to say that the task of economic development, the sole basis of political legitimacy, was assumed to be the primary responsibility of the state. The limits of this state dominance began to be revealed in the mid-1970s, to be followed by the Thatcher/Reagan experiment of combining private enterprise with enhanced state power and finally by the collapse of Stalinism. In the meantime, most of the 'Third World' has effectively dropped out of the world economy and governments there draw a thin veil of power over generalised misery. Now that the euphoria over 'winning' the Cold War has evaporated, the West is witnessing on its own home ground the last phase of national capitalism's moral bankruptcy and economic exhaustion.

Africa was the last recruit to the twentieth century's national capitalist system and its first victim. Ghana, the continental leader, had already, by the early 1960s, torn up the social contract between state and people that had animated the independence years. The military coup that ousted Nkrumah was based on recognition that, in a climate of economic failure, force rather than consent would now have to be the state's explicit foundation. This was the situation I encountered as a fieldworker. I went to Ghana to study the political associations of migrants as citizens; but, in the face of political apathy, I soon turned to the economic vitality of the streets. That is, I followed the people of Nima who, knowing that they were excluded from (and victimised by) the state's monopolies, were busy making lives for themselves in the cracks between. This early moment of what later became a general dialectic gave me insight into what people do when the state's 'macro-economics' fail. In this sense, Ghana's 'informal economy' was leading the world.

For it is indisputable that the drive to control society from the top (through governments, international agencies and large corporations) has over-reached itself since the Second World War. Informalization of the world economy has long been its most dynamic feature, with corrupt arms deals, the drugs traffic, offshore banking, political rackets, tax evasion and inner city crime uniting people at all levels of society. Civil society, the principled separation of public and private interests, has broken down and, as a consequence, the intellectual credibility of economics is in tatters.

One mistake I made in formulating the concept of an 'informal economy' was in treating the paired opposition, formal/informal, as static. In the early 1970s the polarities of the Cold War seemed inevitable and the state's dominance was still taken for granted. So, although I recognized that the people were fighting back through their self-generated economic activities, I assumed that they were condemned to do so only in the minor interstices of society left unsupervised by an omnipotent state. The other mistake lay in sacrificing what was original in my field-work experience – relationships and personalities, the enterprise, the social experiments – for a mechanical worldview that could never see the embryonic democracy contained in these activities.

Things are different now. The old black market hustlers of the Brezhnev era are now riding BMWs round the streets of Moscow. 'Enterprise' is in favour once again. The collapse of the state is so far-gone in many countries (Jamaica and Zaire come to mind) that it hardly seems useful any more to point out that the 'informal economy' is dominant there. But what once seemed a kind of heroic resistance takes on a different odour when it is the only game in town. We are reminded what civil society was invented for, to do away with the mess of political corruption and economic violence that was normal then and now haunts us once again.

This leads me back to the Nima years, to ask what I really learned there that might be useful now, as 'the informal economy' concept no longer is. I began this process in a paper written for a seminar on trust (Hart 1988); and I will not rehearse the arguments here, beyond pointing out that much of my mature thinking on 'African enterprise' can be found there. I posed the problem once again in the form that it originally appeared to me: how do individuals project their enterprises into a future that is mediated by their social relations with others?

Frafra migrants lacked the kinship ties of their homeland and were excluded from state-sanctioned contracts; so they fell back on an ethos of friendship and trust that is quite well-suited to dealing in the short-term, but not to the organisation of production over time. Their dilemma is one we all share, namely how to insert our persons effectively into a world governed by impersonal social forces. It is out of the millions of individual responses to this dilemma that the social material of democracy and development must be emerging now, even as the world's ruling powers prepare to hold off popular government at all costs.

But the main lesson I draw from my experience of fieldwork three decades ago concerns the actual social processes of learning to live in Nima that shaped so much of my future thinking and informs my academic practice today. Nima was a 'no-go area' for the police, who made occasional raids in force to pick up known criminals. I was a natural suspect as an informer whenever one of these raids took place. I was also under surveillance by the Special Branch who often harassed people I spoke to. Shortly before the 1966 coup I learned that I was on the list for deportation as a probable CIA spy. I was drawn into local society in a number of ways; but by far the most intriguing were the economic relations I was obliged to establish. I had to exchange currency; to pay rent; to hire employees; to negotiate with bureaucracy; to handle requests for loans and gifts. All of these transactions tested my basic assumptions about economic life. I discovered that, as a Manchester man, they went to the heart of what I considered society to be.

I never sat back and simply recorded how Frafra migrants thought the world works, their economic culture, if you like. Instead, I entered active relations with them in which my opinions were felt and often modified when I found out why my companions did otherwise. I had significant assets (money, contacts, knowledge) that were put to use; and I had to figure out how to cope with the social consequences, such as being arrested. This is how I became a criminal entrepreneur. Let us just say that there was an 'elective affinity' (Weber from Goethe) between my own proclivities and what Nima society really was. It seems pointless now to seek to distinguish one from another.

The true significance of all this was that I acted out anthropology's modern project, to cross the boundary separating the state and intellectuals from the people. I had to make society, not from scratch, but under extremely alien circumstances; and the people who took me in helped me to find a way through the contradictions of our twentieth century world. I learned to integrate (only partially, of course) the divisions of race, class and culture that initially separated us. Above all, I found friendship and reciprocity in a grossly unequal world that placed a boy in a position of power over men twice his age.

I have spent much of the intervening period trying to make sense of that moment, soon after Ghana's emancipation from colonial rule. I had to live in America and the Caribbean for many years; and I belatedly found the mentor I had been looking for in another world traveller, C. L. R. James (1992). From him I finally understood that modern world history is all of a piece; and I am now once again reaching out to Africa, this time as director of an African Studies Centre in my old university, hoping that Marx's line on history repeating itself as farce might not apply this time.

When I made my original journey to Accra, I imagined that I was bringing world civilisation to the periphery. Since then Ghanaians have spread all over the globe, as just one part of Africa's new diaspora, adding to the old one formed by that earlier migration, 'the middle passage' of slavery. Accra has come to Cambridge, in numbers. Under these circumstances, 'African Studies' must be a collaborative enterprise, pooling the resources, knowledge and initiatives of Africans everywhere and their friends. The lessons of Nima, the difficult practice of equal exchange under unequal conditions, are not captured in marketable phrases; they live on in our faltering attempts to remake society.

Note

1   This text, lightly edited from the original, was published in French as 'Entreprise africaine et l'économie informelle' in Hart (1994). See also Hart (2006).

References

Fortes, Meyer (1949) *The Web of Kinship among the Tallensi*, Oxford: Oxford University Press.

Hart, Keith (1973) 'Informal Income Opportunities and Urban Employment in Ghana', *Journal of Modern African Studies* 11(3): 61–89.

——(1975) 'Swindler or Public Benefactor? The entrepreneur in his community', in J. Goody (ed.) *Changing Social Structure of Modern Ghana*, London: International African Institute, 1–35.

——(1982) *The Political Economy of West African Agriculture*, Cambridge: Cambridge University Press.

——(1988) 'Kinship, Contract and Trust: the economic organisation of migrants in an African city slum', in D. Gambetta (ed.) *Trust: making and breaking social relations*, Oxford: Blackwell, 176–93.

——(1992) 'Market and State after the Cold War: the informal economy reconsidered', in R. Dilley (ed.) *Contested Markets*, Edinburgh: Edinburgh University Press, 214–27.

——(1994) 'Entreprise africaine et l'économie informelle', in S. Ellis and Y. Fauré (eds) *Entreprise et entrepreneurs africains*, Paris: Karthala, 115–24.

——(2005) *The Hit Man's Dilemma: or business, personal and impersonal*, Chicago: Prickly Paradigm Press.

——(2006) 'Bureaucratic Form and the Informal Economy', in B. Guha-Khasnobis, R. Kanbur and E. Ostrom (eds) *Linking the Formal and Informal Economy: concepts and policies*, Oxford: Oxford University Press.

James, C. L. R. (1992) *The C. L. R. James Reader*, ed. A. Grimshaw, Oxford: Blackwell.

Conclusion

Ethnography in the human conversation: a final remark

> In the world of anthropology we are always faced with the worry of
> how to handle 'chaos' in our data. In our fieldnotes there inevitably
> lurks a certain amount of material that we perceive as 'disorderly',
> 'illogical', and 'contradictory'. We ponder over such data, feel guilty
> about their presence; and in the end must make a decision about how
> we are going to deal with them. Many, in bafflement, ignore the delin-
> quent items and treat them as problem children who come from other
> neighbourhoods; others turn, in hope, to the arena of figurative language
> to demonstrate, not delinquency, but the presence of a favoured child,
> the poetic one . . .
>
> We often protect ourselves from handling alien truths that are
> disturbing to us by turning to the more 'solid' ground of tropes. I do
> not mean more 'solid' in the analytical sense; rather, I am speaking of
> an emotional response. It is easier for us to accept the poetic informant
> than to accept (even intellectually) a person who claims to believe
> what is totally crazy, untrue, and irrational according to our own
> empirically based truth conditions and formal rules of logic.
>
> (Overing 1985: 152)

In the introduction to an essay on Amerindian (Piaroa) kinship and myth,
Joanna Overing (1985) explores a basic problem in ethnographic inquiry.
As anthropologists we must expect that, and indeed frequently encounter
the fact that, other people's understandings of reality overlap only partially
with our own. Our socially learnt expectations place limits on our ability
to assimilate certain kinds of alien cultural assumptions and practices. It is
easy, indeed facile, to write off other people's beliefs as meaningless if they
are unfamiliar to us. Almost as simple is treating the 'disorderly' ethnographic material we meet with as merely a poetic trope, or figure of
speech. The harder path lies in stepping outside the customary parameters
and universalising assumptions of our own knowledge. To take this step
may well imply negating our fundamental standards of validity or **relativising** truths that we hold to be self-evident.

In the same essay, Overing offers one kind of view of ethnography as knowledge:

> I [have] expressed my own suspicions of any attempt in anthropology to develop an 'objective' unified language of observation: our problem in anthropology is not the attainment of proper definitions nor even that of translation; rather it is that of learning, attaining the knowledge and understanding of, a framework of thought and action based upon an entirely different set of universal principles . . . than any previously known to us.
>
> (Overing 1985: 156)

Anthropologists differ radically over these kinds of issues and yet ethnography is still considered fundamental to anthropological knowledge. One thing is clear, though. Whether we concur with Overing's suspicion of creating a 'unified language' for assessing ethnographic findings, the historical truth is that anthropology never has established one. Anthropologists have not, and do not seem likely to, agree on a shared set of assumptions in the same way as, for instance, physicists agree on basic laws. And here there arises an inevitable and invidious comparison between anthropology (social science, more generally) and 'hard' science. If ethnography, and by extension anthropology, does not yield a continuously expanding interrelated body of facts and theories that can be applied in a unified and predictable way, what use is it? Which in turn raises questions about ethnography as a kind of knowledge. If there is ethnographic knowledge, what does it consist in? What does it contribute to?

We will settle in these concluding remarks for presenting three different kinds of approach to, and use of, ethnographic knowledge. First we will discuss ethnography as knowledge in the old-fashioned sense – ethnography can deliver facts, these facts can help to create the basis for asking more and different questions. During the twentieth century, ethnographic methods created a storehouse of knowledge, a memory bank of social forms and practices. However, the way these facts have entered Western knowledge has very often served as a basis for a second kind of knowledge, negative debate or social challenge. This is ethnography as provocation: common sense understandings, for instance about 'human nature', may be held up and found wanting in the light of ethnographic findings.

Beyond simply attacking dogma, a third kind of knowledge lies in ethnography's liberating role within discussions about what it means to be human. By entering into and influencing the terms of the conversation, the specialist knowledge of ethnography can act as a thought experiment, opening out possibilities, not only for understanding human experience but also for being human. This, after all, is clearly one of the features that draws people to study ethnography and to join the anthropological conversation in the first instance. All these three slants on, and deployments of, ethnography are interdependent. And of course, in turn, they rely on institutional resources that make possible the kinds of specialised intellectual conversations within which ethnographic knowledge thrives. In these concluding comments, we will review the three roles we have outlined and point to areas of enduring significance for ethnography and for the anthropological conversations in which it becomes salient.

Ethnography as fact

The idea of ethnography as 'fact' – as true knowledge – has remained stubbornly resistant to attack over the years. In the 1980s post-modern critiques raised the notion that ethnography was 'fiction' in the specific sense that it was a creative construction elaborated through the medium of writing. In retrospect, comments such as those by James Clifford in the introduction to *Writing Culture* seem relatively incoherent on this topic (1986: 6–8). Clifford (not a practising anthropologist) argued for seeing ethnography as 'fiction' because an ethnography is inherently 'partial . . . committed and incomplete' (1986: 7). Earlier theorists such as Leach and Geertz had described the analytical framework of ethnography as a **heuristic** 'fiction' *vis-à-vis* fieldwork experience (Leach 1964 [1954]: xi; Geertz 1993a [1973]: 15). Clifford, by contrast, wished to extend the use of 'fiction' to the ethnography taken as a whole. In his view it was necessary to bring to the fore an implication of the word fiction – the written ethnography as a creative 'lie' (1986: 6–7).

Now that the furore over the post-modern intervention has long dissipated, one question that can be raised is, what kind of knowledge is not constructed in the sense of being 'partial . . . committed and incomplete'? We could consider a biologist studying bacteria in a microscope slide, or eyewitness testimony in a court. If she does not simultaneously study the microscope slide itself, or the workbench, or her colleagues we do not say of the biologist that her work is fiction. In other words, we accept that what she does will involve applying particular theories to the microbes in question and that (a) it will have highly specific parameters of relevance and hence (b) it will be partial, committed and incomplete. Likewise, can an eyewitness' statements to a court be anything other than partial, given that what they have to say belongs solely to their reconstructed memories? Would we call what they say 'fiction'? Not in any ordinary use of the word. Why should we make special use of 'fiction' for ethnography?

One reason that an anthropologist cannot very well present their account as untruth (unmitigated 'fiction') we discussed in Chapter 7. There we pointed out that despite recent experimentation, including the presentation of multiple authorial voices, or the ambiguation/displacement of claims to authorship in other ways, readers of ethnography inevitably treat the ethnographer as answerable for their ethnography. The ethnography will be judged in terms of the reliability of its exposition even after differences in style, rhetoric and narrative genre are taken into account. Ethnographers will be held accountable for misleading statements or misinterpretations, whether they like it or not. Hence, despite some experiments in narrative presentation by writers of ethnography, the authors of this book are not aware of any anthropologist making an enduring reputation out of lying. On the contrary, the whole debate about ethnography as fiction suggests the reverse – an over-active anthropological conscience.

The underlying issue is not whether ethnography is fiction but whether ethnography, and anthropology more broadly, is 'science'. This results from how anthropology (the same is true of other social sciences) is compared with 'hard' science and found wanting in its relationship to 'facts'. Scientists have a visible leverage over facts that social scientists do not – scientists can do things with facts. From this emerges a much older debate on which anthropologist Edward Evans-Pritchard commented as long ago as the 1950s.

> Social anthropologists, dominated consciously or unconsciously, from the beginning of their subject, by positivist philosophy, have aimed, explicitly or implicitly, and for the most part still aim – for this is what it comes to – at proving that man is an automaton and at discovering the sociological laws in terms of which his actions, ideas and beliefs can be explained and in the light of which they can be planned and controlled. This approach implies that human societies are natural systems which can be reduced to variables. Anthropologists have therefore taken one or other of the natural sciences as their model . . .
>
> There is, however, an older tradition than that of the Enlightenment with a different approach to the study of human societies, in which they are seen as systems only because social life must have a pattern of some kind, inasmuch as man, being a reasonable creature, has to live in a world in which his relations with those around him are ordered and intelligible. Naturally I think that those who see things in this way have a clearer understanding of social reality than the others, but whether this is so or not they are increasing in number, and this is likely to continue because the vast majority of students of anthropology today have been trained in one or other of the humanities and not, as was the case thirty years ago, in one or other of the natural sciences.
>
> (Evans-Pritchard 1950: 123–4)

Ethnographic knowledge has no strictly practical outcome, it cannot be employed to plan and control reality in the way science-as-technology can,

Evans-Pritchard argues. Ethnography is knowledge in a different sense: ethnographers draw on their own experience of an ordered and intelligible social world in order to gain access to the ordered, intelligible worlds of others. As he further suggests, they are also likely to be more attracted to the humanistic view of social reality, rather than the positivistic one, because they are usually not trained to apply strict positivist methods. This dispute between ethnography as a humanistic versus scientific knowledge remains contentious. Evans-Pritchard's statements were hotly disputed at the time and answered by figures such as Raymond Firth (1953: 151) from a more positivist viewpoint.

That ethnography has augmented our knowledge of the world with facts is undeniable. Mid-twentieth century anthropology provided, for example, detailed insight into kinship practices in a diversity of contexts. Even so, very often, these facts, well validated within anthropological debate, did not have a secure place in broader Western ways of thinking. A case in point is the work of Polly Hill who, in her book *Migrant Cocoa Farmers of Southern Ghana* (1963), argues that an understanding of economic development in Southern Ghana would benefit greatly from a consideration of the different farm systems practised by matrilineal versus patrilineal farmers.

> This book is largely taken up with this observed distinction: with the facts that strip-farms are typically owned by those who inherit through their fathers and that the mosaic pattern of farm-ownership on the family land has to do with the nature of the matrilineal societies – in which 'blood' is supposed to flow through females only.
>
> (Hill 1963: 3)

But she also recognises that these kinds of facts are probably too difficult to incorporate into dominant ways of thinking about development and are likely to be written off as 'an insult to a modern society' (1963: 3).

We have seen in Chapter 5 that the evidence of ethnography become facts only within a framework of argument. And as Chapter 4 showed, there are different styles of narrating ethnography as knowledge. The arguments in which ethnographic facts emerge are, in turn, given relevance and stability by reference to the big disciplinary conversations going on when an ethnography is written (Chapters 6 and 8). Ethnography as fact depends on these complex framings that endow it with factuality: it cannot escape them. But that does not, of itself, transform ethnography into untruth.

Ethnography as fact is then a rather fragile composite of anthropological conversations, though no more than are the facts of other academic disciplines. Fact is here dependent on the good faith of the conversationalists involved, their maturity and differing levels of sophistication in using ideas and concepts in mutually comprehensible ways. Some kinds of ethnographic fact are often only appreciated by small groups of scholars and then only within relatively esoteric localised sub-conversations. The democratic spirit might wish to extinguish these obscure ways of talking and knowing in their current form, insisting that they be more open to a larger field of questioning and validation. Unfortunately, it is difficult to demarcate in advance very important intellectual conversations taking a complicated form from impenetrable nonsense pure and simple.

Taken as a whole, the features reviewed up to now indicate that other factors play an essential role in how, or whether, ethnography is received as true and reliable knowledge. The knowledge that ethnographers offer will clearly be assessed by readers in terms of its perceived intellectual importance to their own readerly interests. Be it ever so significant for the ethnographer, ethnographic knowledge is unimportant unless it is relevant for a specific someone, usually a cluster of academics or students thinking about related issues. Similarly, if the ethnographer is truly answerable for their knowledge then the final point of reference for this, the source of their authority, is their academic personality. Just as in everyday conversation when we measure a person's fitness for making certain statements, questions concerning the skill, maturity and character of the ethnographer are inevitably present in how readers assess ethnography. In other words, academic facts are embedded in lived, continuously changing, social relationships.

A last point requires emphasis. Ethnographic facts very often appear within the wider anthropological conversation in the **holographic** form we discussed in Chapter 3. There we showed how a 'simple' nexus of relations, such as the Trobriand relationship of father and child, can be expanded, taking on more contextual complexity and detail, or reduced to bare outlines without changing its basic form. These holographic examples are standard reference objects of anthropological dialogue and debate. And, after the discussion of the last chapters, it will be clear that facts of this kind are not innocent descriptions. Instead, they contain within their presentation intersecting strands of comparison, contextualisation, narration, argument and meta-narrative.

Ethnographic knowledge as provocation

Those who like their knowledge clear cut will not take much comfort from what has just been said. Ethnographic facts exist as facts only within socially embedded conversations going on at differing levels of complexity and significance (according to the different perspectives and groupings created within an intellectual network). But there is a further intricacy that follows from this. Ethnographic facts have an emotionally or morally committed aspect to them. John Barnes, in these comments on the kind of people who study anthropology, suggests one dimension of this:

> Anthropology, at least in so far as it retains its traditional role of studying others . . . tends to recruit those who perceive themselves as marginal to their own societies, and certainly promotes this perception in those who study the subject. On the other hand my casual observations suggest that in Western capitalist societies economics recruits mainly students who accept capitalism and wish to learn more about how to operate successfully within it. Students are likewise selectively recruited to the various natural sciences but the selection appears based on attitudes towards structures of knowledge rather than on political attitudes to society.
>
> (Barnes 1990: 19)

He indicates an institutional framework, the university, which channels, shapes and disciplines certain kinds of moral-emotional response making room for a diversity of worldviews. This recognition of institutions and institutional processes is an important counterpoint to our rather abstract picture of anthropologists holding conversations. What it suggests is that academic anthropology has developed, in part at least, an institutionalised role as a provocation to some of the central premises of Western society: that is to say, ethnography is very typically negatively positioned as a challenge to other kinds of taken-for-granted knowledge. Something of this is captured in a stanza from a poem by W. H. Auden, published in the 1940s:

> Malinowski, Rivers,
> Benedict and others
> Show how common culture
> Shapes the separate lives:
> Matrilineal races
> Kill their mothers' brothers
> In their dreams and turn their
> Sisters into wives.
>
> (Auden 1969: 152)

Auden is primarily using ethnographic facts here (poetically and ironically reconfigured) to give voice to a sense of the contingency and existential arbitrariness of Western lives and preoccupations. And this is undoubtedly one of the most common ways in which ethnographic facts enter wider consciousness.

We began this book with an exploration of comparison: ethnography is fundamentally a comparative enterprise. This alone indicates an implicit provocation on anthropology's part. Serious comparison implies symmetry, the comparison of like with like. Since the Enlightenment, Western knowledge and social practices have been assumed (by Westerners) to be unquestionably superior in their efficacy to any others, set apart in scale, structure and value. And this appears to be proven every day by the overwhelming advantages of the technology developed out of Western science. However, it is no accident that ethnography had its most intellectually expansive moments during the period 1914–50, when two all-engulfing wars fragmented the confidence of Euro-Americans in the self-evident relationship between advanced civilization and advanced technology.

Lee Drummond captures some of the recurrent potential of ethnography to provoke in his study *American Dreamtime*. There he argues for a serious comparison between American cinema with Aboriginal Dreamtime mythology. The real life of Americans is as interwoven with myth as the real life of Australian aboriginals, he proposes.

> 'Real life' [in America] is a slippery notion that constantly seems on the verge of becoming 'reel life'. This . . . pun . . . runs through much of what follows and constitutes one of the main themes of this work. 'America' is, interchangeably and inseparably, a political and economic titan and a 'dream factory' that spews out, in addition to the mountains of consumer goods and armaments, the mannerisms, fashions, games, sports, magazines, television programs, and movies of the Dreamtime. And our Dreamtime, just as the Australian aborigines', is so thoroughly a part of the fatefulness of life – of whom one loves and marries (and probably divorces), of how one coexists (is there any other term for it?) with one's children, of whom one kills (or simply dutifully hates) in the name of God and Country, of what one does as daily toil, even of what one has for dinner – that it is impossible to segregate it from a supposedly objective, material reality. Consequently, the questions I pursue in the following chapters are concerned with how, and not whether, popular movies like Star Wars shape and transform our most fundamental values and cherished truths. That, in brief, is the goal of this particular exercise in the cultural analysis of American life.
>
> (Drummond 1996: 9).

Sixty years of peace within increasingly rich Western nation states, along with the complete domination of Western capitalism over other political-economic forms, has made mainstream Western thought rather less vulnerable to ethnographic provocation. At the same time criticism from within anthropology during the last twenty-five years has focused on the degree to which the anthropological conversation has turned inwards on itself, developing increasingly obscure theoretical terms and points of reference. But, as Barnes suggests, the self-assured Euro-American creed of capitalism-plus-individualism-ensured-by-democracy remains less than convincing to all of the people all the time. The implication of this is that many will continue to join the anthropological conversation as long as it satisfies the search for a (convincingly) provocative counter-perspective.

Ethnography's liberating role

In an essay, 'The Sound of Light', Tristan Platt (1997) explores the sound world of an Andean shamanic séance. In these initial comments, he describes how the patron saint of this high plateau village, St James of Pumpuri (Tata Pumpuri), finds his place within the cosmos as understood by the Amerindian Quechua. Platt shows that St James, 'the Tata', acts as a mediator between Catholicism, the religion brought by Spanish conquistadores, and the realm of pre-Hispanic powers invoked in shamanism.

> The Tata goes to battle raised above merely human foot-soldiers on his horse: his most terrifying weapons are lightning (*glurya scintilla*, the Flash of Glory), thunder and thunderbolt (*ravu*), which are imagined as the flash, rumble, and bullets of his arquebus. The thunder also represents the sound of his horse's hooves as he gallops through the clouds. His metallic bullets (*walas*, from Spanish *bala*) streak to earth with the lightning – *k'aj*! in Quechua onomatopoeia – and fulminate animals, houses, church towers, people, and especially those fated to be a shaman, or *yachaj*. For these, the experience is an initiation: they die, but are reassembled at a second flash and resuscitated at a third. The triple imagery of Easter, as well as the pre-Hispanic cults of Charcas, is thus reproduced in their death and resurrection. In their new vocation, they will communicate with Father Pumpuri and place their Indian clients in living contact with him, either channelling his voice directly or through the medium of the condor-mountain spirits which are his servants.
>
> At the point where the initiation took place, now sacralised as *surti parisirun* (the place where the Luck appeared), the future *yachaj* finds one of Santiago's bullets, still smoking with sacred energy, and nurtures it with dishes of sacred foods (*glurya jampis*) while learning to become a shaman. The best way to neutralise its dangerous energy is, indeed, to channel it into a shamanic session, or Council (*kawiltu*) . . .
>
> Spirit possession is itself dangerous and exhausting: the spirit enters in the shape of a bird – generally a condor – and possesses the shaman, giving him extra intelligence (*aswan intilijinti*) and changing his voice to the point where the audience can hear him and the spirit conversing as two separate people.
>
> (Platt 1997: 199–200)

He goes on to describe and interpret the sounds of the séance in the light-less village chapel as captured in a tape-recording.

> Gesture is only available in aural form: actions are etched on the dark-ness. Intonation, murmurs and rustles, hesitations, the clinking and blowing of bottles, the 'whistle' of the shaman's bullet, the slurps of the condor drinking alcohol offered by the yachaj, and especially the rhythmic flapping of his wings as he perches invisible on the altar table – all combine with the distant background noises to make up an overwhelmingly aural field of meaning.
>
> (Platt 1997: 202)

Herein is contained much of what is significant about ethnography. At its best ethnography is not just a sympathetic picturing and argued analysis of a life world. It is also a complex thought experiment: what might it be like to experience the world in these terms? – with these relationships in mind? – within this framework of emotional engagement and sensory responsiveness? – according to these ways of reasoning? It is as a sympathetic thought-experiment that ethnography takes on its potentially liberating role in a generalised conversation about being human.

Many departments or centres of social and cultural anthropology run a seminar series, a series of talks. We could take this as one kind of model for an ethnographically informed conversation about social life and our place in it. Typically each week a different speaker presents quite unique ethnography. So, one week the talk may be on health, witchcraft and medicine in Tanzania, the next week on public spaces in Manchester, England. On each occasion, ethnography and analysis are discussed by listeners and sometimes more insight is gained, sometimes less: it is never clear what the outcome will be. There is the potential here for the diversity of these ethnographic acounts to act, not only as a provocation to our habitual ways of understanding the social world but, going beyond this, as an emancipation from those mental habits.

At this point, ethnography conjoins with the novel and poetry in its provision of an alternative perspective, a distinct life world available for appreciation and engagement. Except that the ethnographer is answerable for their ethnography as true knowledge. This may mean that ethnography is less engaging aesthetically than a novel or a play, but it may also make ethnography more useful for the task in hand. Because, if it is effective, ethnography will not just dramatise life aesthetically, it will also analyse it: it will provide analytical tools for carrying the thought experiment beyond the particular instance. This suggests a process of reflection, of continuing conversation, in which reference to different ethnographic life worlds becomes a central aspect. The ethnographic cases act to trap certain problems of social or cultural experience, giving them a narrative focus and analytical coherence in an attempt to rethink assumptions.

An existing conversation between anthropologist Margaret Mead and novelist James Baldwin provides a flavour of this. Published as *A Rap on Race*, Mead and Baldwin traverse the issues of race and racism in contemporary (early 1970s) America. Their conversation is by turns engaging, banal, insightful, invigorating and frustrating. As conversation tends to, their dialogue moves along meanderingly, losing certain threads and regaining others. One central strand – Baldwin talks in depth about this – is the weight of history, the response to the past, as this impinges on the Black American's identity in a White-dominated society. In this part of the interchange, Mead mentions the differing historical sense of Puerto Ricans and Black Americans, then throws in a distinctive ethnographic example:

Mead: . . . But Puerto Ricans say they come from Puerto Rico. There is nothing back of it, nothing at all. Nothing goes back to Spain. Nothing goes back to Africa. They came from Puerto Rico. Haitian peasants believe they originated in Haiti. . . the peasant picture of Africa is only a mythological homeland. Otherwise, they live in Haiti.

Baldwin: That's a funny place to be, isn't it? I am trying to imagine it.

Mead: Very hard for you to imagine, isn't it?

Baldwin: It's almost impossible to imagine. Strange though we are, the line back is very clear and nothing.

Mead: Very clear. You may not know the individual line, you can't tell whether your ancestors came from Ghana or just where, but the fact that some of your ancestors came from Africa is known.

           In New Guinea, I worked for a people there who had very good memories, but they had no sense of genealogy at all. They would go back about six generations. Grandfather's grandfather was about as far back as they could go, and most people didn't do that. And then when they got the Christian Bible they were delighted. They felt that now they discovered how everything started. They had never known. They said it was very nice to know how things began.

Baldwin: They had no-?

Mead: No origin stories at all. None. And they had no future. You see, when a male died, he became the guardian ghost of the house. The minute after he died he got very important. They put his skull in the rafters and he bossed the whole household. He made people sick if they didn't do what he wanted. He listened to the wives gossiping and punished them for gossiping. As a ghost he ran things until somebody else died because he hadn't looked after him well enough. Then out his skull went into the sea and the skull of another person came in.

The ex-guardian ghosts became low-level ghosts. People still knew their names and they were around somewhere, but they didn't have any place to house them any more. Then they became sea slugs and that was the end of that.

Baldwin: Sea slugs?...

Mead: Literally a sea slug...

(Mead and Baldwin 1971: 114-115)

Mead's final instance (which draws on the ethnography *Manus Religion*, written by her former husband, Reo Fortune (Fortune 1935)) is not of the same order as, say, a philosopher's imaginary case. The philosopher might say 'let us imagine a society of Blue People who have no detailed sense of the past or of the future' then go on to draw out certain logical features of Blue People beliefs. A science fiction writer might produce an equivalent fictional version. Both could make an important contribution to our capacity to re-imagine our social world. Again, the difference is that the ethnographic example is true. These are parameters, a cultural logic, that have been lived out; albeit that, in its recounting, they are here reshaped according to the anthropologist's intentions. That doubts over the factual basis of Mead's first ethnography, *Coming of Age in Samoa* (1928), caused a tremendous tumult in America further attests to the importance of ethnographies as true knowledge.

And this centring in true knowledge is critical to ethnography's liberating potential. As she uses it, Mead's example is not just a provocation equivalent to 'people live lives of other kinds, you should be less cock-sure of your own'. There is an element of this, perhaps, but the aim is otherwise. Within the complexity of interaction in mass society, it becomes relatively easy to fall back on habitual experiences, routines and understandings. These stereotypes, propagated in particular through the news media, persist because they are founded in received judgments and organised according to simple oppositions. Mead's approach, the value of ethnography as an intervention in the human conversation, lies in its provenance outside these knowledge frameworks. Ethnography leads us out of the often trivially dualistic structuring of debate in mass society into considering some alternative ways of being human. To take the ethnographic route is to step off a narrow path in which alternatives to our own phrasings of reality are simply meaningless or merely poetic.

Glossary

Affine, affinal An **affine** is a person related to another through marriage (an 'in-law' in English parlance). The analysis of **affinal** ties has played a major part in debates about kinship in Twentieth Century **social anthropology**. In particular, debate has centred on how marriage enables and necessitates the creation of links with outsider groups (the **affines**), and on the tensions and processes of negotiation and exchange that this instigates.

Agency The kinds and degrees of influence and power social actors have regarding social situations or social relations in which they are engaged. Debates over agency centre on the balance between how much is determined by prior social conditions and how much is subject to acts of choice by the person concerned. In turn these issues take in a plurality of questions about, for example, whether notions of individuality (and hence choice) are universally shared or not.

Agnate, agnatic (see **patrilineage, patrilineal**) A person related to another through descent from a male ancestor. **Agnatic** ties/agnatic groups are created on the basis of this shared descent.

Cognate, cognatic Someone related to another through descent from a shared female or male ancestor, with this descent being traced through both male and female links. **Cognatic** ties can also be called **bilateral** ties. The term **cognate** can also be used to refer to consanguineal relatives (as opposed to **affines**).

Cultural anthropology The tradition associated with mainstream American anthropology and with major figures in that tradition, such as Franz Boas, Alfred Kroeber, Ruth Benedict, Margaret Mead and Clifford Geertz. The emphasis in cultural anthropology has tended to be on culture as a patterned whole and hence on the interpretation of integrated patterns/systems of symbolism and meaning. This is distinct from **social anthropology** which emphasises the organisation of social relationships (see also **social anthropology**).

Diffusionism, diffusionist A theory prominent in the early twentieth century, protagonised in Britain by figures such as William Rivers and

Alfred Haddon. **Diffusionism** emphasised the historical spreading out of cultural traits and social structures across large geographic regions. Even though the **function** of practices was emphasised, this was placed within a larger historical viewpoint emphasising social transformation. This historical **meta-narrative** was strongly criticised by Bronislaw Malinowski from a **functionalist** and **synchronic** perspective.

Ethnographic present Ethnographic description that uses the present tense to emphasise the law-like quality of what is being presented as in 'often disputes emerge around who will play with the red Power Ranger figures' as opposed to 'I saw children arguing over red Power Rangers on numerous occasions'. This presentational style is closely associated with the **synchronic** and **normative** emphases in mid-century anthropology.

Feminism, feminist Feminism is collection of political movements, theories and moral standpoints that focus on the gendered dimensions of social hierarchies and inequalities. The **first wave of feminist activity** took place during the late nineteenth and early twentieth century, mainly in Europe and North America. The **second wave** began in the 1960s and has spread worldwide. Although early second-wave **feminists** concentrated primarily on the subordination of women to men, later **feminists** have emphasised the intertwining of gendered hierarchies and inequalities with others, such as class or colour. The concerns and positions of **feminist** political movements, theories and standpoints may overlap and also conflict with each other.

Functionalism, function Functionalist ethnographies lay emphasis on how social and/or cultural traits have specific **functions** or uses for people. So, as Malinowski explained, Trobriand magic has the **function** of reducing the uncertainty people feel regarding enterprises that are dangerous (fishing at sea) or on which they are fundamentally dependent (horticulture). Malinowskian **functionalism** goes with a pragmatic view that culture and society exist as a response to basic needs (compare **structural functionalism**).

Gatherer-hunters Those whose subsistence depends on gathering vegetable foods from the environment as well as hunting animals. The term has come to replace **hunter-gatherers** as a result of the observation that the bulk of nutrition gained by this kind of group comes from gathering rather than hunting.

Heuristic picture/model/device/fiction A heuristic model is one that extends or formalises certain features of reality in order to help the analyst (and their readers) understand a complicated social situation. Pushing the data to their logical extreme **heuristically**, for instance, can allow us to gain insight into seemingly intractable clusters of information. Often referred to also as an 'as if' model or an 'ideal type' (the latter term was made famous by sociologist Max Weber). It is important not to confuse these **heuristic devices** or **fictions** with ethnographic experience itself.

Historical particularism   Describes the turn-of-the-century style of anthropology protagonised by Franz Boas. Boas saw anthropology as essentially a historical-interpretive, or 'ideographic', enterprise rather than a law-giving or 'nomothetic' one. He wished to give full weight to the historical particularity of specific cultural communities. There are clear points of contact between his view and that of the European **diffusionists**, though Boas rejected large-scale theorising.

Holography, holographic ethnography   The **hologram** has recently become a metaphor for how an ethnographic example can instance its social or cultural context in microcosm. When a holographic image is cut into smaller pieces it presents the same picture, only at a lower level of definition. Often ethnographic examples can be seen to work in the same way: the specific example carries in itself the basic pattern of the socio-cultural macrocosm. This **holographic** view is distinct from, though not necessarily incompatible with, a perspective where particular examples are seen as parts or subsystems within a social or cultural whole.

Hunter-gatherers   Those who gain sustenance from hunting animals and gathering vegetable foods from their environment. See also **gatherer-hunters**.

Interactionism, interaction   A theoretical approach that takes the individual and their strategies and choices as its starting point.

Intersubjectivity   An **intersubjective** viewpoint is important for anthropologists who view the individual as an irreducible element of ethnographic analysis. For these ethnographers, cultural meanings and social practices are grounded in communication between distinct individual (subjects). Hence the need to account for how meaning is made **intersubjectively**.

Lineage   A group whose members consider themselves to share descent from an ancestor.

Marxism   Marxist analysis gained ground in anthropology during the mid-1970s as a response to the lack of analysis of structures of inequality in the classic ethnographies. Marxist anthropologists looked for bases of inequality in how groups gained and consolidated control over material resources. This historical materialist viewpoint influenced a range of ethnographers who might not call themselves Marxist.

Matrifocality   A kinship term coined by Raymond T. Smith to describe the way women in their role as mothers become a focus of relationships in the West Indies. Recognising that his original association of **matrifocality** and household organisation was flawed, Smith then emphasised its importance, more generally, in the formation of social networks. Smith's ethnography was hailed at the time because it undermined assumptions about the universality of the nuclear family. It has, however, been criticised because it leaves a negative space for male kinship activity.

Matrilineage A group whose members consider themselves to share descent from a female ancestor. **Matrilineal** societies have played an important part in anthropology's work of theoretical comparison. They throw up ways of organising human relationships and communicating culturally that have provided stark contrasts with Euro-American expectations. Malinowski's studies of the Trobriand islanders present a key example.

Meta-narrative An overarching or framing intellectual worldview within which specific individual narratives and arguments can be ordered and given wider meaning and relevance (see also **paradigm**).

Metonym, metonymic A form of symbolic relationship where the part stands for the whole as where the cross stands for Christian sacrifice, or the signature stands for the authority of the person.

Nomadic pastoralist Groups whose livelihood depends on the herding of cattle or other ruminant animals across outspread territories.

Norm, normative A feature of social life that is so typical it takes on a law-like quality, as in 'discussion of the weather is a **norm** in conversations between strangers in Britain'. **Normative** analysis has its primary focus on that which is typical in social or cultural life and builds its arguments on that basis. The **normative** approach is associated with mid-century anthropology and sociology and with **positivistic** tendencies in anthropology as well as with the use of the '**ethnographic present**'. The words **normative/norm** have tended to fall into disuse amongst anthropologists, but the idea behind them remains important.

Paradigm, paradigm shift An exemplary pattern or model of intellectual activity that guides the work of scientists. Kuhn describes **paradigm shifts** as being marked by the rapid collapse in confidence in one **paradigm** as the new one gains ascendancy (see also **meta-narrative**).

Patrifocal, patrifocality Where men in their role as father become the focus of kinship relations. M. G. Smith coined **patrifocality** as part of a riposte to R. T. Smith's arguments about **matrifocality**.

Personhood, social person **Personhood** describes the forms of capacity deriving from a position within a network of social relations. The term social person emphasises the distinction between this way of understanding human capacities *vis-à-vis* a psychological emphasis on personality or inherent individual capacity. **Personhood/social person** have tended to take the place of **role** in anthropological writing.

Phenomenology **Phenomenological** approaches came to the fore in the anthropology of the 1990s partly as a way of bridging the gap between cultural and psychological descriptions of human experience.

Phenomenology emphasises process in the building of human experience and culture and is hence opposed both to strong cultural constructionist perspectives as well as to views that assert that experience is essentially shaped by innate features of the mind.

Positivism Usually refers to views elaborated by philosophers such as David Hume and Karl Popper that scientific assertions must be capable of verification by further inquiry. This implies, in the case of ethnography, that the sites for particular kinds of evidence can be revisited by later anthropologists and the veracity of particular claims tested out. This has proven very difficult to achieve because social or cultural situations change, sometimes very rapidly. In anthropology, strong **positivistic** thinking tends now to be found primarily, though not exclusively, amongst those who think that the human mind contains certain innate features and that these can be demonstrated using various kinds of data.

Post-modernism Describes a very loose coalition of ideas that came together during the 1980s and early 1990s and was primarily positioned against positivist or scientific **meta-narratives** in anthropology. Associated in particular with the book *Writing Culture* (Clifford and Marcus 1986), in anthropology, post-modernism is connected with a central idea that ethnographic writing is 'fiction' either in a strong sense (a creative lie) or in a weaker sense (truth within a fictional narrative framework).

Reflexivity Typically a **reflexive** style of ethnography is one where the figure of the ethnographer him or herself becomes key to the contextualisation, narration and argument of the ethnography. Debates over **reflexivity** reflect concerns about the way interactions between ethnographer and informant shape general analysis. They also highlight doubts over whether an ethnographer can create an account that is not a projection or reflection of their personality or autobiography.

Reify Literally the turning of an idea into a thing, hence a confusion between idea and thing. Processes of **reification** are particularly apparent when large aggregations of people are labelled with a group term, such as 'working class', and this concept is then transferred to the individual as something inherent in them – 'you are saying that because you are working class'. The concept has been confused with that individual's concrete behaviour and hence **reified**.

Relativism, relativising Typically a tendency to refer to specific cultural contexts in order to explain particular meanings. There can be no absolute relativism in anthropology because this would rule out the possibility of cultural translation. Strong **relativising** tendencies are opposed by strong universalising ones. Universalism is a tendency to refer to human universals or absolutes to explain particular meanings. Strong universalism may encounter the basic difficulty of finding an explanation for social phenomena that approximates to how actors involved talk about them. Ethnography is invariably a compromise between relativism and universalism.

Role The capacity or capacities taken on as a social actor, as in 'the role of king', the 'referee role', 'the child role'. Has tended to be surpassed by the term **social personhood.**

Segmentary lineage While a large group may recognise shared descent from a common ancestor, this large-scale identification may **segment** into smaller alliances of interest according to whether those involved view themselves as closely or distantly related to each other. In Evans-Pritchard's description, coalition under certain constraints and segmentation under others, within an umbrella of shared kinship, allows Nuer nomadic pastoralists to order their stateless politics.

Social anthropology The tradition of anthropology associated with Britain and France during the twentieth century and often opposed to the American **cultural anthropology** tradition. **Social anthropologists** take social relationships as their point of focus and view cultural behaviours or meanings as a result or facet of relationships rather than as objects in themselves. British social anthropologists, led by William Rivers (1922), developed kinship theory as a way of accessing what they saw as deep structures of social organisation. Kinship retains its place as a theoretical touchstone for **social anthropologists** as seen, for example, in the debates over new reproductive technologies.

Social evolutionism The dominant theory of society between the mid-nineteenth and twentieth centuries, protagonised by figures such as Lewis Henry Morgan and Herbert Spencer. **Social evolutionist** theories ranked societies on a ladder of progress culminating in European, or in Morgan's case American, civilisation. Increasing exposure to diverse socio-cultural frameworks, particularly societies under colonial control, made the **social evolutionist meta-narrative** increasingly unsustainable. With hindsight, **diffusionist** and **historical particularist** theories can be seen as the transit point to the ethnographically informed anthropology that dominated the twentieth century.

Structural functionalism The dominant theoretical approach of the period 1930–60 in **social anthropology.** Derived from Emile Durkheim's sociology and associated with Radcliffe-Brown in anthropology, **structural functionalism** viewed society as a system of interrelated parts. In this analogy each part can be seen as having a **function** within the whole **structure.** This is a different emphasis to Malinowski's **functionalism** which understands culture as a response to the basic needs of individuals. More than most of his followers, Radcliffe-Brown viewed society in organic terms where the different social institutions act akin to particular organs in a body. He derived this analogy primarily from the **social evolutionist** thinker Herbert Spencer.

Structuralism Lévi-Strauss' **structuralist** theories entered Anglophone anthropology during the mid-1960s and onwards. Lévi-Strauss views culture as a product of the generative powers of the human mind. Early enquiries searched for these basic generative principles of culture in the incest taboo which, in his view, drives humans to create increasingly ingenious solutions to the problem of organising relatedness. Later studies focused on myth as, again, a cognitive attempt to solve basic antinomies in human social existence. There are a number of theoretical cross-over points between **structuralism** and **structural functionalism** but the basic assumptions are different, which has led historically to misunderstanding.

Synchronic approach The **synchronic** approach in ethnography is one that treats the social situation encountered in fieldwork as if it represented an interconnected pattern within the present. This present-oriented view is opposed to a **diachronic** approach that analyses society over time. Bronislaw Malinowski and Alfred Radcliffe-Brown emphasised the need for a consistent **synchronic** view of society in order to escape the 'conjectural history' that supported social **evolutionist** and **diffusionist** analyses of 'primitive' societies.

Thick description Borrowed from philosopher Gilbert Ryle, Clifford Geertz deploys the term **thick description** to develop a case for an interpretive approach to culture. He uses the analogy of a rapid contraction of the eyelid. Only an interpretive awareness of the whole situation can tell us whether what we are witnessing is a meaningful wink or an insignificant twitch. The analysis cannot be conclusive but should be convincing. Ethnography should be interpretively full in this sense.

Writing culture The title of a book edited by George Marcus and James Clifford (1986) which has become synonymous with the post-modern trend in anthropology. A central stance of the book was that ethnography was, above all, a kind of writing and that ethnographies need to be analysed as literary constructions.

Bibliography

Abrahams, R. (1991) *A Place of Their Own: family farming in eastern Finland*, Cambridge: Cambridge University Press.

Abu-Lughod, L. (1986) *Veiled Sentiments: honor and poetry in a Bedouin society*, Berkeley: University of California Press.

Antze, P. (1987) 'Symbolic Action in Alcoholics Anonymous', in M. Douglas (ed.) *Constructive Drinking: perspectives on drink from anthropology*, Cambridge: Cambridge University Press.

Auden, W. H. (1969) 'Heavy Date', in *Collected Shorter Poems (1927–1957)*, London: Faber and Faber.

Barnes, J. (1990) *Models and Interpretations: selected essays*, Cambridge: Cambridge University Press.

Barth, F. (1966) *Models of Social Organisation*, London: Royal Anthropological Institute.

Bateson, G. (1958) [1936] *Naven: a survey of the problems suggested by a composite picture of the culture of a New Guinea tribe drawn from three points of view*, Stanford: Stanford University Press.

Battaglia, D. (1997) 'Ambiguating Agency: the case of Malinowski's ghost', *American Anthropologist* 99(3): 505–10.

Behar, R. (1993) *Translated Woman: crossing the border with Esperanza's story*, Boston MA: Beacon Press.

Benedict, R. (1989) [1946] *The Chrysanthemum and the Sword: with a new foreword by Ezra F. Vogel*, Boston MA: Houghton Mifflin.

Bird-David, N. (1990) 'The Giving Environment: another perspective on the economic system of gatherer-hunters', *Current Anthropology* 31(2): 189–96.

Blackwood, E. (2005) 'Wedding Bell Blues: marriage, missing men, and matrifocal follies', *American Ethnologist* 32(1): 3–19.

Bouquet, M. (1993) *Reclaiming English Kinship: Portuguese refractions of British kinship theory*, Manchester: Manchester University Press.

Bourdieu, P. (1984) *Distinction: a social critique of the judgement of taste*, London: Routledge and Kegan Paul.

——(2003) 'Participant Objectivation', *Journal of the Royal Anthropological Institute* 9(2): 281–94.

Bourgois, P. (1995) *In Search of Respect: selling crack in El Barrio*, Cambridge: Cambridge University Press.

Bourgouignon, E. (1973) 'Introduction: a framework for the comparative study of altered states of consciousness', in E. Bourgouignon (ed.) *Religion, Altered States of Consciousness, and Social Change*, 3–35, Columbus OH: Ohio State University Press.

Brettell, C. B. (1993) 'Fieldwork, Text and Audience', Introduction to C. B. Brettell (ed.) *When They Read What We Write: the politics of ethnography*, Westport CT and London: Bergin and Garvey.

Briggs, J. L. (1970) *Never in Anger: portrait of an Eskimo family*, Cambridge MA: Harvard University Press.

Brown, K. (1991) *Mama Lola: a vodou priestess in Brooklyn*, Berkeley and London: University of California Press.

Busby, C. (2000) *The Performance of Gender: an anthropology of everyday life in a south Indian fishing village*, London: Athlone.

Carsten, J. (1995) 'The Politics of Forgetting: migration, kinship and memory on the periphery of the Southeast Asian state', *Journal of the Royal Anthropological Institute* 1: 317–35.

Clifford, J. (1983) 'On Ethnographic Authority', *Representations* 2: 118–46.

——(1986) 'Introduction', in J. Clifford and G. E. Marcus (eds) *Writing Culture: the poetics and politics of ethnography*, Berkeley: University of California Press.

Clifford, J. and Marcus, G. (eds) (1986) *Writing Culture: the poetics and politics of ethnography*, Berkeley: University of California Press.

Cowan, J. (1990) *Dance and the Body Politic in Northern Greece*, Princeton NJ: Princeton University Press.

Crapanzano, V. (1977) 'Introduction', in *Case studies in spirit possession*, V. Crapanzano and V. Garrison (eds), 1–40, New York: John Wiley & Sons.

——(1986) 'Hermes' Dilemma: the masking of subversion in ethnographic description', in J. Clifford and G. E. Marcus (eds) *Writing Culture: the poetics and politics of ethnography*, Berkeley: University of California Press.

Crook, T. (2006) *Anthropological Knowledge, Secrecy and Bolivip, Papua New Guinea: exchanging skin*, London: The British Academy.

Di Leonardo, M. (1987) 'The Female World of Cards and Holidays: women, families and the work of kinship', *Signs* 12(3): 440–53.

Dilley, R. (1999) *The Problem of Context*, Oxford: Berghahn.

Douglas, M. (1975) *Implicit Meanings: essays in anthropology*, London: Routledge and Kegan Paul.

Drummond, L. (1996) *American Dreamtime: a cultural analysis of popular movies, and their implications for a science of humanity*, London: Littlefield Adams Books.

Evans-Pritchard, E. E. (1950) 'Social Anthropology: past and present', *Man* L(198): 118–24.

——(1969) [1940] *The Nuer: a description of the livelihood and political institutions of Nilotic people*, New York and Oxford: Oxford University Press.

Fardon, R. (1990a) 'Localizing Strategies: the regionalization of ethnographic accounts', General Introduction to R. Fardon (ed.) *Localizing Strategies: regional traditions of ethnographic writing*, Washington DC and Edinburgh: Smithsonian Institution Press and Scottish Academic Press.

——(1990b) *Between God, the dead and the wild: Chamba interpretations of religion and ritual*, Edinburgh: Edinburgh University Press.

Fauset, A. H. (1971) *Black Gods of the Metropolis: negro religious cults of the urban north*, Pennsylvania PA: University of Pennsylvania.

Feld, S. (1990) *Sound and Sentiment: birds, weeping, poetics and song in Kaluli expression*, 2nd edn, Philadelphia PA: University of Pennsylvania Press.

Firth, R. (1953) 'The Study of Values by Social Anthropologists', *Man* LII(231): 146.

——(1964) [1954] 'Foreword' to Edmund Leach, *Political Systems of Highland Burma: a study of Kachin social structure*, London: Athlone.

——(1983) [1936] *We the Tikopia: a sociological study of kinship in primitive Polynesia*, abridged by the author, with a preface by B. Manilowski, Stanford: Stanford University Press.

Fortune, R. (1935) *Manus Religion: an ethnological study of the Manus natives of the Admiralty Islands*, Philadelphia PA: American Philosophical Society.

——(1947) 'The Rules of Relationship Behaviour in One Kind of Primitive Society', *Man* 47: 108–10.

Freedman, M. (1966) *Chinese Lineage and Society: Fukien and Kwangtung*, London: Athlone Press.

Gay y Blasco, P. (2001) ' "We Don't Know Our Descent": how Gitanos manage the past', *Journal of the Royal Anthropological Institute* 7 (4): 631–47.

Geertz, C. (1973) *The Interpretation of Cultures: selected essays*, New York: Basic Books.

——(1988) *Works and Lives: the anthropologist as author*, London: Polity.

——(1993a) [1973] *The Interpretation of Cultures: selected essays*, New York: Basic Books.

——(1993b) 'Religion as a Cultural System', in *The Interpretation of Cultures: selected essays*, London: Fontana.

——(1995) *After the Fact: two countries, four decades, one anthropologist*, Cambridge MA: Harvard University Press.

Gingrich, A. and Fox, R. G. (eds) (2002) 'Introduction', in A. Gingrich and R. G. Fox (eds) *Anthropology, by Comparison*, London and New York: Routledge.

Gregor, T. (1980) [1977] *Mehinacu: the drama of life in a Brazilian Indian village*, Chicago and London: University of Chicago Press.

Gudeman, S. and Rivera, A. (1990) *Conversations in Colombia: the domestic economy in life and text*, Cambridge: Cambridge University Press.

Hart, K. (1973) 'Informal Income Opportunities and Urban Employment in Ghana', *The Journal of African Studies* 11(1): 61–89.

——(1998) 'The Place of the 1898 Cambridge Anthropological Expedition to the Torres Straits (CAETS) in the History of British Social Anthropology', presented at the conference 'Anthropology and Psychology: the Legacy of the Torres Strait Expedition, 1898–1998', St John's College, Cambridge, 10–12 August 1998.

——(2006) *African Enterprise and the Informal Economy: an autobiographical note*, available at http://www.thememorybank.co.uk/papers/african_enterprise

Helliwell, C. (1996) 'Space and Sociality in a Dayak Longhouse', in M. Jackson (ed.) *Things as They Are: new directions in phenomenological anthropology*, Bloomington and Indianapolis IN: Indiana University Press.

Herskovits, M. J. (1941) *The Myth of the Negro Past*, New York: Harper.

Herzfeld, M. (1985) *The Poetics of Manhood: contest and identity in a Cretan mountain village*, Princeton NJ: Princeton University Press.

Hill, P. (1963) *Migrant Cocoa Farmers of Southern Ghana*, Cambridge: Cambridge University Press.

Hobart, M. (1987) 'Summer's Days and Salad Days: the coming of age of anthropology?', in L. Holy (ed.) *Comparative Anthropology*, Oxford and New York: Blackwell.

Hodge, H. A. (1944) *Wilhelm Dilthey: an introduction*, London: Kegan Paul.

Hugh-Jones, C. (1979) *From the Milk River: spatial and temporal processes in Northwest Amazonia*, Cambridge: Cambridge University Press.

Hugh-Jones, S. (1979) *The Palm and the Pleiades*, Cambridge: Cambridge University Press.

Hunter, M. (1937) 'Bantu on European-owned Farms', in I. Scapera (ed.) *The Bantu-Speaking Tribes of South Africa*, London: Routledge and Kegan Paul.

Hutchison, S. E. (1996) *Nuer Dilemmas: coping with money, war and the State*, Berkeley: University of California Press.

Hymes, D. (ed.) (1974) *Reinventing Anthropology*, New York: Vintage Books.

Jackson, M. (1989) *Paths Toward a Clearing: radical empiricism and ethnographic inquiry*, Bloomington IN: Indiana University Press.

Junod, H. A. (1962) *The Life of a South African Tribe*, New York: University Books.

Kaberry, P. (1939) *Aboriginal Woman: sacred and profane*, London: Routledge.

Kaneff, D. (2004) *Who Owns the Past? The politics of time in a 'model' Bulgarian village*, Oxford: Berghahn.

Kondo, D. K. (1990) *Crafting Selves: power, gender, and discourses of identity in a Japanese workplace*, Chicago: University of Chicago Press.

Kucklick, H. (1991) *The Savage Within: the social history of British anthropology, 1885–1945*, Cambridge: Cambridge University Press.

Kuhn, T. (1962) *The Structure of Scientific Revolutions*, Chicago: University of Chicago Press.

Kulick, D. (1998) *Travesti: sex, gender and culture among Brazilian transgendered prostitutes*, Chicago: University of Chicago Press.

Latour, B. (1996) *Aramis or the Love of Technology*, Cambridge MA: Harvard University Press.

Lawrence, P. (1984) *The Garia: an ethnography of a traditional cosmic system in Papua New Guinea*, Manchester: Manchester University Press.

Leach, E. (1964) [1954] *Political Systems of Highland Burma: a study of Kachin social structure; with a foreword by Raymond Firth*, London: Athlone Press.

Lévi-Strauss, C. (1966) *La pensée sauvage (The Savage Mind)*, London: Weidenfeld and Nicolson.

——(1984) [1955] *Tristes Tropiques*, trans. John and Doreen Weightman, Harmondsworth: Penguin.

Lewis, I. M. (1989) *Ecstatic religion: an anthropological study of spirit possession and shamanism*, London: Routledge.

Majnep, I. S. and Bulmer, R. (1977) *Birds of My Kalam Country*, Auckland and Oxford: Auckland University Press and Oxford University Press.

Malinowski, B. (1927) *Sex and repression in savage society*, London: Routledge and Kegan Paul.

——(1967) [1957] 'Preface', in R. Firth, *We, The Tikopia: kinship in primitive Polynesia*, 2nd edn, Boston MA: Beacon Press.

——(1974) [1925] 'Myth in Primitive Psychology', in *Magic Science and Religion: and other essays*, London: Souvenir Press.

——(1978) [1922] *Argonauts of the Western Pacific: an account of native enterprise and adventure in the archipelagos of Melanesian New Guinea*, London and New York: Routledge and Kegan Paul.

Marcus, G. E. (1998) *Ethnography Through Thick and Thin*, Princeton NJ: Princeton University Press.

Mead, M. (1928) *Coming of Age in Samoa: a study of adolescence and sex in primitive societies*, New York: Morrow.

——(1963) [1935] *Sex and Temperament in Three Primitive Societies*, New York: Morrow.

Mead, M. and Baldwin, J. (1971) *A Rap on Race*, London: Michael Joseph.

Metraux, R. (2000) 'Resonance in Imagery', in M. Mead and R. Metraux (eds) *The Study of Culture at a Distance*, vol. I, New York: Berghahn.

Milton, K. (2002) *Loving Nature: toward an ecology of emotion*, London and New York: Routledge.

Moore, H. (1986) *Space, Text and Gender: an anthropological study of the Marakwet of Kenya*, Cambridge: Cambridge University Press.

Morgan, R. (2002) *Altered Carbon*, London: Gollancz.

Munn, N. (1992) *The Fame of Gawa: a symbolic study of value transformation in a Massim*, Cambridge: Cambridge University Press.

Nourse, J. (1996) 'The Voice of the Winds versus the Masters of Cure: contested notions of spirit possession among the Laujé of Sulawesi', *Journal of the Royal Anthropological Institute* (n.s.) 2, 425–43.

Obeyesekere, G. (1981) *Medusa's hair*, Chicago: University of Chicago Press.

Okely, J. (1983) *The Traveller-Gypsies*, Cambridge: Cambridge University Press.

Olwig, K. F. (1981) 'Women, "Matrifocality" and Systems of Exchange: an ethno-historical study of the Afro-American family on St John, Danish West Indies', *Ethnohistory* 28(1): 59–77.

Ong, A. (1988) 'The Production of Possession: spirits and multinational corporation in Malaysia', *Annual Review of Anthropology* 15, 28–43.

Overing, J. (1985) 'Today I Shall Call Him Mummy', in J. Overing (ed.) *Reason and Morality*, London: Tavistock.

Parkin, D. (1972) *Palms, Wine, and Witnesses: public spirit and private gain in an African farming community*, San Francisco: Chandler Publishing Company.

Piasere, L. (1985) *Mare Roma: catégories humaines et structure sociale: une contribution à l'ethnologie Tsigane*, Paris: Etudes et Documents Balkaniques et Méditerranéens.

Pina-Cabral, J. de. (1992) 'Against Translation: the role of the researcher in the production of ethnographic knowledge', in J. de Pina-Cabral and J. Campbell (eds) *Europe Observed*, Basingstoke: Macmillan, in association with St Antony's College, Oxford.

Placido, B. (2001) 'It's All To Do With Words': an analysis of spirit possession in the Venezuelan cult of María Lionza', *Journal of the Royal Anthropological Institute* 7: 207–24.

Platt, T. (1997) 'The Sound of Light', in *Creating Context in Andean Cultures*, Oxford: Oxford University Press.

Radcliffe-Brown, A. R. (1979) *Structure and Function in Primitive Society: essays and addresses*, London: Cohen and West.

Rapport, N. (1993) *Diverse World-Views in an English Village*, Edinburgh: Edinburgh University Press.

——(1994) 'Trauma and Ego-Syntonic Response', in S. Heald and A. Deluz (eds) *Anthropology and Psychoanalysis*, London: Routledge.

Rattray, R. S. (1927) *Religion and Art in Ashanti*, Oxford: Clarendon Press.

Rivers, W. H. R. (1914) *The History of Melanesian Society*, vol. 1, Cambridge: Cambridge University Press.

——(1924) *Social Organization*, London: Kegan Paul.

Rosaldo, M. Z. and Lampher, L. (1974) 'Introduction', to M. Z. Rosaldo and L. Lamphere (eds) *Woman, Culture and Society*, Stanford: Stanford University Press.

Rosaldo, R. (1980) *Knowledge and Passion: Ilongot notions of self and social life*, Cambridge: Cambridge University Press.

——(1986) *When Natives Talk Back: Chicano anthropology since the late sixties*, Tucson: University of Arizona, Mexican American Studies and Research Centre, Renato Rosaldo Lecture Series Monograph, vol. 2.

Rumsey, A. (2004) 'Ethnographic macro-tropes and anthropological theory', *Anthropological Theory* 4(3): 267–98.

Scheper-Hughes, N. (1992) *Death Without Weeping: the violence of everyday life in Brazil*, Berkeley: University of California Press.

Scheper-Hughes, N. and Sargent, C. (1998) 'Introduction', in N. Scheper-Hughes and C. Sargent (eds) *Small Wars: the cultural politics of childhood*, Berkeley: University of California Press.

Schieffelin, E. (1976) *The Sorrow of the Lonely and the Burning of the Dancers*, New York: St Martin's Press.

Sen, A. (1976) *Poverty and Famines: an essay on entitlement and deprivation*, Oxford: Clarendon Press.

Smith, M. G. (1962) *West Indian Family Structure*, Washington WA: Washington University Press.

Smith, R. T. (1998) [1956] *The Negro Family in British Guiana: family structure and social status in the villages*, London: Routledge.

Strathern, M. (1981) *Kinship at the Core: an anthropology of Elmdon, a village in north-west Essex in the nineteen sixties*, Cambridge: Cambridge University Press.

——(1984) 'Subject or Object? Women and the circulation of valuables in Highlands New Guinea', in R. Hirschon (ed.) *Women and Property, Women as Property*, London: Croom Helm.

——(1988) *The Gender of the Gift: problems with women and problems with society in Melanesia*, Berkeley: University of California Press.

——(1991) *Partial connections*, Savage MD: Rowman and Littlefield.

Talle, A. (1993) 'Transforming Women into "Pure" Agnates: aspects of female infibulation in Somalia', in V. Broch-Due, I. Rudie and T. Bleie (eds) *Carved Flesh, Cast Selves: gendered symbols and social practice*, Oxford: Berg.

Tambiah, S. J. (1990) *Magic, Science, Religion and the Scope of Rationality*, Cambridge: Cambridge University Press.

Tsing, A. L. (1993) *In the Realm of the Diamond Queen: marginality in an out-of-the-way place*, Princeton NJ: Princeton University Press.

Vogel, E. F. (1989) 'Preface', to R. Benedict, *The Chrysanthemum and the Sword*, Boston MA: Houghton Mifflin.

Wardle, H. (1999) 'Gregory Bateson's Lost World: the anthropology of Haddon and Rivers continued and deflected', *Journal of the History of the Behavioural Sciences* 35(4): 379–89.

——(2000) *An Ethnography of Cosmopolitanism in Kingston, Jamaica*, New York: Edwin Mellen.

Weber, M. (1962) 'The concept of social relationship', in *Basic concepts in sociology*, London: Peter Owen.

Weiner, A. B. (1976) *Women of Value, Men of Renown: new perspectives in Trobriand exchange*, Austin TX and London: University of Texas Press.

Wharton, E. (2006) [1920] *The Age of Innocence*, Oxford: Oxford University Press.

Whyte, W. F. (1943) *Street Corner Society*, Chicago: University of Chicago Press.

Williams, P. (2003) *Gypsy World: the silence of the living and the voices of the dead*, Chicago and London: University of Chicago Press.

Index

Related titles from Routledge

Arguing with Anthropology:
An Introduction to Critical Theories of the Gift
Karen Sykes

'It is something of a stroke of genius to make gift exchange the guiding thread of an introductory book... Sykes introduces many of the most important debates that dominate anthropology today. As that rare book that accessibly introduces students to the discipline without talking down to them, I think this book will be widely used.'
    Joel Robbins, *University of California San Diego*

Arguing with Anthropology is a fresh and original guide to key elements in anthropology, which teaches the ability to think, write and argue critically. Through an exploration of the classic 'question of the gift', which functions in anthropology as a definitive example of the entire human experience, it provides a fascinating study course in anthropological methods, aims, knowledge and understanding. The book's unique approach takes gift-theory – the science of obligation and reciprocity – as the paradigm for a virtual enquiry which explores how the anthropological discipline has evolved historically, how it is applied in practice and how it can be argued with critically. By giving clear examples of real events and dilemmas, and asking students to participate in arguments about the form and nature of enquiry, it offers working practice of dealing with the obstacles and choices involved in anthropological study.

- From an experienced teacher whose methods are tried & tested
- Comprehensive and fun course for intermediate-level students
- Clearly defines the functions of anthropology, and its key theories and arguments
- Effectively teaches core study skills for exam success & progressive learning
- Draws on a rich variety of Pacific and global ethnography

Karen Sykes is a Senior Lecturer in anthropology at the University of Manchester, where she teaches a popular introductory course in anthropology. She received her doctorate from Princeton University in 1995 and has conducted research in Melanesia since 1990.

ISBN10: 0-415-25443-4 (hbk)
ISBN10: 0-415-25444-2 (pbk)

ISBN13: 978-0-415-25443-4 (hbk)
ISBN13: 978-0-415-25444-1 (pbk)

Available at all good bookshops
For ordering and further information please visit:
www.routledge.com

Anthropology: The Basics
Peter Metcalf

The ultimate guide for the student encountering anthropology for the first time, *Anthropology: The Basics* explains and explores anthropological concepts and themes in a highly readable and easy to follow manner.

Making large, complex topics both accessible and enjoyable, Peter Metcalf argues that the issues anthropology deals with are all around us – in magazines, newspapers and on television. Engaging and immensely interesting, he tackles questions such as:

- What is anthropology?
- How can we distinguish cultural differences from physical ones?
- What is culture, anyway?
- How do anthropologists study culture?
- What are the key theories and approaches used today?
- How has the discipline changed over time?

A strong addition to this established and successful series, this exciting text presents students with an overview of the fundamental principles of anthropology, and also provides a useful guide for anyone wanting to learn more about a fascinating subject.

ISBN10: 0-415-33119-6 (hbk)
ISBN10: 0-415-33120-X (pbk)

ISBN13: 978-0-415-33119-7 (hbk)
ISBN13: 978-0-415-33120-3 (pbk)

Available at all good bookshops
For ordering and further information please visit www.routledge.com